# ENGLISH LITERARY CRITICISM:
# THE MEDIEVAL PHASE

# ENGLISH LITERARY CRITICISM: THE MEDIEVAL PHASE

by

## J. W. H. ATKINS, M.A.

*Formerly Fellow of St John's College, Cambridge; Emeritus Professor of English Language and Literature, University College of Wales, Aberystwyth*

GLOUCESTER, MASS.

PETER SMITH

1961

*Originally published by the Cambridge University Press, 1934*
*Reprinted, 1961, by permission of the Cambridge University Press*

PRINTED IN UNITED STATES OF AMERICA

# PREFACE

THIS volume is in some sort a continuation of the plan outlined in an earlier work, *Literary Criticism in Antiquity*, in which an attempt was made to recall the views on literature and literary theory current in ancient Greece and Rome. A narrower and less promising field is here explored, that of medieval England. In it, it may at once be said, to look for original and lasting contributions to literary theory, or for illuminating appreciations of literary works themselves, would be alike unavailing and fruitless. What, however, will be found is a running commentary on literature, made up of a few definite studies together with a number of occasional remarks scattered throughout works of various kinds; and as evidences of a growing literary consciousness, which found expression in theorising and in attempts at forming judgments, this material is not without its significance. Representing as it does the first attempts to deal with literary questions in England, it marks the beginnings of English critical activities, forms an integral part of the native critical tradition, and thus constitutes a chapter in the history of English criticism which cannot well be omitted from a survey of that development as a whole. In short, its significance is that which is attached to all beginnings; as Roger Bacon (quoting Cicero) points out in another connexion, *difficile...est aliquem scire pauca nisi cui nota sunt pleraque aut omnia.*

In the pages that follow, an attempt has been made to sketch in outline this first phase of the critical development. And in the survey are included the main efforts made by writers of English origin to further literary interests by varied discussions of literary matters not necessarily confined to the vernacular. The movement in its earlier stages formed part of a larger European movement, against the background of which the English contribution is best appreciated; and attempts have therefore been made to provide in some measure the necessary historical setting. At the same time, intended though this theorising was for educated circles not confined to English shores, treating also of expression in a medium other than that of the vernacular, it has nevertheless a definite bearing on English intellectual life; and, as such, its full significance only emerges when viewed also in its relation to native activities. Certain aspects of the subject, those bound up with metric and *ars dictaminis*, for instance, have perhaps received less attention than they deserve. An adequate treatment of those special studies, however, lay outside the scope of the general sketch proposed. On the other hand, the main interest undoubtedly lies in the recurring efforts to arrive at some conception of poetry, its nature and art, in the concern also with expression in prose and with outstanding developments in contemporary literary history. Altogether this medieval criticism will be found to be lacking neither in general interest, nor in interest more especially of a historical kind. It embodies a section of the ancient teaching on the literary art, provides in a sense a key for the interpretation of contemporary literature, and also helps in the understanding of what really happened at the sixteenth-century Renascence.

It remains to record my indebtedness to earlier writers; and here, as elsewhere in critical ventures, tribute must first be paid to the honoured name of Saintsbury, who, having hewn out a path in what was then a strange country, has since pointed out the road for others to follow. To Dr Edmond Faral also a special debt of gratitude is due for his scholarly study *Les Arts Poétiques du XIIᵉ et du XIIIᵉ Siècle*, by which he has placed under obligation all who are interested in medieval letters. Apart from this I owe much to authorities in kindred studies, and notably to historians of medieval culture, including among others Sandys and Haskins, Lane Poole and Raby, Rashdall and Paetow; while among the specific works that have also been of service are C. C. J. Webb's illuminating editions of John of Salisbury's texts, C. S. Baldwin's *Medieval Rhetoric and Poetic*, C. G. Osgood's *Boccaccio on Poetry*, and *Roger Bacon, Commemoration Essays*, edited by A. G. Little. To the late Professor R. W. Chambers (whose grievous loss to English studies is deeply deplored by all), to Professors H. B. Charlton and J. F. Mountford I am further indebted for their kindness in reading the work in proof and for helpful comments: to the Librarians and Staffs of the National Library of Wales and the University College of Wales, Aberystwyth, for many willing services and unfailing courtesies: and finally to the Staff of the Cambridge University Press for their skilled craftsmanship in presenting what I have written to those who may read.

J. W. H. A.

ISLWYN
ABERYSTWYTH

*September* 1943

# CONTENTS

Is it not a most apparant ignorance, both of the succession of learning in *Europe* and the generall course of things, *to say, that all lay pittifully deformed in those lacke-learning times from the declining of the Romane Empire, till the light of the Latine tongue was reuiued by* Rewcline, Erasmus and Moore?...It is but the clowds gathered about our owne iudgement that makes vs thinke all other ages wrapt vp in mists....The distribution of giftes are vniuersall and all seasons hath them in some sort.

SAMUEL DANIEL, *Defence of Ryme* (1603)

# CHAPTER I

## INTRODUCTION

IT is generally taken for granted that literary criticism in England really began at the sixteenth-century Renascence. And this assumption, it must be allowed, has at least this amount of justification, that then for the first time there appeared in English a considerable body of works definitely devoted to literary problems, and represented by the *Artes*, the *Discourses*, and the *Apologies* of Elizabethan writers. Yet it does not follow that with these works critical activities in England had their actual beginnings, or that then for the first time Englishmen concerned themselves with problems of literature. The Middle Ages, we have learnt, were less dark than was once supposed. They reveal to-day much eager search after knowledge, besides considerable creative activity in art, literature and institutions. It is therefore worth inquiring, in view of the unbroken efforts at literary criticism from the Elizabethan age onwards, whether such critical activities were a product solely of modern times, or whether any evidence exists of earlier attempts to engage in those many-sided activities now known as literary criticism.

It is usually maintained, with some amount of truth, that intellectual conditions during the Middle Ages were such as to militate against the adoption of a critical attitude towards life in general. It is claimed, for instance, that the rule of the Roman hierarchy, having imposed the fetters of religious dogma on the medieval mind, compelled thought to move within the limits prescribed by an earlier authority, thus establishing a regime from which the free play of intellect was banished. It is contended, further, that the age being one of intellectual childhood, it was therefore incapable of that detachment and reflexion which all critical thought demands. In short, 'whatever the Middle Ages were or were not', so writes one authority, 'they were certainly not ages of criticism'. Yet there are considerations which suggest that the matter is not as simple as this, and that such generalisations should be accepted with some amount of reserve. In the light of the activities of John of Salisbury and Roger Bacon in England, for instance, of Abelard in France, and Petrarch and others in Italy, it would at any rate seem that the spirit of free inquiry had not altogether become a lost tradition in Western Europe. Moreover, there is the fact that if, as is surely the case, a satirical element in literature implies a critical attitude to life, then there was no lack of the critical temper in England during this period. From the eleventh century onwards satire appears and reappears in the works of Jean de Hanville and Nigel Wireker, in the Goliardic poems, in Langland, in Chaucer and Skelton; and, indeed, nothing is more characteristic of contemporary writings than the constant attacks made on ecclesiastical and social abuses of the time. Nor can it be doubted, further, that the charge of immaturity can easily be overstated. So far from being an age of simple childhood, the period, it may justly be claimed, was one in which men's wits had been sharpened by intensive logical studies, and when scholars gave evidence of an 'eagerness in thinking' which has rarely been surpassed in later ages. So that to describe the Middle Ages as wholly uncritical would seem to be something like a misreading of history. This at least is the inference to be drawn from the statement of a modern historian, that 'there was never a time when the life of Christendom was so confined within the hard shell of its dogmatic system that there was no room left for individual liberty of opinion'.[1]

At the same time there were undoubtedly factors which made an application of the critical spirit to literature in England a matter of some difficulty at this particular date. For one thing there was the unsettled state of the vernacular, which finally triumphed over medieval Latin as the recognised literary medium, but not before the fourteenth century; and this tardy triumph, together with the slow emergence of literary genius, resulted in the production of no great quantity of material for critical comment. Apart from this, there was an absence of clear ideas concerning the nature of poetry in particular, its

[1] R. L. Poole, *Illustrations of the History of Medieval Thought*, p. 3.

aims and its standards; while further obstacles to a free and rational discussion of literature existed in the deep-seated reverence for the *littera scripta*, the distorted views of poetry resulting from allegorical interpretation, or again, the predominance of logical studies in the medieval curriculum, with their tendency to divert interest from literary matters. Most serious of all, however, was the intellectual isolation of the Middle Ages, and the prevailing ignorance of much that was best in the teaching of antiquity. A youthful age or nation cannot afford to neglect the guidance of its predecessors, least of all in matters of art; and yet little assistance of this kind was available for medieval writers, apart from a certain amount of ancient thought which had come down in summary and mutilated form. Except for this, the avenues to classical art and theory were practically closed; and altogether the period would seem to have been one of confused thinking in literary matters, one from which could therefore be expected no great contribution to literary criticism.

Despite these manifold disabilities, however, there are grounds for thinking that this medieval period will be found to be not entirely lacking in the discussion of literary questions, and that in it, on the contrary, may even be traced the tentative beginnings of literary criticism in England. In the first place it has been remarked, and not without truth, that 'man has seldom long been content to create art without also attempting to understand what he was doing—sometimes with a vague intention of furthering those activities, but sometimes also from a purely theoretic impulse'; and this statement is not without its bearing on the intellectual exercises of the Middle Ages. It suggests the existence of some amount of literary theorising as the inevitable accompaniment of medieval efforts at literary creation. Then, too, whatever truth may lie behind this generalisation, one thing seems certain, and that is, that a tendency to discuss matters of literary import was definitely fostered by the nature of medieval education. From Roman culture had been inherited an educational system of a literary kind, comprising among its main studies the subjects of grammar and rhetoric, in which the art of expression generally, and the interpretation of poetry, were duly cultivated; and in this way encouragement and direction were given to a treatment of literary problems, and to studies which in an elementary form represented criticism in the making. Furthermore, it is worth noting that most of the conditions which were to lead to the appearance of critical works in Elizabethan times were also present during these earlier centuries, though in less active and intensive form. In the sixteenth century, for instance, critical activities developed owing primarily to the ardent desire for artistic expression in words, and to the recovery of a considerable body of ancient literary theory; partly also as a reply to Puritan hostility to art, and as a result of the appearance of an increasing volume of works of literature. And none of these factors was wholly absent from the preceding centuries. Nor were there wanting yet more definite incentives to critical inquiry at this date. Far-reaching changes in literature were taking place during the Middle Ages, among the more important being the change-over from the quantitative to an accentual system of verse, the development of the love-theme in literature, the recognition of the vernacular as the normal literary medium; and in the light of these developments it would have been strange if some amount of comment had not been forthcoming. Moreover, in the half-light which then prevailed, certain questions presented themselves with some urgency to medieval minds, questions relating for instance to the nature of poetry and the poetic art, or again to the processes of translation and the proper methods of attaining an effective prose. All these were recurring problems which called for attention; and they rendered some amount of discussion almost inevitable.

Under conditions such as these it is therefore not surprising to find that a critical tradition was in reality slowly forming in medieval England. And in attempting now to trace the growth of that tradition it will be necessary to take into account the multifarious efforts that were being made to pronounce on literature and literary matters, whatever their origin or their immediate purpose. Much of the running commentary thus obtained will be found to be couched in the earlier literary medium of medieval Latin, the rest in the vernacular. But this difference of medium involves no essential break in the critical development. All pronouncements alike form part of one continuous movement, representing attempts of Englishmen to throw light on the literary craft, either by an exposition of literary principle and method, or by a discussion of literature and literary values. So that at this stage the contribution of early Latinists is no less significant than that of later writers in the vernacular. To confine the attention to vernacular work alone would be to obtain a distorted perspective of medieval literary interests and activities. Then, too, it will be found, in contrast with modern developments, that most of the critical material available consists, not of formal works of criticism, but of detached and occasional comments on literature generally, together with fragments of literary theory scattered indiscriminately throughout works of various kinds. Some few short treatises definitely devoted to literary matters do actually occur, as, for instance, the grammatical and rhetorical works of Bede and Alcuin, or again, the thirteenth-century manual known as *Poetria Nova*. Such works, however, are comparatively rare; and the relevant material for the most part is to be sought in digressions and remarks of a casual kind, introduced, after the discursive fashion of medieval writers, into poetic productions, treatises on morals and education, prefaces to translations, sermons. tractates and the like. In short, literary criticism during this formative period was largely an unconscious exercise, a sort of by-product of other activities, intermittent in its appearance.

There were, on the other hand, certain definite stages at which such remarks acquired an added momentum, when substantial and noteworthy contributions were made to the critical advance. First came the age of Bede (675–735) when contact, however imperfect, was established with the art and learning of the Mediterranean world; and Bede, and subsequently Alcuin, educators of the clergy, expounded the elements of grammar and rhetoric, as well as certain aspects of Biblical and Christian poetry. Then, with the twelfth-century Renascence, came a wider vision of literature and its potentialities; and John of Salisbury, with the help of ancient classical theorists, gave new life and meaning to literary studies, revealing principles that govern artistic expression in words, while displaying with infectious enthusiasm the value of literature, as represented by the achievements of classical Rome. Fresh developments followed in the thirteenth century when, influenced by the new culture, attempts were made by Geoffrey of Vinsauf and John of Garland to provide instruction in poetic technique by means of school manuals, those of Geoffrey being the most systematic, perhaps also the most significant historically, of all the medieval attempts at theorising on literature in England. Meanwhile the influence of Scholasticism was successfully diverting interest from literary matters; and although Roger Bacon and others were incidentally opening up new lines of literary study, it was left for Richard of Bury in the century following to rekindle in part the earlier enthusiasm for literature. Then with the triumph of the vernacular in the fourteenth century, critical activities entered on yet another and a final stage; and, from now on, discussion was concentrated on problems of English literature itself. This change of direction had been foreshadowed more than a century previously by the debate in *The Owl and the Nightingale*; but at this later date Chaucer, and in a lesser degree Wiclif, extended this tradition, more especially in their efforts to inculcate a more natural mode of expression, in place of the artificial methods then current in both poetry and prose. In the fifteenth and early sixteenth centuries this same critical interest in vernacular literature was still active, though assuming at this date a somewhat different form. An attempt was made by Hawes, for instance, to formulate a conception of the poetic art, according to which poetry was defined as allegorical in form, highly decorative in style; and in addition, efforts for the first time were being made to evaluate the works of contemporary poets.

Such then were the outstanding stages of the critical progress in medieval England; and from this outline may be gathered some idea of this early phase of critical activity and the course of its development. That it originated from no inward self-generated energy, no conscious effort at discussing literature as such, this, to begin with, may be safely asserted. At first a movement concerned primarily with literature as a factor in education, both religious and secular, it was only at a comparatively late date that it assumed direct and more or less independent form, in treating of literature in and for itself, and as an art presenting definite problems of its own. Moreover, its teaching throughout will be found to be based on doctrines drawn from an earlier civilisation, from post-classical ideas of literature modified by Christian tradition; and in assimilating and translating these doctrines into English thought lay perhaps the main part of the critical achievement. Yet this process of adaptation was not accomplished without some amount of modification; and this was due in part to agencies shared by the rest of Western Europe, partly also to the workings of the national genius, and to influences derived from foreign sources. So that the resultant theories were to some extent distinctive and medieval in character. If not the outcome of first-hand observation or free reflexion, they are also something more than the fruit of mere repetition. And as for the worth of the performance as a whole, this much may at least be claimed, that it represents a contribution to literary theory of considerable historical, if not of intrinsic, value.

# CHAPTER II

## THE MEDIEVAL INHERITANCE

ANY attempt at throwing light on the critical activities of
the Middle Ages must inevitably begin with some
account of the literary traditions handed down from
the centuries immediately preceding. Whether we assume that
the Middle Ages in Western Europe began at the close of the
eleventh century, or, as some historians suggest, when Charlemagne was crowned Emperor at Rome (800), with the Dark
Ages representing the birth-throes of the medieval era, in either
case it is to the cultural conditions of the Imperial and succeeding ages that we must turn for some idea of medieval
origins, and more particularly for the medieval inheritance in
literary matters. Since the time of Augustus the Roman world
had undergone momentous changes, both political and social,
during which a great empire had moved to its decline and fall.
The first two centuries of the Christian era were centuries of
consolidation. They were followed by a period of widespread
anarchy, by a series of shocks from without and within.
In the meantime Roman world dominion had split up into
Eastern (Greek) and Western (Roman) sections; barbarian
inroads in the fifth century had completed the disruption; and
Christianity, from being proscribed, had become the faith of
the Imperial house, the recognised state religion. Thus was
transformed the political face, the civilisation of Europe; a
transition, in short, was being effected from the old world to
a new. And as a result of these upheavals Imperial Rome had
become little more than a provincial city, while Roman
provinces were reduced to Germano-Roman kingdoms, semi-
barbarous in kind. Hellenistic life and traditions were still
preserved in Eastern Europe, more especially at Constantinople,
which had grown in importance at the expense of Rome. But
in the West, after the fifth century, an impenetrable darkness
gradually fell, accompanied by political chaos and an intel-

lectual paralysis, to which the coming of Charlemagne for the time being put an end.

Highly significant, however, were the cultural changes involved in these transitional centuries (400–800), which witnessed a confused clash of races and traditions that threatened the extinction of all that was valuable in the past. For the first four centuries of the Christian era the resources of ancient culture had to some extent persisted; modified, it is true, by changes in the Roman genius, still more by provincial developments in northern Africa, Gaul and Spain. But after this period learning languished, ancient texts disappeared, and the Roman educational system, which had kept alive in the West the ancient scheme of studies, came abruptly to an end. For this collapse the breakdown of Roman administration, together with barbarian influences, was mainly responsible; though the fear and distrust of pagan learning betrayed by the Church were also contributory factors. By the sixth century, however, the effects were everywhere plainly seen. In Italy and Gaul, and throughout Western Europe generally, earlier traditions of learning succumbed before the exigencies of an iron age, and intellectual activities ceased to occupy the minds of men.

Yet during these Dark Ages the links with ancient culture were never entirely broken; and the task of education, on the disappearance of the Roman schools, was taken up by the Church. Despite the uncompromising opposition of Tertullian and others, more liberal counsels in the end prevailed, and profane studies were fostered as a means of fitting ecclesiastics for the discharge of their duties. With this object in view ancient studies were subjected to some amount of modification; and this was done with the help of monasticism, a social organisation founded in Gaul in the course of the fourth century, and representing originally a reaction against pagan culture. Now, however, it was instrumental in giving new life and direction to educational effort, by providing centres of study as well as works of instruction adapted for that specific purpose. Centuries before in the Graeco-Roman world a synthesis of culture had been current in what became known as the Liberal Arts. This scheme had embraced in an elementary form well adapted for

teaching purposes the traditions of Greek literature and science
reduced to a system; and whereas its origin went back at least
as far as Plato, it had subsequently been developed by Varro,
commended by Cicero and Quintilian, and had also been
utilised by writers like Aulus Gellius, Macrobius and Augustine
in Imperial times. When therefore monastic schools took the
place of the schools of Rome, this encyclical discipline became
the basis of their instruction. The Seven Liberal Arts, made up
of the Trivium (grammar, rhetoric and dialectic) and the
Quadrivium (arithmetic, geometry, music, and astronomy),
from now on became the staple of education, and all alike were
made to converge on sacred studies. Already in northern Africa
before the coming of the Vandals, Martianus Capella had
produced his allegorical treatise *De Nuptiis Philologiae et Mer-
curii* (*c.* 410–27), in which, in pedantic and fantastic fashion,
he treated for the first time the Seven Arts as an organic unity.
A century later he was followed by Cassiodorus, one-time
minister of Theodoric, who in his *Institutiones Divinarum et
Saecularium Lectionum* (543–55) dealt with the same theme in
his exposition of secular learning. Still later, from Isidore,
bishop of Seville (*c.* 570–636), came the encyclopaedic work
known as *Origines* or *Etymologiae*, which treated in some twenty
books of the Liberal Arts and much else besides. Thus from
northern Africa, Italy and Spain came evidence of the same
encyclopaedic trend in contemporary teaching, a development
of the taste for summaries and epitomes which had characterised
the Latin-speaking world since the close of the first century;
and as monastic and cathedral schools were to be the main
centres of liberal study up to the close of the eleventh century,
it was now that the foundations of medieval education were
really laid. The works of Capella, Cassiodorus and Isidore were
to remain the most popular of manuals for centuries to come,
and they preserved at least some elements of ancient learning.
But it was learning made subservient to ecclesiastical ends;
learning codified, methodised, and therefore sterilised; and the
resulting system of education was one from which the spirit of
ancient culture had inevitably been withdrawn.

Such, then, in brief, were some of the main aspects of the

intellectual conditions prevailing at the birth of the Middle Ages; and it now remains to recall those conceptions of literature then current, which were subsequently to form part of the medieval inheritance of critical theory. That not a few of the doctrines were handed down from antiquity through the medium of the schools, both Roman and monastic, is in the first place undoubted. Others, again, were obviously generated by the literary conditions and activities of the time; while the prevailing attitude to literature was dictated by the Church, especially after Constantine's day, when it was admitted to a share in the government of the state. Here, then, if anywhere, will be found the key to such literary theorising as followed; the explanation, for instance, of the medieval views on literature and of the fragmentary theories discussed; the causes, too, of the prejudices, the errors and limitations which marked medieval comments on literature. So that our first task is to inquire into the literary traditions handed down from these formative centuries, and, in particular, those modifications of Graeco-Roman doctrine which were to constitute the main body of later theorising.

Of fundamental importance, to begin with, is the fact that Latin, as distinct from Greek, culture lay at the root of all subsequent literary developments—a point nowadays often taken for granted, though its full significance is sometimes missed. That during the opening centuries of the Christian era some measure of Roman culture had permeated the whole of the Western Empire is of course true. From the first century Roman conquests in Western Europe were everywhere accompanied by a diffusion of the Roman way of life, its language, its system of education, its religion and customs; and while from the *coloniae* and the schools was spread something of the higher learning, further contact with Roman merchants and soldiers brought to the various peoples some knowledge of the popular Latin speech. Yet such conditions in themselves did not necessarily decide the cultural future of Western Europe. Already in the second century the Latin literary genius was showing signs of exhaustion, and its short-lived revival two centuries later was due to external and temporary causes.

More than this, at Rome itself during this same second century, Greek, not Latin, traditions were palpably in the ascendant, Imperial patronage having given to Greek culture a new lease of life. Thus Athens had once more become the chief centre of intellectual life; and the outstanding literary development of the time was the New Sophistic, a revival of the artificial stylistic effects of the early Greek sophists. In the meantime Roman writers like Suetonius and Fronto indifferently made use of both Greek and Latin; whereas Marcus Aurelius, it is significant, employed Greek for preference. Moreover, Greek, the then universal language and the language of the New Testament, was for generations the only medium recognised by the Western Church for liturgical purposes. So that altogether it must have seemed at the time that the future in cultural matters lay rather with Greece than with Rome; and, as the sequel was to show, it was indeed a parting of the ways, full of significance for later history. The final decision was incidentally made when, in the middle of the third century, Latin became the liturgical language of the Roman Church, and therefore the literary language of Western Europe. In Gaul and elsewhere there forthwith sprang into being a vast Latin Christian literature; and a knowledge of Greek became rare in Western lands. Greek literature and culture, it is true, continued to flourish elsewhere in the Empire, in regions east of the Adriatic; and after the fourth century Byzantium, the new Imperial capital, became the centre and custodian of Greek learning. But by then, the political division of the Empire into East and West had taken place; and from now on, the break with Greek traditions in the West was final and complete. Western Europe, already Romanised, adopted Latin as its literary medium, along with Latin cultural traditions and Latin learning;[1] while Greek influences and Greek ideas were now discarded, to be revived, though only in part, at the sixteenth-century Renascence. On the far-reaching consequences of this decision there is no need to dwell. It is sufficient to say that to the Middle Ages, not only the masterpieces of Greek literature,

---

[1] See M. L. W. Laistner, *Thought and Letters in Western Europe A.D. 500–900* (1931), *passim*.

but also the teachings of Plato, Aristotle and others on literature, remained closed books; and the guidance in critical matters which had proved so effective at Rome, had in fact inspired much that was best in the Graeco-Roman literary tradition, was no longer available. It was upon Latin learning practically alone that medieval writers were to draw.

But this is not all; for if the literary influence of Greece was wanting at this stage, so also was the influence of what classical Rome had to teach in literary matters. The truth was that only an imperfect conception of Rome and its literary traditions was handed on during these transitional centuries; and indeed, by an early date, the vision of antiquity itself had sensibly faded. In late Roman times distorted versions of ancient history had already appeared, notably Dares's story of Troy, which Cornelius Nepos was pretended to have translated, but which was probably a forgery of the fifth or the sixth century; and whereas to writers like Ausonius and Claudian Rome meant simply Imperial Rome, as distinct from Rome of the Republic, to later medieval minds it represented little more than a pilgrim city, a home of strange legends and stranger magicians. Similar limitations marked also the transmission of the literary traditions of Rome, its literature and its literary theory. Up to the end of the fourth century a fairly wide acquaintance with Latin literature may be generally assumed. Prudentius, for example, was not alone in his extensive borrowings from Virgil and Horace, Lucretius and Ovid, Statius, Lucan and Juvenal; and such knowledge, there is no reason for doubting, was largely based on an acquaintance with actual texts. After the fourth century, however, in the political disturbances that followed, a multitude of texts was undoubtedly lost. The transmission of Latin culture from that time onwards was seriously hampered; though with the copying of manuscripts that went on in the monasteries of the West—a work inaugurated by Jerome and Cassiodorus—the loss, it is true, was partly to be made good. In the meantime, however, it was the literary influences and standards of the Imperial age that survived and were handed on to succeeding centuries; the influences embodied, for instance, in the works of Suetonius and Apuleius,

Ausonius, Macrobius and Claudian, all with their marked rhetorical colouring. Of the writings of Republican Rome but little was known; while of the classical period the works most cherished were those which stood nearest in spirit to Christianity, and were therefore of use for doctrinal purposes. It is not without its significance, for instance, that part of Virgil's fame already rested on the current interpretation of his fourth Eclogue; and among the works most familiar by reason of their moralistic teaching were the writings of the two Senecas, and the *Satires* of Horace, Persius and Juvenal. Of the dramatic legacy of antiquity, on the other hand, practically nothing was preserved, owing to the fierce opposition of Christian authorities to all stage performances. Apart from some acquaintance with the plays of Plautus and Terence, which were but imperfectly understood, there was little to remind future generations of earlier dramatic traditions;[1] and it was left for medieval writers to work out new dramatic forms of their own. Then, too, there was the loss of the earlier tradition of historical writing, which now assumed the form of epitomes, biographies and chronicles, under the influence of Florus, Suetonius and the like. Of these the chronicles of Eusebius and Jerome, and the *History* of Orosius, were striking examples; works written to supersede the records of Hellenic culture, and with doctrinal aims in view. In short, the earlier philosophic conception of history was now discarded; and the tradition of Livy and Tacitus was in practice lost to the Middle Ages.

Most important of all, at least for our present purpose, was the neglect of the valuable output of literary theory which had distinguished the classical period at Rome, when by a series of critics many of the underlying principles of ancient art had been duly formulated. Of these Latin theorists, Cicero and Quintilian alone were well known at this date, though their achievements were far from being adequately appreciated. Augustine, it is true, in his *De Doctrina Christiana*, had made an excellent use of Cicero's *De Oratore* in his exposition of oratory. But, apart from this, the critical influence of Cicero was almost

---

[1] Cf. however the six plays of the tenth-century nun, Hroswitha, written in imitation of Terence, but in prose and with moralistic intention.

wholly confined to his early and immature *De Inventione*; and, in addition, to him was falsely attributed the yet earlier *Rhetorica ad Herennium*,[1] a school-book of anonymous authorship, apparently rediscovered in northern Africa *c.* 350. Quintilian's work, on the other hand, supplied the broad plan for the instruction that went on in the Roman schools; but since his scheme no longer corresponded to the needs of the age, it was but an attenuated form of his teaching that was handed on to later ages. For the rest, the classical teaching of Rome may be said to have been ignored during these early centuries; and with it went the Augustan sense of the value of literature, the lofty ambitions cherished for a poetry that was new, as well as a host of principles based on the highest artistic ideals then known. Those principles had embodied a firm grasp on the essentials of both poetry and prose, while affording valuable insight into matters of technique and workmanship—all of which would have cleared the vision at this particular date, and have altered materially the course of literary history throughout Western Europe.

As it was, the guidance that was forthcoming was of a vastly different kind. It came mainly through the Roman schools and the text-books of post-classical rhetoricians and grammarians, conspicuous among whom was that galaxy of (mainly) fourth-century philologians, including Donatus, Victorinus, Charisius, Diomedes and Fortunatianus. To such sources must also be added those *compendia* of the Arts in which the earlier teaching on letters had been reduced to decadent form, suited to barbaric understandings and the exigencies of the schools; and to all alike may be assigned the merit of having kept alive in days of darkness some of the rudiments of letters, though such works had but slight bearing on literature itself. On the other hand the influences they represented were of a narrowing and degenerate kind. Their studies were confined to outlines of grammar and rhetoric, to conceptions of those subjects which, far removed from the teaching of classical Rome, had as their basis pre-Ciceronian standards, and above all to reactionary doctrines bound up with the false rhetoric or

[1] Ed. F. Marx; see also W. Kroll, *Rhetorik*, § 29 (Mél. Bidez [1934], 555).

Sophistic of the second century A.D. Thus, in grammar, their teaching was drawn from the arid theories of Varro, Palaemon, and Q. Terentius Scaurus; and in rhetoric their one aim was that of Hermogenes and his school—the inculcation of an inflated and exaggerated style. Their methods were like-wise in keeping with their subject-matter. What was aimed at was not the enunciation of broad general principles based on human nature, but rather the provision of elaborate systems of devices, with ample divisions and subdivisions, capable of mechanical application. The result was thus a travesty of the humane studies of the classical period, which now assumed the form of barren, cut-and-dried theories, based on Hellenistic and early Roman school-books, and on those rhetorical heresies against which all the great critics had inveighed, from Plato to Quintilian.

With the loss of practically all that was valuable in the literary criticism of Greece and Rome it was inevitable that no great interest was displayed in literary discussions and theorising during these early centuries. Indeed, it would be true to say that the very conception of literature became faint and con-fused at this date; for while the ancient literary tradition was being handed down in strangely mutilated form, new conditions were giving rise in practice to definite modifications of Graeco-Roman doctrines. With regard to the current views concerning literature, in the first place, the Church doubtless exercised considerable influence; though to say, as is sometimes said, that it was wholly responsible for the breakdown of the ancient literary tradition—and incidentally for the loss of its literature —is far from being in accordance with the facts. For one thing, it was under the auspices of the Church that the copying, and therefore the preservation, of classical texts began; moreover, it was Christian inspiration mainly that led to the temporary revival of a moribund Latin literature in the fourth century. So that ecclesiastical influence, even in these early centuries, was no mere destructive agency where literature was concerned.

At the same time it cannot be doubted that the Church from the first hindered an appreciation of literature at its true worth, its attitude for the most part being one of definite hostility. The

position thus adopted was due to certain utterances of the Latin
Fathers, made in the first flush of religious enthusiasm, and
handed on to later ages as final and dogmatic pronouncements.
Thus Tertullian had begun by describing literature as 'foolish-
ness in the eyes of God'.[1] He condemned it in impassioned
fashion on theological, moral and psychological grounds, and
was the first to raise the question, 'What has Athens to do with
Jerusalem?' He also reminded his readers of Plato's attitude
to poetry, how that famous philosopher had rejected from his
ideal state even the much-honoured (*sane coronatum*) Homer;[2]
and similar utterances came from Jerome, Augustine and
Gregory, embodying in substance Plato's objections of a moral,
metaphysical, and psychological kind. Thus Jerome in one
place states poetry to be 'the food of devils' (*daemonum cibus*);[3]
in another he narrates his famous dream, in which he was
rebuked before the throne of Heaven for his excessive love of
the classics (*Ciceronianus es non Christianus*);[4] and following
Tertullian he asks 'What concern has Horace with the Psalter,
Virgil with the Gospels?' Augustine, again, attacks poetry on
the moral side, pointing out that poets had impiously assigned
vices to the gods.[5] Gregory, too, maintained (following Jerome
in this) that 'the praises of Christ could not be uttered by the
same lips as the praises of Jove';[6] and Boethius, it might be
added, adopted much the same attitude when he represented
Philosophy as driving from his couch the Muses with their false
and comfortless counsels. These then were among the pronouncements which were to furnish arguments for the dis-
crediting of literature throughout the Middle Ages; though at
no stage in practice was the rejection of secular literature
complete. To this, however, there is one exception; and that
is in connexion with the drama, for which the attacks of
Tertullian and others were responsible. From the first, plays
were viewed with special abhorrence; they were held to excite
the passions, to counterfeit what did not exist, and to be wholly
contrary to Holy Writ. The idea of the drama as a school of
morality was not unknown; but, as Tertullian put it, 'the

---

[1] *De Spectaculis*, XVIII.    [2] *ad Nationes*, II, 7; cf. also Augustine, *De Civitate
Dei*, II, 14.    [3] *Ep.* XXI, 13.    [4] *Ep.* XXVIII, 30.    [5] *Ep.* XI, 34.    [6] *Ep. ibid.*

moral good induced was only a drop of honey, mixed with the poison of toads'.[1] For the rest, numerous decrees of the Church were directed against players and playgoing, thus giving rise to a tradition of hostility which survived until the seventeenth century.

Such then was the attitude towards literature ostensibly fostered by the Church during these early centuries; and had these utterances stood alone, the views of the Church would have been clear and unmistakable. As it was, however, the situation was complicated by a deeply rooted consciousness of the value of classical literature; a sense, visible in Jerome and Augustine, of its aesthetic and humane qualities, and an aliveness even on the part of Tertullian to its uses as a preliminary to theological studies (*studia quibus sine divina non possunt*).[2] And in this more liberal attitude they were supported by the Greek Fathers of the third and fourth centuries, by Origen and Clement of Alexandria; while Basil the Great also wrote an address to young readers, pointing out the positive value of pagan literature. Among the Latin Fathers, however, it was the practical, rather than the aesthetic, argument which prevailed; and both Jerome and Augustine were at pains to point out the wholesome results that would accrue from a wise use of ancient literature. Thus Augustine boldly proclaimed that 'truth wherever found should be accepted' (*profani si quid bene dixerunt non aspernandum*);[3] that pagan writings contained useful teaching, even glimpses of God; and that these good things belonged to those who could use them. Hence the duty of Christians to cherish and study all that was good in antiquity, even as the Israelites of old, he added, had 'spoiled the Egyptians'.[4] Similar arguments were also advanced by Jerome for utilising profane literature in the service of the Church. He held, for instance, that the best in ancient literature and thought might well be adapted to Christian needs; and then, appealing to authority, he gave a list of sacred writers from Moses and Solomon downwards, who had successfully 'spoiled the Egyptians'. Thus he noted in particular how St Paul in his

---

[1] *De Spect.* xxvii.
[2] *De Idololatria*, x.
[3] *De Doctrina Christiana*, 18.
[4] *Ibid.* 40.

Epistles had embodied reminiscences of the Greek poets Aratus, Menander and Epimenides;[1] and such treatment he commended for the use of edifying. He further recalled the fact that David on occasion had seized the sword of Goliath; and in this same letter, which was widely read in the Middle Ages, he likened classical literature to 'the captive woman' mentioned in *Deuteronomy*,[2] who by fitting treatment could be made a goodly matron in Israel.

Thus far, then, it may be said that, despite earlier prejudices, positive value as time went on was attached to the Graeco-Roman tradition in literature, the aesthetic merits of classical literature being to some extent appreciated, and still more its usefulness for practical and educational purposes. At the same time changing conditions were bringing to light literary ideals and forms which had constituted no part of those of antiquity, thus modifying in definite fashion the literary traditions of Greece and Rome; and this is seen, first, in the aesthetic value now attached to Biblical literature, which, except for the brief reference of 'Longinus' in his work *On the Sublime*, had fallen outside the province of ancient criticism. In this field Jerome was the chief inspiration; and his claim rests not only on his production of the Latin Vulgate and his sixty-three works of Biblical exegesis, but also on his skill in appreciating literary qualities which had hitherto escaped notice. Thus he comments with enthusiasm on the harmoniousness (*canor*) of the *Psalms*, the sheer beauty (*pulchritudo*) of the Prophetic writings, the dignity (*gravitas*) of *The Song of Solomon*, and the perfection (*perfectio*) of *Job*.[3] David, again, he describes as 'our Pindar and Horace'; and elsewhere he significantly adds that 'if I can but teach what I have learnt there will be born something unknown to Greece'. Nor was the lead thus given altogether impaired by certain erroneous ideas also set forth; as when, for instance, he asserts that *Job* for the most part was written in hexameter verse, relieved at times by rhythmical passages (*numeris lege solutis*).[4] He even goes further and states that

[1] *Ep.* LXX, 2; cf. *Acts* xvii, 28; 1 *Cor.* xv, 33; *Titus* i, 12.    [2] xxi, 11–13.
[3] Pref. letter to Bk. II of his trans. of Eusebius's *Chronicon*; cf. also *Ep.* LIII and Augustine, *De Doc. Chr.*, for further appreciation of Biblical literature.
[4] Pref. to *Job*.

nearly all the *cantica* of the Bible were metrical after the manner of Horace and Pindar, Alcaeus and Sappho—a false conception of Hebrew verse apparently derived from Philo, Origen, and Eusebius. Then, too, in commenting on certain obscure passages of the Bible Jerome implies that such obscurity was inherent in poetry itself. The poet's (and the prophet's) business, he asserts, was not to speak plainly, but to speak in such terms as only the initiated could understand.[1] This, he explained, would prevent the poet's truths from becoming cheap and vulgar; it would also render his truths more precious, seeing that they were won only after effort. And traces of such doctrine are not wanting in later ages.[2]

In this extension of the range of vision in literary matters so as to include Biblical poetry, the traditional conception of literature had, however tentatively, been considerably widened; and further modifications were indirectly suggested by the emergence of that Christian literature which flourished from the third century to the seventh, and which embodied elements foreign to classical standards. Such literature from the first subserved the needs of the Church; and the use of Biblical themes in the epics of Juvencus, Avitus, Arator and others, represented, to begin with, a distinct departure from classical usage. Further literary possibilities were also being revealed in the hymns of Ambrose and his followers, which rivalled with some difference that lyrical note, which, conspicuous in Greece, had latterly been silenced at Rome. Meanwhile striking changes were taking place in the form of poetry itself, changes of the highest significance in regard to later developments. Of these the appearance of a new system of verse in place of the accepted prosody based on classical metres was perhaps the most important. By the second century metrical quantity had ceased to be a vital element of the Latin language; and with the feeling for quantity lost, it became necessary to find new principles of verse structure. This Commodian had first tried to do; and subsequently there was evolved a new verse form, no longer based on elaborate rules of quantity, but on the

---

[1] *Ep.* LIII; cf. also Augustine, *Contra Mendacium*, I, 5, 5. Professor Chambers notes Lucretius, *De rerum natura*, I, 638 ff.

[2] Cf. Boccaccio's teaching, see p. 172 *infra*.

principle of an equality in the number of syllables together with recurring accentual effects. Hence the creation of a new accentual poetry, essentially different from the metrical poetry of the classical period. For a time, it is true, the appearance of the old hexameter, elegiac and sapphic measures was to some extent retained. But in appearance only; for in the absence of an observance of quantity, all forms alike tended to fall into the simpler trochaic and iambic measures of the Latin hymns of the Church. Indeed, the part played by the Church in this development seems to have been considerable; though other influences have also been adduced, such as the examples provided by Syriac hymns, or by the popular, mainly trochaic and semi-accentual, Latin verse. On the significance of this change there is no need to enlarge; it represented a development in prosody which was to affect all the future literatures of Western Europe. The same also holds true of rhyme, which now for the first time was being utilised in Christian poetry. Whether originally it came from Syriac religious poetry, or whether it was merely a rhetorical device adapted for poetic purposes, remains uncertain. What at any rate is clear is that it represented an innovation of these early centuries, and that it modified in lasting fashion the conception of literature received from antiquity.

Among the innovations of this period, however, none is more significant in its bearing on literary theory than the place that was now assigned to allegory in the sphere of literature, and the unwritten doctrine that in consequence resulted. The conception of allegory as an integral element of poetry had formed no part of ancient theory; though its use had been foreshadowed in the *Thebaid* of Statius, where the abstractions resulting from the personification of pagan gods were in the main the outcome of a changed attitude towards Roman religion.[1] At the same time a vogue for personification was being fostered by contemporary rhetoricians; and later on, the allegorising tendency derived support from Christian writers, with their increased inwardness and their feeling for a hidden world behind the world of sense. These then were among the conditions which at this date conduced to the emergence of allegory in literary works. And the

[1] See C. S. Lewis, *The Allegory of Love*, pp. 49 ff.

movement was one that affected literature generally, its fruits being already seen in the allegories underlying such works as the *Psychomachia* of Prudentius, and Martianus Capella's *De Nuptiis*.

But while a drift towards allegory thus becomes perceptible in these early centuries, the idea that all literature contained an allegorical element was also slowly forming as a result of the exegetical methods pursued by the Church in its interpretation of sacred literature. An allegorical interpretation of literature was no new thing. It had previously arisen out of the need for accommodating sacred writings to altered conditions which brought in their train new ethical standards; and its use had been widespread. It had been employed by Homeric critics, particularly the Stoics, also by Jewish rabbis in expounding their Scriptures; and it was in accordance with this procedure that the allegorical method of interpretation was adopted by the Church in introducing its sacred literature to a new and hostile society. Thus Origen had first introduced the method into the Christian schools of Alexandria, since the Old Testament contained elements that were discordant with the thought and morality of a later age; and in this he was following the precedent of Philo Judaeus, who had read allegorical meanings into many of the Bible stories. From Alexandria it passed into the West through the instrumentality of Hilary of Poitiers and Ambrose of Milan; was subsequently adopted by Jerome, Augustine, Gregory and others; until at length it became the accepted mode of Biblical exegesis, with its three-fold interpretation, the literal, the typical and the moral. Nor was its application confined to Biblical writings. Virgil's works, for example, had reached Augustine already laden with inner meanings; and of these the interpretation of Virgil's fourth Eclogue (ll. 6–7) as a prophecy of the coming Messiah was perhaps the most familiar. Equally significant, however, was the *Continentia Virgiliana* of Fulgentius (sixth century), a detailed exposition of the *Aeneid* as an image of human life, and the first systematic application of the allegorical method to secular poetry by a Christian grammarian. Thus in these early centuries was inculcated the doctrine according to which all literature was capable of allegorical interpretation; though

Jerome uttered a warning against its excessive use and the absurd results that might ensue.[1] From this it was but a short step to the position that allegory formed part of all literary creation. This doctrine, which represented a departure from the Graeco-Roman tradition, was to impress the Middle Ages as did perhaps no other part of its inheritance; and its genesis is therefore a matter of some interest. If its origin may be traced to certain intellectual tendencies of these early centuries, its recognition as a theory was doubtless influenced by the attitude of the Church, which was to play so great a part in the instruction of later generations. Subsequently it was to enter into the medieval conception of poetry, giving colour to not a little of the work actually produced; and significant in this connexion is Petrarch's later definite pronouncement that 'allegory is the very warp and woof of all poetry'.[2]

In considering the medieval inheritance handed down from these early centuries attention has so far been drawn to certain limitations and modifications of the ancient literary theory thus received. And it now remains to recall briefly what actually survived, the extent to which ancient literary traditions were preserved, and the significance of those doctrines that became current. It has been already stated that of the ancient theory all that came down was some amount of that grammatical and rhetorical teaching upon which Roman education had been mainly based, and that the channels through which such teaching reached the Middle Ages were the works of Cicero and Quintilian, imperfectly understood, the rhetorical and grammatical treatises of fourth-century philologians, together with the encyclopaedic works of Capella, Cassiodorus and Isidore. As the main text-books of these early centuries, it was from these works that the prevailing conceptions of literature were derived; and confined as they were to rhetorical and grammatical studies, it is obvious that their teaching could be none other than of a narrow and limited kind, though by no means devoid of historical interest.

Of prime importance, to begin with, was the theory drawn from rhetorical sources; for in keeping with earlier educational

---

[1] *Ep.* LIII.    [2] *Ep.* CXVIII.

practices, rhetoric remained the paramount study in Roman schools down to the end of the fourth century. Wherever Roman arms had penetrated, rhetoric was wont to be taught; and its study was everywhere the all-absorbing concern of writers, both pagan and Christian. By the fourth century, moreover, its teachers in the West had come to form a class apart, honoured by Imperial and municipal patronage; and as late as the time of Theodoric, when force reigned supreme, Ennodius declared it to be 'the first of the arts, fit to govern the world'. But while rhetoric thus retained much of its earlier importance, a marked decline in its treatment and significance became visible, involving changes which were not without their effects on later studies. From the time of Aristotle and Isocrates onwards, classical rhetoric had stood for what was essentially a course in the humanities, a system of general culture based on the art of speaking and writing well on all subjects; and these ideals had been maintained at Rome by Cicero, Quintilian and others. In the meantime Hellenistic influence had produced a form of scholastic rhetoric which was finally to displace this larger treatment. Concerned solely with a lifeless analysis of the technique of style and the processes of argument, such works had nevertheless the merits of a brief and systematic treatment suitable for teaching purposes; and to the adoption of the doctrine contained in school manuals of this kind may be attributed the decline of rhetoric as an educational force, as well as not a few of the defects of the theory that came down.

One of the main characteristics of the prevailing rhetorical theory was its use of conventional precepts and stock definitions drawn from earlier sources. That the aim of rhetoric was 'persuasion', the orator a *vir bonus dicendi peritus*, and that oratory itself was of three kinds (forensic, deliberative, and epideictic); these commonplaces formed the groundwork of most treatments. After this the subject was treated in rigid and systematic fashion. Oratory was said to consist of five elements (*inventio, dispositio, elocutio*, etc.); a speech of four, sometimes more, parts (*exordium, narratio, argumentatio*, and *conclusio*). Three styles were indicated (grand, middle and plain); and the requisite skill was held to be acquired by natural gifts (*natura*), a knowledge of art (*doctrina*) and practice (*usus*). In addition, advice was given for the formation of an effective style. Certain vices, in the first place, were to be avoided, the clash of consonants, ambiguity, tautology, and the rest. On the other hand, the use of personification (*prosopopoeia*) was specially commended; and attention was drawn to the importance of 'decorum' (*ethopoeia*), to the necessity for adapting words and style to differences of age, sex, rank, and the like. Most important of all were, however, the effects of the figures (of speech and thought), which were described as the chief ornaments of style, giving variety and colour to expression. Their number was unlimited; they were expounded with meticulous care, and were ultimately regarded as the main object of rhetorical teaching. Such then were the chief elements in the orthodox rhetoric of the time; a series of generalities, couched in conventional terminology. And its defects are obvious; they were those of an arid and schematic treatment from which all vitality had vanished, and which embodied but the dry husks of earlier classical doctrine.

Another outstanding feature of the rhetorical teaching of the time was the tendency to limit its application to the political sphere and to political themes. In classical antiquity the scope of rhetoric had been wide and general. It had implied an education, based on literary studies, which was regarded as a preparation for life as a whole, and not merely for activities of a political kind. Already in the second century B.C., however, so we learn from Quintilian,[1] the definition of rhetoric had been narrowed to a treatment of *quaestiones civiles* by Ariston, pupil of Critolaus; and this conception, accepted by later rhetoricians—Fortunatianus, Sulpicius Victor, Victorinus and others—was subsequently adopted by Cassiodorus and Isidore, by whom the doctrine was handed on to later generations. This then accounts in part for the decline in the importance of rhetoric after the fourth century, and for its neglect in the centuries that followed. But while the study of rhetoric in its true sense thus became extinct, this limited conception was not without its effect on later history. When, in the schools of the ninth and tenth centuries, attempts were made to restore

[1] *Institutio Oratoria*, ii, xv, 19.

ancient studies, rhetoric was once more revived in this limited and political sense; and thus gave rise to *ars dictandi* or *dictamen*, the art of composing state letters or legal documents, which then became an important part of the school curriculum.

The most far-reaching influence on the rhetorical teaching of the time was, however, that of the New Sophistic, that morbid revival of Asiatic tendencies in rhetoric which had marked the opening centuries of the Christian era throughout the Empire, and which had drawn its inspiration ultimately from the traditions of Gorgias and the early Greek sophists. This movement was of a widespread kind. It not only coloured the styles of early writers like Florus and Apuleius; its effects are also seen in the later writings of the Christian Fathers, in the works of Ausonius, Claudian and other Latin poets, as well as in the fourth-century *Panegyrics*, that 'last phase of Roman eloquence'. All fields of intellectual activity, in short, came under its influence; and its main exponents had been Hermogenes in his *Progymnasmata*, Theon, Libanius and others, who thus gave to literary studies a false direction for ages to come. Of the main principles underlying this New Sophistic it has already been said that they embraced most of the errors against which the best thought of antiquity had persistently striven. In the first place it is significant that in its system rhetorical study was confined to occasional (or epideictic) oratory; that is, to displays of verbal skill on great occasions when panegyrics were usually looked for. Oratory of the forensic and deliberative kinds was thus ignored; and, as a result, attention in matters of composition was directed solely to points of style, to those details which made for novel and striking utterance. At the same time earlier and important injunctions ceased to be emphasised; those relating, for instance, to the need for sound subject-matter (*inventio*), or for orderly arrangement of thought (*dispositio*). In their place demands were made for mere ingenuity of expression, for the use of fixed patterns for structural purposes; and in this way were neglected not a few of the basic principles of good speaking (or writing) laid down by antiquity, the value of coherent structure, for instance, that organic quality inherent in all good prose, or again, the importance of psychological factors in all matters of expression. In short, rhetoric as a result became little more than a barren study of a fixed and elaborate technique. Nor was this all; for in the treatment of style, upon which attention was now concentrated, there was much that was positively harmful, the result being the establishment of an artificial and vicious way of writing. It is not without its significance, for instance, that now once again flourished in the teaching of rhetoric that evil practice of declamations, against which the elder Seneca and Quintilian had inveighed in no uncertain terms. This practice consisted of scholastic exercises in which fictitious themes were invested with a false glitter of style for show purposes; and, as before, the system was chiefly notable as a means of inculcating an inflated and exaggerated mode of expression. Apart from this, however, such tendencies were fostered by the actual teaching of the rhetoricians. Viewing style as mere verbal artistry, to be attained by the mechanical application of certain specific devices, they aimed mainly at expounding such means as were calculated to add a meretricious glamour to expression. Hence the importance attached to episodic descriptions, prolix amplifications, neat antitheses, pointed epigrams, far-fetched and paradoxical expressions, which now became the main ingredients of an attractive style. It was not that such figurative devices were inherently wrong; but, used mechanically and indiscriminately, they led to sheer absurdity, providing little more than specious ornament and artifice, and a burlesque exaggeration of 'the pomp of Roman speech'.

Nor must the wider and more lasting effects of this influence be allowed to pass unnoticed; one of which was the false conception of rhetoric that was thus perpetuated, and was to be still active in the persistent attempts at an elaboration of style characteristic of both medieval poetry and prose. In Capella's *De Nuptiis* this idea of rhetoric had been set forth in a fashion that was destined to influence literary studies for centuries to come. There Rhetorica is depicted in fantastic and allegorical fashion as one of the seven handmaids presented by Mercury to his bride. She enters, significantly enough, with an alarming flourish of trumpets, and appears as a stately woman of lofty stature, self-assured in bearing, and armed at point-device. On her vesture are embroidered all the figures of speech; she is girt about with *colores*[1] as jewels; and as she strides on her way her accoutrements are said to clash as if it thundered. Thus in exaggerated Byzantine fashion was rhetoric represented to later ages; and it is not strange to find that the false glamour obtained by stereotyped ornament was subsequently the chief quality associated with rhetorical and poetic effects.

While, however, the rhetorical teaching of these early centuries thus accounts for much in medieval literary doctrine, of interest, too, is the work of contemporary grammarians, which also gave guidance to later literary studies. As in antiquity, grammar, or 'the art of speaking correctly', was still held to prepare the way for rhetoric; and as an important, though ancillary, study, it was represented by Donatus, Diomedes, Priscian and others, whose works, based on earlier text-books, shared with their predecessors the deadening effects of classifications, definitions and rules. Thus it was that the matters mainly treated were the technical laws of language, namely, definitions of the parts of speech, expositions of the nature of letters, syllables and feet, discussions on the use and misuse of words, while figures and tropes also came in for detailed treatment. At the same time, traces of a more liberal conception of the subject were generally to be found in the close association maintained with literary study. The earlier Romans had given life to grammar by the interpretation of poetry; they had sought their standards of correctness in the works of poets, orators and historians; and in this way some consideration had been given to literary matters. Nor were such features wanting in these post-classical treatises. Most grammars embodied discussions on metric and style, abundantly illustrated from classical authors; and attempts were also made at explaining and evaluating poetry. In this way a commentary of sorts on literature was provided; and it is not without its significance that Diomedes in one place defines grammar as *litteralis scientia*,[2] or the study of literature.

[1] See p. 109 *infra*.  [2] *Ars Gram.* II (H. Keil, *Grammatici latini*, I, 421).

But it was not only in a general sense that grammar kept alive at this date some interest in literature and literary theory. Of special historical value are the doctrines concerning poetry found scattered in the works of these grammarians and the later encyclopaedists; for they represent practically all of the ancient theory that survived. Already in these early centuries the conception of poetry as an art had become vague and indistinct. Poetry had ceased to be studied as an independent subject, or as an intellectual activity with principles of its own; and consequently, nothing corresponding to the earlier *Poetics* or *Artes* is to be found at this date. When, in addition, it received any sort of consideration it was viewed as little more than a subordinate study, a branch of one or other of the major departments of learning; and an illustration of this is its association with grammar, of which it was regarded as a mere hand-maid, useful mainly as a guide to correct expression. Other treatments of the subject were associated with studies for which there was, however, less warrant. Isidore,[1] for instance, included poetic in his exposition of theology, on the ground that poetry sprang originally from the religious instinct; though he, to be sure, was practically alone in this peculiar grouping. More general was the conception of poetry as a branch of rhetoric; and if for this there were more specious reasons, the resulting consequences were also of a more serious and lasting kind. Since the first century, poets had practised with increasing zest all the rhetorical devices. Orators had imitated poets, and poets orators; and already in the second century Florus had raised the question whether Virgil was really a poet or an orator. At the same time, rhetoric was being limited to a con-sideration of style, and its treatment was held to embrace the style of poetry as well as that of oratory or prose. Hence poetry came to be regarded as a sort of versified rhetoric; and rhetoric assumed in some sense the function of the earlier poetic. Such views, however, represented a complete break with the classical tradition; for whereas in ancient rhetorical treatises frequent references had been made to poetry with a view to illustrating the effective use of this or that figure, yet nowhere had rhetoric

---

[1] *Etymologiae,* VIII, 7.

legislated for poetry, nor had rhetoric and poetic ever been confused. Now, however, as a result of the loss of the older conception of rhetoric, and in the absence of clear ideas concerning the essence of poetry, the earlier distinction between rhetoric and poetic became blurred and unmeaning, with disastrous consequences for later study. In short, rhetoric throughout the Middle Ages was to absorb poetic; and the study of poetry was to be limited by the current rhetorical teaching, to the exclusion of matters of more essential import.

In the light of these conditions such poetic doctrines as filtered through to these early centuries are therefore not without their value, however inadequately they preserve the teaching of classical antiquity. Indeed, most of the doctrines being ultimately of Hellenistic origin, they are far removed from the enlightened theories of ancient Greece, though still of historical interest. In the first place widely different views were held concerning the nature and function of poetry. Thus Jerome, it has already been stated,[1] conceived of poetry as an esoteric art, a means of conveying hidden truths to the initiated; while Augustine, having caught, it would seem, some distant echo of Aristotle, declared it to be none other than 'an art of telling lies skilfully' (*rationabilium mendaciorum potestatem*).[2] From Diomedes, again, came a definition of yet another kind; to him it was 'an art of true and fictitious narrative, with suitable rhythm and metrical in form, conducing to utility and pleasure alike'.[3] And Isidore, who traces its origin to primitive worship, when fit words in pleasing numbers were uttered for the glory of the gods,[4] also calls attention to its more formal aspects, when he describes the poet's main function as that of 're-fashioning true stories into something new by means of fancy and ornament'.[5]

Apart from these definitions, however, further traces of poetic theory are found in the various expositions of poetry itself; as

---

[1] See p. 20 *supra*.  [2] *De Ord.* II, 14, 40.

[3] *Ars Gram.* III (Keil, *op. cit.* I, 473): 'Poetica est fictae veraeque narrationis congruenti rythmo ac pede composita metrica structura ad utilitatem voluptatemque accommodata.'  [4] *Etym.* VIII, 7, 2.

[5] *Ibid.* VIII, 7, 10: 'Ea, quae vere gesta sunt, in alias species obliquis figurationibus cum decore aliquo conversa transducant.'

when, for instance, the old distinction between *poesis, poema*, and *poeta* is reiterated by Diomedes,[1] Isidore[2] and others. This three-fold category was taken from Hellenistic poetic;[3] it had stood for the three main heads under which poetry was treated. At this later date, however, the original significance of the terms is lost; thus *poesis* is defined as the art of poetry generally or a work of many books like the *Iliad*, while *poema* is reserved for a single work of lesser magnitude. Then, too, there is extant some amount of theorising on the formal aspects of poetry, also derived mainly from Hellenistic sources. Thus three styles are in general associated with poetry;[4] the narrative, the dramatic, and the mixed, in accordance with the degree in which the personal utterance of the poet is represented. And these three styles are said to give rise to three distinct 'kinds' of poetry: the narrative, as represented by Virgil's *Georgics*, the dramatic, consisting of tragedies and comedies, and the mixed or epic kind, of which Virgil's *Aeneid* was quoted as an example. Nor were these the only 'kinds' expounded at this date. The 'kinds' already mentioned were further subdivided into certain species. A list was added, embodying poetic forms such as lyrics, *saturae*, bucolics or pastorals, epigrams, hymns, epithalamia, and the rest;[5] and in this way was formulated the doctrine of the 'kinds' as representing the teaching of antiquity on the subject of poetry.

Beyond these generalities the theorising on poetry did not go far, though what is said regarding certain literary forms is of undoubted interest. To begin with, there are those definitions of tragedy and comedy, the influence of which was to persist even after the sixteenth-century Renascence. These, too, were probably of Hellenistic origin,[6] having been handed on by Varro and Suetonius to fourth-century grammarians, in whose pages the conceptions appear, though in slightly different forms. Thus tragedy, according to Diomedes, is 'a narrative of the fortunes of heroic (or semi-divine) characters in adversity' *(est-*

---

[1] *Ars Gram.* III (Keil, I, *op. cit.* 473).　　[2] *Etym.* I, 39, 21.
[3] See Atkins, *Literary Criticism in Antiquity*, I, 170.
[4] Diomedes, *Ars Gram.* III (Keil, *op..cit.* I, 482 ff.). Isidore, *Etym.* VIII, 7, 11.
[5] Diomedes, *Ars Gram.* III (Keil, *op. cit.* I, 482). Isidore, *Etym.* I, 39; VIII, 7.
[6] See Atkins, *op. cit.* I, 159.

*heroicae fortunae in adversis comprehensio*),[1] a statement based on a Greek definition[2] which he ascribes (on doubtful grounds) to Theophrastus; and the same conception is likewise characteristic of Isidore, who defines tragedy as 'sad (*luctuosae*) stories of commonwealths and kings' (*res publicae et regum historiae*).[3] Comedy, on the other hand, is defined by Diomedes as 'a narrative concerning the fortunes of men in private or public life, and dealing with action of a harmless kind' (*est privatae civilisque fortunae sine periculo vitae comprehensio*),[4] a statement also based on an earlier Greek definition.[5] Isidore, again, explains that comedy deals with 'the deeds of private individuals' (*privatorum hominum acta*), and that its stories are of a joyful (*laetus*) kind.[6] His further division of *comici* into two classes, however, the old and the new, led to later confusion. Plautus and Terence he described as representatives of the old, the satirists Horace, Persius and Juvenal as representatives of the new; and in the absence of any clear idea of ancient dramatic form these two classes were later on confused. *Comoedia* came to be regarded as a narrative in elegiac verse, written in familiar style and with a happy ending; and this conception resulted in the appearance of a new literary genre in the twelfth century, namely, the medieval comedy which was none other than a versified tale. Yet another statement regarding comedy is due to Donatus,[7] who, while pointing out that its characters are drawn from ordinary life, further defines that form as a story 'containing diverse teaching concerning everyday life, from which may be learnt what is useful in life and what is to be avoided'. In addition he quotes the statement (ascribed to Cicero) that comedy is 'an imitation of life, a mirror of manners, and an image of truth' (*imitatio uitae, speculum consuetudinis, imago ueritatis*).[8] Thus was handed on the tradition that tragedy consisted of stories of 'the sad falls of princes', comedy, of

---

[1] *Ars Gram.* III (Keil, *op. cit.* I, 487).
[2] τραγῳδία ἐστὶν ἡρωϊκῆς τύχης περίστασις (tragedy is an action involving a reversal in the fortunes of heroic characters).
[3] *Etym.* VIII, 7, 6.          [4] *Ars Gram.* III (Keil, *op. cit.* I, 488).
[5] κωμῳδία ἐστὶν ἰδιωτικῶν πραγμάτων ἀκίνδυνος περιοχή (an episode of everyday life involving no serious dangers).
[6] *Etym.* VIII, 7, 6.
[7] Kaibel, *Comicorum Graecorum Fragmenta*, p. 67.          [8] *De re publica*, IV, 13.

stories of ordinary men which ended happily; and at the same time the way was prepared for the non-dramatic forms of both medieval tragedy and comedy.

Of lesser interest was the importance attached at this date to yet another narrative form, the fable. It is defined by Macrobius, for instance, as 'a form of discourse which, under the guise of fiction, illustrates or proves an idea';[1] by Isidore as 'a fiction in which, through the conversation of dumb animals, an image of life is presented';[2] and in virtue of its fictitious character it is invariably contrasted with 'history', which is defined as 'a narrative of actual facts'. Here again may be detected a relic of Hellenistic doctrine, though somewhat changed in meaning. According to earlier theory the subject-matter of poetry might consist of what was probable ($\pi\lambda\acute{a}\sigma\mu a$), what was absurd and fabulous ($\mu\hat{v}\theta os$: fabula), or what was real and actual ($\iota\sigma\tau o\rho\acute{\iota}a$: historia).[3] This classification was now taken to refer to narrative 'kinds', rather than to the subject-matter of poetry; and an inordinate value was therefore attached to the fable form—a point not without its interest, in view of the later popularity of that form, notably in the twelfth century.

These, then, were among the main literary theories preserved by grammarians during these early centuries; and some statement must finally be made concerning the critical judgments of this period, and their value for later generations. In accordance with earlier tradition, the evaluation of poetry ($\kappa\rho\acute{\iota}\sigma\iota s$ $\pi o\iota\eta\mu\acute{a}\tau\omega\nu$) was still recognised as part of the grammarian's function;[4] but nothing tangible had resulted, apart from illustration of points of technical interest, the use of figures and the like. Of anything resembling an aesthetic appreciation the period is practically devoid; and Augustine's testimony to the moving influence of Virgil, how he wept for Dido, or again, was stirred to higher life by Cicero's Hortensius, stands almost alone at this date. At the same time efforts were made at literary commentary of sorts, Virgil in particular receiving close attention; and the estimates thus formed were characteristic of the critical standards and methods of the time, while they

[1] Somnium Scipionis, I, 2.　　[2] Etym. I, 41.　　[3] See Atkins, op. cit. I, 174.
[4] Cf. Diomedes, Ars Gram. I (Keil, op. cit. I, 421).

exercised a marked influence on the views of later ages. Among the outstanding Virgil-studies were Servius's *Commentary on Virgil*, and certain sections of Macrobius's *Saturnalia*,[1] in which the merits of the poet were discussed at a symposium. Both works belonged to the fourth century; and they were followed two centuries later by Fulgentius's *Continentia Virgiliana*, with its elaborate and far-fetched allegorical interpretation of the *Aeneid*. This work of Fulgentius was destined to inspire many later writers, including Bernard Silvestris, Dante and others; though it can scarcely be said to have added anything to the true appreciation of the poet. More significant are the contributions of Servius and Macrobius, who, drawing on the same authorities and adopting similar methods, have consequently not a little in common.

In the first place their work marks a definite change in the attitude adopted towards Virgil, whose fame during the preceding centuries had undergone many vicissitudes. From the first century onwards, criticism of that poet had been not uncommon. It had embodied attacks by *obtrectatores*, and much praise from admirers; and while others held him to be inferior to Ennius, to Hadrian the *Aeneid* was already a sacred book, capable of inspiring the *sortes Virgilianae*.[2] By the fourth century, however, things had changed, and Virgil's position had become firmly established. He was to receive from now on unbounded praise; and with Servius and Macrobius began that Virgil worship which was to culminate in sixteenth-century enthusiasm. Nor are the grounds that are given for this new estimate without their interest; for they witness once again to Hellenistic influences at work in the tests applied and the standards of poetic excellence adopted. In general it may be said that the main effort was devoted to showing that Virgil was a learned (*doctus*) poet, and that, as such, he was a master of technique, besides being possessed of a wealth of learning. In the matter of technique his all-pervading eloquence is primarily stressed. He is shown to have observed faithfully the laws of rhetoric, to

[1] End of Bk. I and Bks. III–VI.
[2] See E. E. Sikes, *Roman Poetry*, p. 90; also pp. 66–92 for an account of post-Augustan criticism generally.

have made above all an excellent use of the figures; and, compared with Cicero and other orators, he is declared to have surpassed them all in versatility and propriety of style. Then, too, he is judged to be supreme in the field of learning, and in the use he makes of traditional lore, that 'literary vice of Alexandrian poetry', as it has fittingly been described. Thus attention is drawn to his reminiscences of Homer, his frequent indebtedness to earlier Latin poets, his vast knowledge of the religious ritual of ancient Rome, and the use he makes of Greek mythology as an element of refinement in the classic style. To him in short is attributed encyclopaedic knowledge; he is hailed as an authority in all branches of learning. And upon these unaesthetic criteria the fame of Virgil was mainly to rest for centuries to come, since the medieval estimate of the poet was largely based on that of Macrobius and his followers.

# CHAPTER III

## EARLY GRAMMARIANS: BEDE AND ALCUIN

FOR the earliest definite traces of the discussion of literary matters in England we must turn to the seventh century, to that 'golden age' of Anglo-Saxon scholarship, when England moved out into the main cultural stream of Western Europe, and entered for the first time into the inheritance of Greece and Rome, sadly attenuated though that tradition was at that particular date. Concerning earlier literary teaching on these shores we can but conjecture. How far, for instance, did the Romanisation of Britain include some amount of instruction in Roman literary culture? That schools and rhetoricians arrived wherever Roman armies penetrated, this much is certain; and that Roman Britain shared with Gaul in the educational policy of the Roman conquerors, this incidentally may be gathered from Tacitus's account of Agricola's campaigns. Thus in *Agricola* (A.D. 98) we learn of the efforts made at instructing the sons of British chieftains in the Liberal Arts, for which we are told they had a natural genius, as compared with the more plodding qualities of the Gauls; so that before long the Britons had not only adopted Latin, but had even aspired to eloquence in that language.[1] Moreover, there are grounds for thinking that included in Agricola's staff was a famous scholar, Demetrius of Tarsus, a friend of Plutarch and author of an extant treatise *On Style*, who may well have shared in the education of the Britons, if indeed his identity is established.[2] Evidence of further literary interests comes from yet other quarters; as when Martial in A.D. 96 boasts that he is being read in Britain,[3] or when Juvenal some twenty years later refers to British lawyers trained by Gallic teachers.[4] Altogether, then, it may be surmised that in Roman Britain of the first century, as in the rest of the Western Empire, some

[1] *Agricola*, c. 21.
[2] See Demetrius, *On Style*, ed. W. R. Roberts (Loeb Cl. Lib.), Intro. pp. 271–5.
[3] *Epig.* XI, 3, 5.   [4] *Sat.* XV, 110–12.

amount of Latin culture was being communicated to the conquered people, including those rhetorical studies characteristic
of Rome. Of similar activities in the succeeding centuries of
the Roman occupation the evidence is yet more scanty. It
would seem that Latin culture took root less firmly in Britain
than in the neighbouring Gaul; for whereas Latin was employed by the Roman Britons, no record exists of any British
poet or writer. The truth would seem to be that there had been
no real assimilation of the conquered people by the Romans,
such as had occurred in Gaul; and the native language never
wholly gave way to the Latin tongue. At the same time the
influence of Christianity, which had spread to Britain through
the Gallic Church, cannot have been altogether negligible from
the educational point of view. Already in the year following
the edict of Constantine (A.D. 313) three British bishops were
present at the Council of Arles; and up to, and after, the
removal of the Roman legions from Britain (A.D. *c.* 410) the
British Church was doubtless instrumental in keeping alive some
knowledge of Latin letters. Nevertheless, if anything is certain,
it is that little or nothing of these cultural traditions was handed
on from Roman Britain. The Anglo-Saxon invasions followed;
all centres of Roman life were extinguished; and in the darkness
that fell in the fifth and sixth centuries—the 'two lost centuries
of Britain'—what earlier teaching of rhetoric and literature
there had been was completely lost.

Nor can anything definite be gleaned concerning the new
artistic principles introduced later by the Anglo-Saxon invaders
from overseas. It may indeed be inferred from the evidence of
contemporary Latin writers that the Angles and the Saxons
brought with them the tradition of an oral poetry, sung by
*scopas* or minstrels to courtly or popular gatherings, with both
subject-matter and forms that differed vitally from those of
Latin poetry. Apart from this, the appearance in the eighth
century of a written vernacular poetry, notable for its conscious
art, also goes to suggest the existence of earlier Anglo-Saxon
traditions in poetry, developed and perhaps modified at that
later date. And of this the *Beowulf* affords the best illustration,
with its elaborate metrical technique and its ever-present

rhetorical devices, suggestive surely of a long anterior development. Nor is it without its significance that such features recur in the poetry of other peoples of the Germanic stock, which likewise gives evidence of the same metrical rules, the same functional uses of alliteration and the like. It would therefore seem that a definite though unwritten poetic had been brought over by the Anglo-Saxons from their continental homes, a poetic evolved by professional minstrels and developed in some measure on British soil. But for any statement of the underlying principles we shall seek in vain. The Anglo-Saxon poetic, like the earliest poetry itself, was no doubt handed down in oral form, and all traces of that primitive code have thus completely disappeared.

With the seventh century, however, great and momentous changes took place; changes as fruitful in the intellectual life of Britain as the advent of Germanic heroic traditions, and even yet more far-reaching in their ultimate effects. First came the introduction of Christianity to the peoples of the Anglo-Saxon kingdoms; then the revival of Latin culture in their midst. Thus were Englishmen enabled for the first time to share in the legacy of the ancient world, and to hand on to later generations the elements of that culture. Nor was the importance of these developments confined to England alone; from a European standpoint they were possessed of no less significance. Throughout the Imperial provinces of Gaul, Spain and Africa ancient learning at the time was being ruthlessly extinguished. It was now cherished in England and Ireland alone, in what had hitherto been regarded as unknown and backward regions. Hence it came about that English scholars at this date represented one of the main bulwarks against the barbarism that flooded Western Europe, the chief guardians of letters in a distracted age. And 'never before nor since', adds a recent historian, 'has England occupied a similar position in European civilisation'; a truth, it would seem, that is nowadays often forgotten.

For the full significance of this Latin revival, however, we must turn to the activities of Northumbrian scholarship from 650 onwards. There in the north, in the peace brought about by the supremacy of the Northumbrian kings, the movement culminated in a strange, almost miraculous fashion, though fostered by influences from several sources. First came the inspiration of Irish missionaries, who, like Aidan at Lindisfarne (635), had established in the north certain centres of religious instruction, wherein were imparted elements of ancient learning which had long been preserved in Irish monastic schools. In the meantime new cultural interests had been stirring in the south, and they too were to play their part in the general awakening. Augustine's mission (597), it is true, had been concerned with conversion rather than with culture, though it had also been instrumental in forming new ties with Rome; and the full tide of the revival was finally seen when Theodore of Tarsus and Hadrian arrived on these shores and established at Canterbury (669) their monastic school, which was to remain one of the great centres of ancient learning. Both were men of outstanding erudition, scholars imbued with Byzantine lore; and by them were laid the foundations of English scholarship, as a result of their enlightened teaching and the zeal they inspired in a host of disciples. Nor was their influence confined to the south; for within a few years Benedict Biscop, a notable figure among the retinue of King Oswy of Bernicia, had transmitted the new learning to Northumbrian centres, and had set up schools at Wearmouth (674) and Jarrow (681), the libraries of which he endowed with vast stores of Latin texts, the fruits of his travels to monasteries abroad. There in the north under the guidance of Ceolfrid, Wilfrid, John of Beverley and others, the new learning flourished. With Wearmouth and Jarrow was associated the great work of Bede, which in due course inspired the cathedral school of York, and still later, through Alcuin, the Carolingian revival, upon which the culture of the Middle Ages was ultimately to rest. Thus in the north as well as in the south before the close of the seventh century a new era of letters was ushered in, full of significance in the history of English thought. A vigorous movement of rapid growth, it embodied what was in effect an eclectic culture, being based on Italian rather than on Irish tradition, and representative of Imperial culture in its later Christian days. And not least of the achievements was the impulse given in the north to activities other than the mere study of letters; the copying of manuscripts, for instance, and the production of the *Lindisfarne Gospels*, more especially, with its exquisite illuminated script, or again, the creation of the sculptured scenes of the famous Bewcastle and Ruthwell crosses.

It is, however, in the beginnings that were made with the discussion of literature and literary matters that this movement has for us its chief interest in our present inquiry; and however elementary and tentative such efforts may nowadays appear, they are still of considerable historical importance in view of what was to follow. In general it may be said that the scope of literary study at this date was mainly determined by the facilities that were available, and the more immediate needs that claimed attention. Now for the first time the Anglo-Saxon peoples were made acquainted with books, and with an education based on books, which opened up for them new ideas and arts handed down from an earlier civilisation. Thus access was now obtained to many of the writings current in Imperial times —the Latin Vulgate, for instance, the works of the Latin Fathers, the treatises of fourth-century grammarians, the encyclopaedic writings of Cassiodorus and Isidore, the main body of Christian poetry, as well as works of Cicero, Virgil, Lucan, Statius and other classical authors. Here then was abundant material for a revival of learning and literature. Indeed, it has been said, not without reason, that this period, more truly than the sixteenth-century Renascence, 'gave to Englishmen a new heaven and a new earth'.

At the same time it cannot be doubted that the use made of this material was largely conditioned by the circumstances of the time. That literary study should assume an elementary form, was, to begin with, inevitable. The key to these newly acquired treasures was a knowledge of Latin, a language foreign to Anglo-Saxon tongues; and the mastery of the rudiments of grammar was bound to be the main concern at this particular date. Then, too, not without its influence was the fact that the sole educational centres were the monastic schools, with their traditions inherited from Jerome and Augustine,

Cassiodorus, Gregory and others. In those schools the earlier compromise arrived at by the Latin Fathers was still maintained, the main object being not so much the creation of Latin *littérateurs* as the training of ecclesiastics for the performance of their duties, notably, the reading of the Scriptures, the Latin services, patristic writings and the like. To that end the study of secular literature, and more particularly its grammatical principles, was deemed necessary, since sacred knowledge demanded a culture that patristic writings alone were unable to give. Hence grammar, which at Rome had prepared the way for rhetoric, became now the recognised preliminary to the understanding of the Scriptures. It took the place in the scheme of studies which in Imperial times had been assigned to rhetoric. But it was a somewhat narrow conception of grammar that now became current. It had lost the larger meaning that Quintilian had given to it, no place in its treatment being given to the interpretation of poetry. Nor did it comprise the philosophical inquiry bound up with the work of Priscian. It was, in short, a limited and technical study, with special importance attached to certain sections. Its aim was purely utilitarian; and it became the means of adapting ancient culture to religious education, and of introducing men to the language and literature of the Church.

Significant of what was to come was the work of Aldhelm (*c.* 640–709), abbot of Malmesbury, England's earliest man of letters, and the first Englishman of whom any literary remains are preserved. Educated at Malmesbury under Maildulf, its Irish founder, and subsequently at Canterbury under Theodore, he embodied the main features of both the Irish and Roman disciplines; and his teaching at Malmesbury was destined to be of an influential kind. Of his numerous Latin writings one alone is concerned with literary matters; and that is his *De Septenario*, or the *Letter to Acircius* (695?) (i.e. to Aldfrith, King of Northumbria), which consists of a short treatment of Latin metre, enlivened by a number of riddles in verse. The work is of no great value intrinsically. It is a confused compilation of notes on the hexameter, which fails to reveal any guiding principles. On the other hand, it affords definite. evidence of the condition of Anglo-Saxon scholarship at the time; and it also witnesses to the methods and interests of Anglo-Saxon grammarians. Most of its doctrines, for instance, are taken from Donatus, Priscian, Audax and others; and it thus foreshadows the derivative character of most of the later theorising. Then, too, it illustrates the interest taken in metrical matters, mainly on religious grounds. The tradition that metrical verse was found in the Scriptures had previously been developed by Jerome,[1] while some knowledge of metric was held to be necessary for the reading of Christian poetry; and these were among the causes of the place now given to prosody in grammatical studies. Apart from this, the work of Aldhelm in general has this further interest; it goes to show the imperfect conception of ancient culture that existed at this stage. With him, for example, the cultivation of letters was ancillary to religious studies; he knew but little of classical authors; and his florid, grotesque style, his *verborum garrulitas*, embodied elements far removed from the true classical manner. These defects of style were perhaps due to the exaggerated rhetorical tradition handed on by late Latin writers, or else to that strange Hisperic Latinity cultivated in Celtic centres of learning; for he was not alone in these extravagances. His contribution to literary theory was therefore slight; though of his scholarship and wide reading there can be no doubt. He was a noteworthy pioneer in a sterile age; and among his disciples was included Wynfrith (Boniface), the apostle of Germany, and author of a short grammatical treatise *On the Eight Parts of Speech*.

Of greater interest is the work of Bede (673–735), the saintly scholar-monk, most venerable of pre-Conquest figures, who passed his days in the cloisters at Jarrow, 'reading, writing, and teaching', and whose erudition survives in a vast library of Latin writings, fragrant still with the charm of a gracious personality. Least apparent, perhaps, are those qualities in his critical writings; whereas they emerge more clearly from his *Ecclesiastical History of the English People*, and are present also in his *Commentaries*, his *Letters* and elsewhere. Yet his works which deal with literary studies are far from devoid of value, though,

---

[1] See p. 19 *supra*.

it is true, they were nothing more than elementary text-books. Written in his early years (691–703) for use in school, they nevertheless preserve something of the contemporary teaching on letters, and are otherwise significant in their bearing on later work. Of these writings the least important is the work *On Orthography*, written in imitation of treatises by earlier scholars, Cassiodorus, for example. Bede's treatment, however, differs from that of his predecessors, who had aimed at supplying an introduction to Latin for those to whom Latin was not unknown, inasmuch as his work is a mere glossary of Latin words intended for beginners. He draws freely on the works of Charisius and Diomedes; but he has simplified their teaching and adapted it to the needs of his time. Greater importance is attached to his work *On the Metrical Art*,[1] a short treatise addressed to Cuthbert, his 'fellow-deacon', to whom incidentally we owe an account of the death of Bede. The work opens with some explanation of letters, syllables and feet (§§ 1–9), and then proceeds to deal with the various kinds of metre used by the ancients and later Christian poets (§§ 10–23). A short discussion on rhythm (§ 24) follows, perhaps the most interesting part of the treatment; and the work is brought to a close by a brief statement on the three kinds of poetry (§ 25). Here again Bede draws on a host of earlier grammarians, and among others on Donatus, Servius, Audax, Victorinus, Diomedes and Mallius Theodorus—a list that affords eloquent testimony of his wide reading. The work is thus mainly of the nature of a compilation; and its significance lies primarily in its choice of material, and in its use of illustrative passages drawn from Christian poets. The third and last contribution of Bede to literary theorising was the work *On Figures and Tropes in Holy Writ*.[2] It was a sort of appendix to his work on metre, demonstrating the presence of figurative expressions in Scripture, and making use for this purpose of two chapters from the *Ars Grammatica* of Donatus. Whereas Donatus, however, had employed Virgilian and other classical illustrations, Bede, in

---

[1] H. Keil, *Grammatici latini*, VII, 219–60.
[2] K. Halm, *Rhetores latini minores*, 607–18 and Migne, *Patrologia Latina*, XC, 175ff.

accordance with his plan, makes use of Scriptural passages only. Altogether some seventeen figures and twenty-eight tropes (thirteen from Donatus) are discussed; and the work is of distinct interest in critical history.

When we turn to consider Bede's actual teaching, what he has to say on prosody first calls for attention. That he held with Jerome that Biblical precedents existed for the use of metrical verse is clear; and he further notes with approval the statement of Arator[1] that 'metrical effects are not unknown in Holy Writ' (*metrica vis sacris non est incognita libris*). But while this was his special reason for treating the subject, the example of earlier grammarians also counted. One conception of the poetic art (*poetica*) was that it consisted of true and fictitious stories in metrical and rhythmical form, which conduced to both pleasure and profit;[2] and most of the preceding grammarians had dealt with versification, as representing one, if not the chief, of the elements of poetry. In writing his tractate *On the Metrical Art* Bede is therefore following in the steps of these earlier writers; and in the main body of that work he supplies an analysis of Latin metres—the dactylic hexameter and pentameter, sapphic and anacreontic verses, the various forms of the tetrameter, and the like—and he finally refers his readers for further information to Servius's *De Centum Metris*. Of his treatment of these matters this much may be said, that it is characterised throughout by good sense and discretion. He does not attempt a scientific theory of metrical verse; but he selects with judgment, avoids needless complications, and concentrates on the more important forms. Nor does he slavishly follow the grammarians in their theories, which were intended to account for and systematise the practice of classical poets. Attaching equal value to the later Christian poets, Bede occasionally defends faults of quantity found in Arator and Sedulius, while also renouncing certain licences sanctioned by classical poets. Thus the metrical rules of the grammarians, he maintained, had necessarily to be modified by later achievements; the last word on metrical verse had not been pronounced by Virgil. This position he adopted, however, not so much from a sense of

[1] *Ad Vigilium*, v, 27. See Keil, *op. cit.* vii, 260.
[2] See Diomedes, p. 30 *supra*.

historical development, as from a conviction of the authority attached to Christian poetry. Gregory had refused to comprise under the rules of Donatus 'the words of the Heavenly Muse'; and the same principle had already been applied by Bede to matters of orthography. He had admitted as of equal validity words drawn from writers sacred and profane alike; and on questions of word-form the Scriptures were for him the final authority.

Useful, however, as this exposition of metrical technique was for contemporary readers, the chief value of his treatment of prosody for later ages lies rather in his concluding remarks on rhythmical verse. Here, as elsewhere, he embodies material from an earlier scholar, in this case, Victorinus; and the passage is taken over by Bede practically as it stands. Thus rhythm, it is explained,[1] is like metre, in that it is a harmonious arrangement (*modulata compositio*) of words, attained, not by metrical law, but by a recurrence of syllables (*numero syllabarum*) satisfying to the ear, as in the songs of popular poets (*carminum vulgarium poetarum*). There can be rhythm, it is added, without metre; but no metre without rhythm. In other words, metre is system (*ratio*) resulting in harmony, whereas rhythm is harmony without system. At the same time, in rhythm a certain element of system may often be found, resulting not from controlling law (*artifici moderatione*) but from the nature of sound-qualities and harmony itself (*sona et ipsa modulatione ducente*); and this effect popular poets were said to achieve of necessity somewhat crudely (*rustice*), trained poets more expertly (*docte*). This, then, is Bede's statement on rhythm as distinguished from metre; and in thus emphasising the principle laid down by Victorinus that verse-forms based on quantity were not the only kind, Bede calls attention to a new poetic device that had already established itself in the fourth century, and had entered largely into Christian poetry. The innovation had come about primarily through the decay of classical Latin, and the loss of the distinction between long and short syllables. With the partial breakdown of classical artifice, however, the earlier principle of linguistic vitality (i.e. accent) was once more revived. It had characterised Latin popular poetry even in classical times;

---

[1] § 24. See also C. S. Baldwin, *Medieval Rhetoric and Poetic*, p. 111.

it still survived in the verses of *vulgares poetae*; and from the fourth century onwards a new dignity was acquired by this accentual verse. To it was given the name of *rhythmus* as distinguished from *metrum*, which stood for quantitative verse; though *rhythmus* might also include verse in which classical forms were adopted, but without the observance of quantity. Such then was the new verse to which Bede gave his approval as a valid and effective poetic medium. And these remarks he follows up with an appreciation of Ambrosian hymns, commending especially that stately hymn which begins, with a defiance of strict numbers, *Rex aeterne Domine Rerum creator omnium*. Judged by classical rules such verse was inaccurate. Yet Bede finds in it much that was pleasing and effective; and in the approval he thus gives to Christian rhythmical verse he was incidentally recognising an important literary development of his age—the establishment of a versification which was ultimately to play a great part in modern poetic expression.

Hardly less important was Bede's attempt to deal with another section of grammatical studies in his treatise on the use of figurative expression in the Bible. Here again his main object was the elucidation of Christian literature; for, as Cassiodorus had pointed out, many things in the Scriptures had been presented in images; and since a term misunderstood meant a falsification of the word of God, a correct understanding of such passages called for some knowledge of tropes and figures. Apart from this, figures at the time were regarded as essential elements of poetry; and Bede further justifies his study on the ground that figures existed in the Scriptures before the grammarians drew up their theories.[1] For his list of figures and tropes he draws on Donatus and Isidore.[2] Hence his particular classification of figures (*schemata*) and tropes (*tropi*); the former relating to changes in the order of words, the latter, to changes of meaning. It was a distinction that had been discountenanced by Quintilian, though retained and expanded by later grammarians; and Bede adheres closely to the later tradition. To begin with, he deals with seventeen figures,[3] including *prolepsis, anadiplosis, hypozeuxis,* and the like—

---

[1] Halm, *op. cit.* 607.     [2] *Etym.* i, 36–7.     [3] Halm, *op. cit.* 608–11.

terms more or less unmeaning to modern readers, though there
are others more familiar. Thus the various effects of repetition
are pointed out. There may, for instance, be repetition of a
word (*epizeuxis*) as in 'Comfort ye, comfort ye, my people';[1]
or repetition of a word at the beginning of different verses
(*anaphora*);[2] or again repetition of an initial word at the end of
a verse (*epanalepsis*), as in 'Rejoice in the Lord always, and
again I say rejoice'.[3] Then, too, the effective use of many
conjunctions (*polysyndeton*) is pointed out;[4] as is also the effect
of their omission (*asyndeton*).[5] Elsewhere the conclusion of
phrases with similar endings (*homoeoteleuton*) is noted, as in
*Melius est a sapiente corripi quam stultorum adulatione decipi.*[6] And
again, instances are given of play upon words (*paronomasia*),
as in *in te confisi sunt et non sunt confusi*;[7] or in *expectavi ut faceret
iudicium et ecce iniquitas, et iustitia, et ecce clamor.*[8] In the latter, so
Bede subtly explains (with the help of Jerome), the play of
words occurs in the Hebrew original, that is, between *iudicium*
(Heb. *mishpat*) and *iniquitas* (Heb. *mispah*), and *iustitia* (Heb.
*sedaqah*) and *clamor* (Heb. *se'aqah*).

Yet more detailed is Bede's exposition of tropes in the Bible.
The thirteen kinds mentioned by Donatus he expands to twenty-
eight by means of further refinements and subdivisions derived
from Isidore.[9] Thus among others is included the use of
*metaphora* which he illustrates by 'the wings of the morning',[10]
and 'who hath measured the waters in the hollow of his hand'.[11]
An expression embodying the part for the whole (*synecdoche*) is
likewise noted and illustrated by the phrase 'The Word was
made flesh';[12] while as an instance of *onomatopoeia* is given the
well-known phrase 'as sounding brass or a tinkling cymbal'
(*ut cymbalum tinniens, clangor tubarum*).[13] *Periphrasis*, too, is included, that device of circumlocution which, we are told, may
either add dignity or gloss over indecencies of expression. As
an instance of the former is quoted 'a building of God, an
house not made with hands, eternal in the heavens';[14] while
the latter is illustrated from St Paul's description of morals at

[1] *Isaiah* xl, 1.      [2] *Ps.* xxvii, 1.      [3] *Phil.* iv, 4.      [4] *Ps.* xli, 2.
[5] *Ps.* lxvi, 2.      [6] *Eccles.* vii, 5.      [7] *Ps.* xxii, 5.      [8] *Isaiah* v, 7.
[9] *Etym.* I, 37.      [10] *Ps.* cxxxix, 9.      [11] *Isaiah* xl, 12.      [12] *John* i, 14.
[13] 1 *Cor.* xiii, 1.      [14] 2 *Cor.* v, 1.

Rome.[1] Then there is the device of exaggeration (*hyperbole*), of which the passage 'swifter than eagles, stronger than lions'[2] is quoted as an example; or again, *allegoria*, with its suggestion of a hidden meaning, seen for example in 'Look on the fields for they are white already to harvest'.[3] Closely akin to *allegoria*, however, are said to be other tropes such as *ironia*, which is illustrated by Elijah's scoffing reference to Baal, 'either he is talking,... or peradventure he sleepeth, and must be awaked'.[4] Another trope of the same kind is *aenigma*, an obscure form of allegory, as represented in 'the wings of a dove covered with silver and her feathers with yellow gold'.[5] Other kindred devices also noted are *paroemia*, the use of proverbial utterance, as 'Is Saul also among the prophets?';[6] or again *sarcasmos*, as in 'He saved others, himself he cannot save';[7] and among the last to be mentioned is *parabola*, a comparison of dissimilar things, as in 'the kingdom of heaven is like to a grain of mustard-seed'.[8]

These remarks on prosody and figurative expressions may therefore be said to constitute the main substance of Bede's teaching in the sphere of literature. Scattered throughout his works, however, are other details of interest which also call for passing mention. In the first place, reference has already been made to his note on the poetic 'kinds',[9] which he takes over from Diomedes;[10] first, the dramatic 'kind', in which persons are introduced speaking without the interlocution of the poet, then the narrative 'kind', in which the poet alone speaks, and thirdly, the mixed 'kind', in which both the poet and his characters speak. It is true that Bede's object here is to show that all three 'kinds' are present in Biblical literature; that *The Song of Songs* is of the nature of a drama, that *Ecclesiastes* and the *Wisdom of Solomon* are narrative poems like that of Lucretius, and that *Job* is of the mixed 'kind' like the *Odyssey* or the *Aeneid*. But whatever may be thought about the justice of his comparisons, it is not without its interest that here is the first reference to the literary 'kinds' made by an English scholar.

[1] *Rom.* i, 26.  [2] 2 *Sam.* i, 23.  [3] *John* iv, 35.
[4] 1 *Kings* xviii, 27.  [5] *Ps.* lxviii, 13.  [6] 1 *Sam.* x, 12.
[7] *Matt.* xxvii, 42.  [8] *Matt.* xiii, 31.  [9] *On the Met. Art,* § 25.
[10] See p. 31, *supra.*

Concerning Biblical literature he has also further notions; that *Job* for instance was originally written mostly in hexameter verse, and that Hebrew writers (not the Greeks) were the discoverers of such devices as figures and tropes.[1] Such conceptions were lacking in historical truth; but they formed part of the accepted learning of the time, being borrowed from Jerome and others. Apart from this, there is also abundant evidence that Bede accepted the doctrine of the allegorical interpretation of Biblical literature. In one place he describes the process as 'a stripping off the bark of the letter to find a deeper and more sacred meaning in the pith of spiritual sense';[2] and his *Commentaries* are full of such interpretations, revealing a three-fold and sometimes a four-fold sense of Scripture. Nor must we overlook his references to vernacular poetry, and in particular his account of the 'divinely-inspired' Caedmon,[3] the earliest reference to the cultivation of poetry in England. As was shown by his remarks on rhythm, and by his own contributions in that measure, Bede had no pedantic scruples about forms of classical verse devoid of quantity; and he gives evidence of a like broad-mindedness in commending the efforts of the Old English poet in the native alliterative measure.

From what has now been said of Bede's literary theorising it is evident that with him critical activities in England really begin. That his efforts, moreover, were of a modest and limited kind is equally obvious. His elementary teaching on metre, figures and the like, do not take us far in an appreciation of the sources of literary excellences; and except for his recognition of an important change in the prevailing verse-systems, he has but little of interest in the way of doctrine for modern readers. At the same time the historical interest of his teaching is considerable; for it affords a valuable insight into the critical doctrine and method current at the time. With him is inaugurated, for example, the tradition of grammatical study in England, which for centuries was to remain the chief avenue to the understanding and appreciation of literature; and his work supplies the earliest instance of that concern with the

---

[1] *On the Met. Art*, § 25.
[2] Pref. to *Commentary on Ezra* (Giles, VIII, 360).　　[3] *Eccles. Hist.* IV, 24.

more formal aspects of poetry, which was to be a feature of later studies throughout the Middle Ages. Then, again, to his task he brought the learning of fourth-century grammarians, the representatives for the time being of classical tradition in literature; and with them he shares an imperfect conception of that tradition. Viewing ancient literature through the eyes of Donatus and others, he is limited in his teaching to their particular doctrines, while his methods are also confined to their systematic codifications of art. Apart from this his theorising is further influenced by his monastic environment and training, which supplied an inadequate perspective of earlier literature at Rome. Thus to Christian poetry he attached an exaggerated importance on account of its subject-matter; whereas such classical literature as came within his ken he failed to value adequately because of its pagan spirit. Most of his illustrative passages are taken from Christian poets, notably, Sedulius, Prosper, Juvencus, Prudentius, Fortunatus, Arator; and though references are made to Virgil, Lucan, and Terence, the poems of P. Optatianus Porphyrius he refuses to consider, because of their pagan character (*quia pagana erant*). The truth was that as yet there existed no idea of classical standards in literature. Augustine and Prudentius were to him models for imitation as suitable as Cicero and Virgil, the former being described as *moderni, recentiores*, the latter as *antiqui, veterani*.

Yet in spite of all limitations Bede stands for something positive in critical history. His enthusiasm for letters, his disciplined and concrete studies, and the freshness with which he invests such knowledge as was available, all these are evidences of a new spirit stirring. Nor did he fail to inculcate something of the ancient literary tradition, more especially in his good sense and the clearness of his style; while the false rhetoric of Hisperic Latinity he in some measure counteracted, in his efforts ' to express statements tersely ', on the ground that 'plain brevity rather than prolix disputation is wont to stick in the memory '.[1] That he fails to deal with problems of the native literature was perhaps inevitable; for his scholarship, newly acquired, was confined to academic grooves, and he

[1] See A. H. Thompson, *Bede*, p. 155.

lacked the qualities needed for judicial criticism. He is the first, however, to attempt an appreciation of Biblical literature; and his efforts, though formal and mechanical, are not without their interest to-day. He further enlisted grammar in the service of religion; a task of piety in keeping with the rest of his literary labours. And what is more, he helped to bridge the gap between antiquity and the Middle Ages. Fulbert of Chartres, for instance, was still making use of his works on literary theory in the eleventh century; by Roger Bacon he is described as *literatissimus in grammatica*;[1] and for centuries to come his influence was felt in the schools of the West.

For the next attempt to deal with literary matters we must turn to the work of Alcuin (735–804), yet another product of the Northumbrian revival of learning, and one who, like Bede, was to achieve a European reputation. Already during Bede's lifetime there had come into being a cathedral school at York, which, rivalling the fame of Canterbury and Jarrow, soon became in its turn a centre of learning, characterised by an unselfish devotion to letters. It was there, under archbishop Egbert, a pupil of Bede, that Alcuin was educated, receiving instruction in the Liberal Arts, and acquiring vast stores of learning from the famous York Library,[2] a collection unrivalled at the time, though destroyed by the Vikings in 867. As in the previous generation, Latin culture was still the sole subject of study at York; but the eighth century was to witness fresh interests and activities, seen first in the emergence of a native English literature, and again in the missionary work of Boniface (678–755) in Germany. It was towards the close of the seventh century, for instance, that English poetry had begun with Caedmon, and that *Beowulf* most probably had assumed written form, to be followed a generation later by Cynewulf's Christian verse, all of which constituted a development of vernacular literature unparalleled at the time in any continental country. And further evidence of the growing vitality of the native spirit is to be found in the spread of Anglo-Saxon culture

[1] *Opus Minus* (Rolls Series), ed. J. S. Brewer, p. 332.
[2] For details of the Library see Alcuin, *Versus de Sanctis Eboracensis Ecclesiae*, vv. 1535 ff. (*Poetae Latinae Aevi Carolini*, I, 203); also A. F. West, *Alcuin*, pp. 34–5.

abroad by Boniface and his English priests, whose work left definite traces on Germanic life and civilisation, influencing indirectly both its language and literature,[1] founding schools at Fulda and elsewhere, while also preparing the way for an alliance between the Pope and the Frankish rulers. With such developments as these, however, Alcuin was not concerned; his interests from the first were centred in Latin culture, and it is as one of the transmitters of ancient learning that he figures in the history of literary theorising.

Of the story of his life-work the details have often been told. His meeting with Charlemagne at Parma in 780, his consenting to take part in the revival of learning in Gaul, and his subsequent labours, first at Aachen at the court school (782), and later on at Tours (796)—these are familiar facts, but none the less worth recalling, since they conditioned his work in education, and incidentally in literary theorising. Charlemagne's aim was none other than a revival of letters throughout his wide dominions, which in 800 embraced practically the whole of Western Christendom. By that date the earlier educational system of Gaul had completely disappeared. The Frankish clergy had shared in the decline of the Merovingian dynasty; and in the famous proclamation of 787 (drawn up probably with Alcuin's aid) Charlemagne had outlined his scheme, which had for its main object the inculcation of right speaking as well as right living. Noting the prevalence of illiteracy everywhere, he feared that without skill in letters the Scriptures would not be understood; and he exhorted all men therefore to submit to the proper discipline, so as to be able to read in their spiritual sense those 'images, tropes and figures' of which the sacred pages were full. This, 'the first general charter of education for the Middle Ages', explains likewise the animating purpose of Alcuin's activities. To him are attributed numerous works on the Liberal Arts written for Charlemagne's school; and among others are the treatises *On Orthography*,[2] *On Grammar*,[3] and *On Rhetoric*.[4]

---

[1] See Braune, *Beiträge zur Geschichte der deutschen Sprache*, XLIII (1918), 361–445.

[2] Keil, *op. cit.* VII, 295–312; Migne, *P.L.* (vols. C and CI), 901–19.

[3] Migne, *P.L.* CI, 847–901.      [4] *Ibid.* 919–49; Halm, *op. cit.* 523–50.

It is in these works that Alcuin's contribution to literary theorising will therefore be found; and elementary and even trivial as in places it appears, out of all proportion to the great reputation of the writer, it is nevertheless not without its interest in historical perspective. Of the work *On Orthography*, in the first place, but little need be said; like Bede's earlier production, it was a concession to the widespread illiteracy of the age. A short manual, with a list of words drawn partly from Bede's treatise, its main objects were to secure accurate spelling and the proper use of Latin words, while at the same time attempting to free Latin from its many barbarisms. Etymological explanations are given, often of a startling kind, as when *caelebs* (bachelor) is defined as one who is on his way to heaven (*ad caelum*). Yet the treatment is not without a certain philological interest; it throws light on the condition of Latin, at a date when the *lingua Romana* was in process of forming, the earliest extant specimens of which have come down from the century following.

Nor can the treatise *On Grammar* be said to possess any great substantial value, apart from the light it throws on the educated intelligence of the time. Its elementary character, to begin with, is shown by its catechetical form, the work consisting of a dialogue between a young Saxon and a young Frank, with occasional interpolations of *Magister* (the author himself). By way of introduction, Alcuin opens with some remarks on the value of the Seven Liberal Arts. They are described as the seven pillars of the House of Wisdom, the seven steps to ascend to the heights of Theology, in accordance with Solomon's statement in *Proverbs*.[1] And here, in giving Biblical sanction to such study, Alcuin is modifying the position of earlier teachers like Augustine, who had accepted the Arts merely as a secular, though useful, means for the interpretation of Scripture. In this way, it has been pointed out,[2] 'the proscriptive utterances of Tertullian' were fairly met; though echoed repeatedly down through the Middle Ages, they never again dominated the practice of the Church. When he turns to deal with grammar as one of the Arts, Alcuin follows closely Donatus, Priscian and

[1] ix, 1.    [2] A. F. West, *Alcuin*, p. 97.

Isidore, presenting their material in a fashion adapted to 'those who had but lately rushed upon the thorny thickets of grammatical density'. Words, syllables and letters are treated at some length; and a conventional definition of grammar follows. It is described as 'the science of letters, the guardian of correct speaking and writing, founded on nature, reason, authority and custom';[1] and its study is divided into twenty-six parts. The rest of the work is occupied with expositions of the parts of speech, figures and the like, into which many fanciful etymologies enter, as when 'feet' in poetry are said to be so called because 'metres walk on them'. The limitations of the work are therefore obvious; and chief among them is the narrow conception of grammar it embodies. To earlier scholars grammar had been the art which taught not only *docte scribere legereque* but also *erudite intelligere probareque*. It had represented what was in fact a critical study of literature; and Cassiodorus had prescribed the reading of 'illustrious poets and orators'. Even Bede had employed grammar as a means of furthering an appreciation, if not of ancient, at least of Biblical and Christian, literature. With Alcuin, however, it becomes a barren science, a technical and mechanical exercise dissociated from all literary interest. In one place, it is true, he concedes that 'fables and histories' traditionally belonged to the sphere of grammar; but he fails to treat that aspect of the subject. With him, in short, the divorce between 'authors' and the 'Arts' is practically complete.

Of greater historical interest, though still wanting in intrinsic merit, is Alcuin's work *On Rhetoric* (793), which was written abroad on his return to Frankland after a short stay in England. Its immediate occasion was a request from Charlemagne for instruction, not in oratory, but in the art relating to the conduct and settlement of civil disputes which were incessantly forthcoming in Imperial affairs; and Alcuin's response took the form of a summary account of the teaching on rhetoric then available, that study which under the Empire had not infrequently been narrowed down to a treatment of *quaestiones civiles*.[2] For his main outline and substance he drew on Isidore and

---

[1] Migne, *P.L.* CI, 857.          [2] See p. 25 *supra*.

also Cicero's *De Inventione*, an early and immature work which represented merely an epitome of the teaching prior to Cicero's day, and contained nothing of his later and more suggestive doctrines. In adapting this material for his particular purpose Alcuin once again makes use of the dialogue form, Charlemagne and Alcuin himself being the interlocutors. Illustrations, moreover, are taken from both classical and Scriptural sources; and the discussion is concluded by an exposition of moral virtues, as being closely bound up with skill in speaking.

It is in the main body of the work, however, that the historical interest chiefly lies; for here will be found a summary of pre-Ciceronian rhetorical theory. Thus Alcuin begins by defining rhetoric as the art of speaking well (*bene dicendi scientia*);[1] after which reference is made to the civilising effects of rhetoric, the power of speech being said to distinguish man from beast. Then follow the definitions and classifications of earlier teachers. In the first place rhetoric is said to consist of five elements or qualitative parts; that is, *inventio, dispositio, elocutio, memoria, pronuntiatio*.[2] It is further described as of three kinds, the forensic, the deliberative and the epideictic;[3] and examples of the respective kinds are indicated in St Paul's defence before Felix,[4] the opposing counsels of Ahithophel and Hushai to Absalom,[5] and the divine acceptance of Abel's offering.[6] The six divisions or quantitative parts of a speech are also enumerated, including *exordium, narratio, partitio*[7] and the rest. Then comes a treatment of the several elements of rhetoric. In the first place the finding of argument (*inventio*) is treated at some length; though equally significant is the fact that the arrangement of that material (*dispositio*) is lightly passed over. A disquisition on style (*elocutio*) is subsequently given, together with some remarks on memorising (*memoria*) and delivery (*pronuntiatio*);[8] and of all these sections that on style is perhaps the most interesting, embodying as it does many of the earlier commonplaces. Thus passing rapidly over the need for the

[1] c. 3.  [2] c. 4.  [3] c. 5.
[4] *Acts* xxiv.  [5] 2 *Sam.* xvi, 15.
[6] *Gen.* iv, 4.  [7] c. 19.
[8] cc. 39, 41; c. 39 contains a passage from Cicero's *De Oratore*, i, 18; c. 41 a passage from i, 132 of the same work.

observance of grammatical rules and the use of plain (*aperta*) words, Alcuin states that style in general was adorned by words single and in combination.[1] The choice of words, to begin with, was to be governed by the practice of the ancients. Rare words and words with unpleasant associations were therefore to be rejected, preference being given to well-sounding words and words *electa et illustria*; and the use of figures such as metaphor was also commended. In the use of words in combination Alcuin notes certain vices which were to be avoided; hiatus, for instance, or again, undue repetition of syllables, as in *ut prima mater*. Among the other precepts of style laid down by Alcuin is his reiterated injunction regarding the observance of *decorum*.[2] This quality, he states, was to characterise both thought and expression; it was as essential in speech as in the conduct of life (*ut vitae quid deceat considerandum*). 'In speaking, as in walking', he adds,[3] 'it is good to go gently (*clementer*) without leaping or delaying'; and he urges the observance of the ancient dictum *ne quid nimis*, since whatever was beyond measure (*modum excedit*) was a vice. Elsewhere, again, he stresses the need for constant practice, without which, he held,[4] neither inborn talent nor the wisest teaching could do much. Moreover, in all arts, he stated, practice gave confidence and led to consistency; and without these qualities no advance in skill was possible. This, then, was the main substance of Alcuin's teaching on rhetoric; and that it was adapted to his Frankish readers is plain, not only from its elementary character, but also from the importance attached to the moral aspects of the literary training, which are emphasised in the concluding discourse on the cardinal virtues.

Such then was the gist of Alcuin's teaching as a literary theorist; and his work was evidently of a preparatory kind, with but slight bearing on literature itself. That he had arrived at no definite conception of the inherent value of literature or of the special merits attached to the earlier classics, so much at least is suggested by references here and there in his *Letters*. He himself had written some amount of Latin verse; Virgil at one time he had regarded as a model for sacred poetry; and in one place he commended the reading of the classics as a

cc. 37–8.      [2] c. 38.      [3] c. 43.      c. 42.

means of acquiring elegance of style. In practice, however, he makes but little use of literary material in his grammatical and rhetorical studies; and, moreover, it is clear that he shared in the prejudices of the early Fathers where pagan literature was concerned. Thus, in spite of his earlier love for Virgil (*Vergilii amplius quam Psalmorum amator*),[1] on one occasion he reproves a friend for too intimate an acquaintance with the *Aeneades*[2] (*sic*); and in decrying the luxuriance of Virgil's language, he adds, that 'the sacred Books are sufficient for you'. Then, too, he apparently condemns the heroic themes of Old English poetry when he asks 'What has Ingeld to do with Christ?' (*Quid Hinieldus cum Christo?*).[3] Here, however, he is palpably adapting the familiar phrase of Tertullian; and the reference, strictly speaking, is not to Old English poetry as such, but rather to its cultivation in monastic communities. A canon of 747 had required that monasteries should not be the homes of poets, musicians, and comedies; and here Alcuin is admonishing the clergy *in sacerdotali conuiuio* against mingling songs on sacred and profane subjects. Even on such occasions, he urges, their concern should be with *sermones patrum* and not with the popular lays (*carmina gentilium*) of ordinary revellers.

In attempting an estimate of Alcuin's contribution as a literary theorist it is important to bear in mind contemporary conditions, the state of learning and the intellectual darkness which then prevailed. Judged by those standards his work is by no means inconsiderable; even though it does not attain the level of fourth-century scholarship, while a great gulf separates it from the critical achievements of classical antiquity. His aim was limited to that of inculcating correct reading and writing. In the first place he carried on the grammatical tradition of Bede, though in so doing he gave to that tradition a yet narrower interpretation; and at the same time he also introduced to his readers ancient rhetoric as represented by Cicero's *De Inventione*. It is true that the epitome of pre-Ciceronian doctrine thus presented was the least valuable part of the ancient teaching on rhetoric; that Alcuin's efforts moreover

---

[1] *Alcuin vita*, c. 1.        [2] *Ep.* CLXIX.
[3] *Letter to Hygebald, Bishop of Lindisfarne*, 797 : see H. M. Chadwick, *The Heroic Age*, p. 41.

were limited by ecclesiastical and political needs; and that his treatment was arid, technical, and full of puerilities. Yet the work was not without its significance. It represented for one thing the earliest direct contact of the Middle Ages with the teaching of ancient Rome. It also acquainted men anew with some of the classical commonplaces, such as the need for plainness and clearness of utterance, for skill in the choice and handling of words, or again, the importance of constant practice and the observance of *decorum*. And whereas these are fundamental requirements in any age, to Alcuin's generation, deficient above all in the sense of form, they undoubtedly came with special meaning and force. It is therefore in this adaptation of rhetorical theory to contemporary needs that Alcuin's main services were rendered; and it is not without its significance, further, that he wrote, not as Bede, with monks primarily in mind, but rather for laymen and men in public life, thus extending literary education to the secular sphere. This is seen more particularly in the attention given to forensic eloquence (*quaestiones civiles*), which he expounds in greater detail than any other branch of the subject. In his treatment, on the other hand, will be found no trace of originality, no new ideas; and since he includes much dead matter in his theorising, doctrines irrelevant to the main purpose, in the end he affords but a glimpse of the spirit of ancient culture. What he stands for in literary history is an intellectual force, one who quickened men's interest in letters at a critical juncture in the development of Western Europe; and his influence is seen in the long line of scholars he inspired, men like Rabanus Maurus and Servatus Lupus, who were to carry on the literary education of the West. With Alcuin, in short, may be said to have culminated the tradition of Northumbrian scholarship, the grammatical studies of Anglo-Saxon writers. An uncritical compiler of earlier literary theory, he extended in a sense the work of Bede, thus preparing the way for a more intimate study of literature; and in both may be detected the influence of Cassiodorus and Isidore, whereas that of Martianus Capella was to be felt more powerfully at a later date.[1]

[1] See pp. 100, 166, 168 *infra*.

# CHAPTER IV

## THE DAWN OF HUMANISM: JOHN OF SALISBURY

WITH the death of Alcuin the tradition of learning in England underwent a prolonged eclipse; and, in particular, the part played by Bede and Alcuin in the transmission of literary culture came abruptly to an end. Three centuries were to elapse before any serious contribution was made to the discussion of literary matters in England; and then, under the changed conditions of Henry the Second's reign, and as a result of influences from abroad, literary problems once again engaged the attention of English scholars. Concerning the causes of this long silence there is no need to say much. They are to be found in the political turmoil which prevailed with hardly a break from the beginning of the ninth century to the close of the eleventh; the outcome, first, of the Danish invasions and settlement (787–1017), and subsequently, of the Norman Conquest (1066) and its aftermath. Thus it was that the earlier centres of education, the monastic schools with their libraries, were now almost wholly destroyed, and the rudiments of culture, painfully acquired during the preceding centuries, were ruthlessly swept away by the Danish inroads. Of these changed conditions eloquent testimony is supplied by Alfred in the famous *Preface* to his translation of Gregory's *Pastoral Care* (890).[1] At the same time not without their significance were Alfred's attempts to educate his people by means of translations of the works of Boethius, Orosius and Bede; an educational movement, which in a different form was continued a century later, as part of the monastic revival inspired by Dunstan, Aelfric and others. Such efforts, however, were animated primarily by aims of a social or religious kind; the furtherance of literary culture at no stage can be said to have formed part of their plans. And this holds true in spite of notable developments in contemporary vernacular literature, of which *The Battle of Maldon*

[1] Ed. H. Sweet (E.E.T.S. 1871–2): also Sweet's *A. S. Reader*, pp. 4–7.

(991) and the *O.E. Chronicle* (892–1154) together with Aelfric's *Homilies* (991–4) were outstanding examples in both poetry and prose. One contribution of value to critical ideas there was, however, which dates from this period. It was Alfred's 'revolutionary' conception, incidentally made, of the need for translation in making known the teaching of the ancient world. In the *Preface* already mentioned he notes the example of the Greeks in translating the Hebrew scriptures, of the Romans also in turning into Latin certain works of the Greeks; and he therefore claims for Englishmen the same right of turning into their native language outstanding works of Latin origin. To this end he suggests the processes of both a literal (*word be worde*) and a freer (*andgit of andgiete*) interpretation;[1] and in so doing he not only inaugurated the many later discussions on the art of translation, but he also asserted the claims of English to recognition as a literary language long before its actual triumph. And both were achievements of a significant kind historically. For the rest, however, the truth remains that during these stirring centuries men's minds were for the most part engaged with urgent political and religious matters, or else with attempts at providing English reading for Englishmen. They had neither the time nor the inclination for speculations on literature, or for preserving the traditions of Latin scholarship inaugurated by Bede and Alcuin; and these conditions remained practically unchanged for some time after the Conquest.

It was not until the twelfth-century Renascence had dawned in Western Europe that the next contribution was made to literary discussion in England; and then it was forthcoming from that famous English man of letters, John of Salisbury (1110–80), friend and secretary of Becket, and one of the greatest scholars of the Middle Ages. With him, it is obvious, literary culture had entered upon a new phase; and in order to understand the significance of his work, some account must first be given of those cultural developments in Western Europe which had taken place in the meantime, and which in a large measure determined the conditions under which he wrote. To begin with, it will be found that the earlier tentative efforts

[1] Sweet's *A. S. Reader*, p. 7.

of scholarship in England had not been altogether in vain. As a result more particularly of Alcuin's work abroad, an intellectual revival took place throughout the vast dominions of Charlemagne, which, while dissipating the darkness of the Merovingian period, was instrumental also in transferring the primacy of letters from England to France and in a lesser degree to Germany. For the next three centuries, therefore, the chief agents in the spread of education were the monastic and cathedral schools scattered throughout the Frankish Empire, notably Fleury, Corbie and Ferrières in the West, Fulda, Reichenau, Trier and St Gall in the East. And although in the tenth century a decline set in, owing to the political confusion caused by the break-up of the Carolingian Empire, and by Scandinavian and Saracen invasions, yet the intellectual activities of these and other centres never wholly ceased. Then with the eleventh century came renewed life and the multiplication of schools in France. This was the period of the efflorescence of the famous school at Chartres, which marked a new stage in the advance of culture. In due course that school as a centre of learning was succeeded by the University of Paris (*c.* 1170); and with its establishment the educational movement of Charlemagne may be said to have fitly closed.

Equally interesting, however, was the nature of the education that was thus broadcast; for, from the ninth century onwards, sporadic attempts were made to free learning from the narrow limits within which it had hitherto been confined. The main instrument of education had been the Seven Liberal Arts. that scheme which was held to embody an indispensable minimum of knowledge, and was intended to supplant the study of the profane writers of antiquity. As early as the ninth century, however, the scope of this scheme was being slowly broadened. It was felt to be impossible to ignore those ancient writers on whose work the scheme was originally based; and already a new sense of the value of ancient literature was in process of forming. This was seen, for instance, in the teaching of Rabanus Maurus (776–856), the most proficient of Alcuin's pupils, and subsequently the distinguished abbot of Fulda. His innovation consisted in attaching to grammar something of its ancient scope and value; viewing it, that is, as primarily a preparation for the critical study of literature, and not, as it had been in the hands of Alcuin, a barren science of words devoid of literary interest. Like tendencies were also betrayed by his pupil, Servatus Lupus, whose later years were spent as abbot of Ferrières (c. 842–62). With him the study of Latin classical literature became a ruling passion; and abundant evidence of this enthusiasm is to be found in his *Letters*, which reveal a wide acquaintance with the ancient classics, and establish his right to be regarded as the precursor of the later Humanists. Nor in the generations that followed was this new literary spirit wanting. Fresh impetus was received in the tenth century from Bruno, archbishop of Cologne (d. 965), in Germany, and from Gerbert (950–1002), subsequently Pope Silvester II, in France; until, with the founding of the school of Chartres under Fulbert (d. 1029) and its later development under Bernard of Chartres (d. 1126), the value of classical literature, in itself and for educational purposes, seemed to be fully recognised.

At the same time, it should be added, this recognition of the value of classical literature was being fostered by yet other agencies, and notably by the attention given to the rescuing and copying of ancient manuscripts. Indeed it is not too much to say that the work thus done on Latin texts during the ninth and tenth centuries was of supreme and lasting importance, being instrumental in preserving for later ages much of the literary legacy of ancient Rome.[1] This task of copying had been made possible by the earlier instruction in orthography provided by Cassiodorus, Bede and others; and the work was carried on throughout the length and breadth of the Frankish Empire. Thus to Servatus Lupus and his circle of friends was due the important part played by France in the transmission of Latin classics. But similar activities were characteristic also of Germany; and certain notable works, including those of Tacitus, Statius, and Lucretius, would seemingly have perished, had it not been for the German manuscripts which date from

---

[1] By a curious coincidence it was during these same centuries that much of Greek literature was preserved by copyists at Byzantium.

this period. Nor can the results be otherwise described than as surprisingly good; and this was due in part to the energy and discretion shown in the choice of manuscripts for copying. Such texts as had survived the darkness of the Merovingian period were few and hopelessly corrupt; but now no effort was spared in seeking out reliable texts in Italy and elsewhere. Then, too, the accuracy and legibility of the copying are also noteworthy; for it was now that the clear 'Caroline minuscule' first came into use, with those forms from which sprang our modern script. To this period, therefore, an immense debt is owed;[1] and of the influence of this work on the period that immediately followed, there can also be no doubt. It is, in fact, only in the light of these activities that the twelfth-century revival of interest in ancient classical literature becomes really intelligible.

But while literary studies were thus slowly gaining ground and the way was being prepared for a sounder knowledge of classical literature, these same centuries witnessed other activities which tended to check this movement, and were to militate against the realisation of the hopes of these early scholars. Chief among these was the growing importance attached to dialectic or logic, which as one of the Seven Arts had everywhere been sedulously cultivated. Hitherto such teaching had been based on Boethius's translations of two of Aristotle's works on logic, his *Categories* and *De Interpretatione*; and in the hands of most writers it had assumed a lifeless and mechanical form. By John the Scot (Erigena) (*c.* 810–75), however, it was later on invested with new life and meaning, which were to influence the work of subsequent thinkers. With his voicing of the claims of reason as opposed to authority, and his opening up of the question of 'universals' with its far-reaching issues, the way was now prepared for an age of inquiry and discussion, for a revolution in the methods of theological study, in which logic was to play an ever-increasing part; and the effects are seen in the intellectual activities of the eleventh and twelfth centuries, which became predominantly speculative and contro-

[1] See F. W. Hall, *A Companion to Classical Texts*, pp. 87 ff.; also M. L. W. Laistner, *op. cit.* pp. 180 ff.

versial in kind. First Roscellinus (*d.* 1106), and still more
Abelard (1079–1142), were conspicuous in the application of
dialectical methods to the discussion of theological problems;
so that disputations, the use of syllogisms, and the marshalling
of arguments for and against this or that thesis, became everywhere the main concerns. Moreover, in the generation after
Abelard, the hitherto unknown books of Aristotle's *Organon*—
his *Topics* and *Analytics*—became for the first time accessible to
Western scholars. They were known for instance to John of
Salisbury; and they too gave fresh impetus to the New Logic,
as it was called. In short, the twelfth century witnessed a
triumph of the study of logic, with results that were lasting in
medieval thought. From this period emerged the new theorising
of Scholastic theology which was to absorb men's energies for
generations to come; while the Humanistic movement, with its
literary studies, received a check from which it was not to
recover until after the close of the Middle Ages.

Such then were the cultural conditions in Western Europe
up to, and including, the twelfth century, namely, a slow
awakening to the value of the literature of classical antiquity,
together with marked developments in the field of logic. And
now once again English scholarship re-entered the main stream
of European culture, to which, through the instrumentality of
John of Salisbury, it was to make its own special contribution.
For the renewal of critical activities in England at this date
there were many causes. Chief among these were the changes,
both political and social, which led to an era of progress and
reconstruction, together with a transformation of the intellectual
position. Thus with the Norman Conquest and the establishment of relations with France, England had begun to share in
that revival of learning, which, while characteristic of Western
Europe generally, had yet found its main inspiration in the
schools of France. At the same time wider intellectual horizons
were being opened up to English scholars. From being an
isolated island kingdom, England now became a great continental power, the greatest of Western powers in the reign of
Henry II (1154–89), whose rule extended from Scotland to the
Pyrenees; and this led to free and frequent intercourse with

foreign states, occasioned not only by Crusading ventures and pilgrimages, but also by embassies and diplomatic activities of various kinds. The effects are seen in the renewed vitality of intellectual and literary interests, which reached its culmination in the second half of the twelfth century. Now for the first time the literary output in England became one of a considerable kind, inspired no doubt by royal and aristocratic patronage, but to a yet greater extent by the spirit of the age, by that growing national consciousness which kept pace with the stirring events of the time. This at least must account in part for the appearance of those Latin Chronicles that illuminate this period; the work of William of Malmesbury, Henry of Huntingdon, and a host of others. Hardly less remarkable, however, were the satirical works of Walter Map and Nigel Wireker, with their searching analysis of men and things; the legal treatises of Ranulf de Glanville and Richard Fitz-Neale, with their records of constitutional principles and practices; or again, the new vogue of letter-writing, of which the *Letters* of John of Salisbury and those assigned (wrongly) to Peter of Blois were outstanding examples. Nor were there wanting signs of a new zeal for scholarship. At the court of Henry II, in the household of Theobald, archbishop of Canterbury, and at other cathedral centres there was to be found a brilliant array of scholars, men learned, acute and versatile; and they too, representatives of an eager and inquisitive age, bore witness to the vitality of the twelfth-century Renascence in England.

Of these Angevin scholars and writers, however, none was more distinguished than John of Salisbury,[1] by whom literary discussions were once more renewed, and Humanistic views regarding literature first propounded in England. For this task he had been well equipped by his early studies abroad (1136–48), notably at Paris and Chartres, where he came under the spell of Abelard and others, including teachers who preserved the traditions of Bernard of Chartres, the pious work of whom he commemorated in later writings. And for the rest of his days

---

[1] See Schaarschmidt, *Joannes Saresberiensis nach Leben und Studien* (1862); R. L. Poole, *Illustrations of the History of Medieval Thought*, pp. 201–25; H. Waddell, *John of Salisbury* (Essays and Studies, Eng. Assoc. XIII, 28–51).

he remained the central figure of English learning, a scholar richly endowed, and alive to all that was best in the intellectual movements of the age. At the same time he played an active and important part in public life. As secretary of archbishop Theobald (1150), and later of Becket (1162), he became immersed in ecclesiastical and political affairs, a wise and trusted adviser to those in power, a close personal friend of the English Pope, Hadrian IV, and a diplomat often engaged in missions both at home and abroad. With Becket he also shared the vicissitudes of fortune. Already in 1159 his friendship with the war-like chancellor had earned for him the king's displeasure; and in that year of enforced idleness he completed his *Policraticus*[1] and *Metalogicon*,[1] works dedicated to Becket, in which were enshrined his views on life and letters. Further offence against the king caused him subsequently to seek refuge in France (1163). He returned with Becket in 1170, was present at the murder in Canterbury cathedral, and finally ended his days as bishop of Chartres (1176–80), that city of dreams, from which had come his earliest inspirations.

For his contribution to the discussion of literary matters we must turn to the works already mentioned, both of which are written in the fluent Latin style of which he was master. Neither, it is true, has literature for its main theme. Both are, in fact, encyclopaedias of the cultivated thought of the age, embracing ancient and contemporary history, a treatise on logic, the earliest of medieval theories on government, some treatment of philosophical, moral and educational doctrine, besides caustic satire on court foibles and scholastic vagaries. As such, they are perhaps the most representative literary productions of the twelfth century, that most vital of medieval periods. At the same time it may be doubted whether any one aspect of these works has greater interest for later ages than that which is concerned with literature and literary theorising. Thus *Policraticus*, as its subtitle (*De Nugis Curialium et Vestigiis Philosophorum*) explains, is concerned primarily with the vanities of courtiers and the traditions of philosophers. It represents, in

[1] Ed. C. C. J. Webb, with Intro. and notes (1909, 1929), to which I am deeply indebted.

fact, a satire on courtiers (Bks. i–iii) followed by a treatise on morals (Bks. iv–viii), in which the principles of government and philosophy are expounded. At the same time it is also something more than this, in virtue of its underlying spirit and treatment. Medieval in its discursiveness, its use of digressions and episodes, it is nevertheless imbued with a new culture, as its author ranges freely among memories of antiquity, touches on matters of literary interest, or brings classical literature to bear at all stages of his argument. And the same spirit informs the *Metalogicon* which deals with another aspect of the intellectual life of the time. Here the ostensible object is a defence of logic; and the greater part of the work (Bks. ii–iv) is devoted to an analysis of Aristotle's *Organon*. Of yet greater interest for our present purpose, however, is the plea made throughout Bk. i for the study of grammar as a necessary preliminary to the study of logic. This implied the need, not only for a study of expression in words, but also for the study of literature as well; and here John of Salisbury's literary sympathies are most clearly revealed. To medieval readers the more elaborate *Policraticus*, with its political and moral teaching, made undoubtedly the greater appeal; but to later ages the *Metalogicon* is equally interesting, on account of its direct bearing on one of the most urgent intellectual problems of the day. From time to time the *Metalogicon* has been variously described; as 'the cardinal treatise of medieval pedagogy', or again, as 'the greatest defence of the scholar's religion that the Middle Ages produced'. That it is the first work written by an Englishman in which the spirit of Humanism appears cannot at any rate be denied; and that honour it shares in some measure with the *Policraticus*.

When we attempt to consider more closely the actual contribution of these works to critical thought we shall find their achievement to consist, first, in an attempt to claim for literature and literary study an essential place in a liberal education; secondly, in efforts made to expound those artistic principles that underlie good writing while also helping in an appreciation of literary values; and thirdly, in illuminating pronouncements on literature in general and on ancient classical literature in particular. And in view of the confused ideas concerning these

matters which prevailed at the time, the teaching thus submitted cannot be otherwise described than as of the first importance. Then, too, it should be added, this vindication of
literature and literary studies was in response to yet more urgent
needs. A growing appreciation of literature and a new sense
of the potentialities of logic had both alike been characteristic
of the ninth and following centuries; and now in the twelfth
century these developments had led to a conflict of educational
interests, the main question being the relative value of those
basic studies which had been comprised in the Trivium, namely,
grammar, rhetoric and dialectic. In the meantime rhetoric in
its ancient sense had ceased to be seriously studied; and the
dispute now centred round the studies of grammar and dialectic.
The ultimate issue was therefore whether education was better
served by a basis of grammatical and literary study, or whether
dialectic or logic in itself provided an adequate foundation;
and it is to this general question in the first place that John of
Salisbury addresses himself.

The problem, to begin with, was not without its difficulties;
for although logic had firmly established itself in the scheme
of things, had become in fact a recognised part of a liberal
education, there were yet certain grave abuses which passed
under the name of dialectic, and which threatened its value as
a serious study. First came the practices of Cornificius[1] and his
followers, who claimed to arrive at truth by the light of nature,
and whose activities took the form of mere futile displays of
casuistry and sophistry—a complete negation, in short, of good
sense and scientific reasoning. Then, too, there was the fruitless

---

[1] Of the identity of Cornificius nothing is definitely known. He may
possibly have been a monk named Reynold, the *Reginaldus monachus* mentioned in the *Metamorphosis Goliae Episcopi* (c. 1142), a poem attributed to
Walter Map, which treats of the state of learning *c.* 1139–42. There Reynold
is described as a contemporary, notorious for his noisy arguments, his
everlasting contradictions and studied obscurity of speech—qualities associated with Cornificius. Yet this identification is mere conjecture. John of
Salisbury does not supply the name of the heresiarch, but merely labels him
as 'Cornificius' (*Pol.* 388 a; *Met.* 827 d), one of the detractors of Virgil
mentioned by grammarians, or 'Lanuvinus' (*Pol.* 388 a), the envious rival
poet and detractor of Terence. See R. L. Poole (*E. Hist. Rev.* xxxv, 336–42);
*Latin Poems attributed to W. Mapes*, ed. T. Wright, pp. 21–30; also Roger
Lloyd, *The Golden Middle Age*, pp. 92 ff.

pedantry of the 'logic-choppers' (*nugiloqui ventilatores*),[1] men who, trained in the lore of the schools, nevertheless spent their days in debating trivial and useless questions, and in collecting differing opinions of various authorities, without ever arriving at definite results. In view of the sterility of such methods of study it was clear that a restatement of the case for logic was needed; and this is supplied by our author himself in his *Metalogicon*, where he concedes its claim as a basic element in an educational scheme.

At the same time there were not wanting those who attached primary importance to grammatical and literary studies, and who maintained that grammar was the portal to all the Liberal Arts, and that the study of ancient literature was a necessary preliminary to instruction in other branches of knowledge. Such views, it is true, were not everywhere acceptable. There were many who still nursed those prejudices against pagan literature which had come down from the early Fathers,[2] and had since been voiced by Alcuin, Odo of Cluni, and others. Echoes of these objections are still heard in the twelfth century, as when Honorius of Autun asks how the soul was profited by 'the strife of Hector, the arguments of Plato, the poems of Virgil or the elegies of Ovid';[3] or when Abelard, again, is found inquiring why bishops did not 'expel from the city of God those poets whom Plato forbade to enter into his city of the world'.[4] Elsewhere the mystic, Hugo de St Victor (*d.* 1142), describes ancient literature as merely an appendix to the more substantial Liberal Arts, the latter being to him serious (*seria*) and fundamental, the former merely amusing (*ludicra*), a pleasant way of smoothing the path to philosophy.[5] Or again, the futility of literary study is the theme of Peter the Venerable (*d.* 1156), abbot of Cluni, when, pointing out that the ways to happiness were otherwise found, he asks a correspondent why, 'vainly studious', he was 'reciting with the comedians, lamenting with the tragedians, trifling with the metricians, and deceiving with the poets?'[6] Yet strong as were the ancient

---

[1] *Met.* 864 b.    [2] See p. 17 *supra*.
[3] Pref. to *Gemma Animae* (*c.* 1120); see Sandys, *History of Classical Scholarship*, I, 618.    [4] *Theologia Christiana*, ii; see Sandys, *ibid*.
[5] *Didascalicon*, III, 4.    [6] Migne, *P.L.* CLXXXIX, 77 D; see Sandys, I, 620.

prejudices at this date, equally strong was the conviction that *grammatica* in its widest sense, including, that is, the study of ancient literature, was an indispensable element in a liberal education. As a ringing challenge, for instance, to twelfth-century scholarship came the oft-quoted dictum of Bernard of Chartres relating to the value of the writers of antiquity. 'The moderns are to the ancients', he had stated,[1] 'as dwarfs on the shoulders of giants' (*nani gigantum humeris insidentes*); and the spirit underlying this pronouncement was fitly enshrined in the literary tradition associated with Chartres. From yet other quarters came further evidence of this new sense of values. 'It is written', so writes a contemporary,[2] 'that knowledge is with the ancients. One does not pass from the shades of ignorance to the light of knowledge except by re-reading with affection the writings of the ancients.' Or again, 'in reading the ancients we revive and renew their most elegant thought, which time and the laziness of men have abolished or treated as dead'.[3] And with the views of this school of thought John of Salisbury was also in complete agreement; more especially as Quintilian (whose work he knew well) had assigned to grammar and literature an important place in his scheme of education.

To reconcile these conflicting views was therefore the task undertaken by John of Salisbury; and the solution he suggests is of the nature of a compromise. For while he stands, first, for a training in logic, he also advocates as a necessary preliminary the pursuit of grammatical and literary studies. This position he arrived at by an appeal to first principles, and to what he regarded as the fundamental needs of man. Thus Nature, he explains,[4] had endowed man with faculties of reason and eloquence, with the object of enabling him to rise to the highest things. By the exercise of reason man was said to attain to wisdom, whereas by eloquence he was enabled to make wisdom fruitful. Both faculties were therefore needed, and both called for systematic training. Skill in reasoning, however, was held to be best attained by the study of logic, the instrument for

---

[1] Cf. *Met.* 900 c; Peter of Blois, *Ep.* xcii; Neckam, *de Naturis Rerum*, c. 78.
[2] Peter of Blois, *Ep.* xcii.          [3] Migne, *P.L.* ccvii, 1127.
[4] *Met.* 825 c.

extending and testing all knowledge (*scientia inueniendi et . . . iudicandi*); and with John of Salisbury, accordingly, logic comes first—but not first in order of time. As a condition precedent for attaining skill in argument, he goes on to assert the need for speaking correctly and effectively; and skill in eloquence, he maintained, was best acquired by studies which gave control of speech, as well as that correctness and facility of expression without which logical activities were impossible.[1] It is therefore as an indispensable preliminary to the study of logic that he advocates the cultivation of grammatical and literary studies in their widest sense. And here he was forestalling the plea for the study of classical literature put forward a century later against the tyranny of the Arts by the French trouvère, Henri d'Andeli, in his lively poem, *The Battle of the Seven Arts*,[2] the precursor, if not the inspiration, of Swift's later work, *The Battle of the Books*.

Not content, however, with mere advocacy of a literary training, our author proceeds, in the second place, to bring to men's notice a body of theory calculated to revive the art of sound writing, while also conducing to a better understanding of what the ancients had written. His teaching on the art of expression in words, on the methods of attaining that 'eloquence', to which the ancients had attached such importance, is therefore a matter of considerable interest. With regard to the value of 'eloquence' he is as enthusiastic as the ancients themselves; indeed, effective speech he asserts to be one of the most potent factors in human life. He recalls, for instance, the ancient commonplace that 'eloquence' had been instrumental in founding cities and uniting peoples.[3] He quotes Horace to support the view that 'eloquence' comes second in order of things to be desired, that is, after 'right thinking' (*sapere*), but before fame, health or riches.[4] Or again, he describes it as an adornment of every phase of life, an unfailing aid to prosperity and power;[5] while he also recalls Cicero's statement on its transforming power, its faculty of rendering

[1] *Met.* 837 b.
[2] Ed. L. J. Paetow, with Intro. and trans. (Univ. of California Press); see also Sandys, *op. cit.* pp. 676–8, for a summary account.   [3] *Met.* 827 b.
[4] *Ibid.* 834 d; cf. Hor. *Epist.* 1, 4, 8–11.   [5] *Ibid.* 835 a.

the improbable probable, and of refining what was uncouth or terrible.[1] In short, Cornificius, he maintained, in opposing the study of 'eloquence' was in reality undermining human society.

He therefore insists anew on the need for a systematic study of the art of expression; and this he does in reply to the strictures of Cornificius, who had contended that 'eloquence' could not be taught, that it was merely a gift of nature, and that while rules were ineffective for this purpose, they also involved more labour than they were worth.[2] That natural gifts, in the first place, were necessary and even indispensable, this much our author readily concedes; without such gifts (*invita Minerva*), he explains, no advance in art was possible.[3] At the same time he denies that in themselves they were all-sufficient, since native powers might become ineffective through various causes; so that it was the function of art to assist nature and to help it to realise the fulness of its powers.[4] In support of his position he recalls the dictum of Horace that both nature and art were necessary for the writing of poetry;[5] and he further asserts that the naturally gifted man but seldom developed fully without some knowledge of art, whereas if genius were wanting, then art, he added, was all the more necessary.

Having thus established his basic ideas, our author proceeds to deal with his task in more detailed fashion, explaining first the various terms he employs. 'Eloquence', for instance, he briefly defines (here following Cicero) as 'skill in uttering appropriately (*commode*) what the mind wishes to express' (*expediri*).[6] Native genius (*ingenium*), again, he describes as a certain force implanted by nature in man, which influences all the activities of the mind.[7] To the explanation of 'art', however, he devotes rather more attention, drawing on Quintilian for that purpose, and defining it in general as 'theory or method (*ratio*) which briefly and in accordance with nature conduces to skill in things that are possible'.[8] Thus art, he explains, has its origin in nature, which inspires genius to certain activities

---

[1] *Met.* 835 a; cf. Cic. *Paradoxa Stoicorum*, Pref. § 3.   [2] *Ibid.* 833 c ff.
[3] *Pol.* 618 c.                                             [4] *Met.* 836 b.
[5] *Ibid.* 836 c; cf. Hor. *Ars Poetica*, 408–11.            [6] *Ibid.* 834 b.
[7] *Ibid.* 838 b.        [8] *Ibid.* 838 a; cf. Quintilian, *op. cit.* II, 17, 9 and 41.

of the mind. These activities without guidance, however, often take the form of laborious roundabout methods; and the function of art is to reduce such activities to rational form, to provide guidance towards the attainment of skill in this or that project, thus helping men to proceed more easily and correctly. Genius uninstructed, he adds, does not necessarily attain that skill; though nature suggests the methods by which art advances and is made perfect. It is by the cultivation of art that artistic skill is most surely acquired; and since nature, he reiterates, is the mother of art, contempt of art is none other than contempt of nature. Then, lastly, he calls attention to yet another fundamental factor, that is, the need for constant practice (*exercitium*). Thus genius, he shrewdly remarks, is rendered more acute by moderate exercise, though it may also be blunted by excessive toil;[1] and elsewhere he demands that all precepts of art should be accompanied by practice, if they are to be effective. In support of this view he quotes the author of *Rhetorica ad Herennium*,[2] adding that if precept and practice are dissociated, then practice without precept must at any rate be retained. At the same time he insists that both are really necessary. Improvement, he states, comes from practice, and perfection from art; and while art, he adds, is sterile without practice, practice without art is uncertain (*temerarius*) of result. Having made these statements our author has in effect presented to his readers some of the representative doctrines of classical antiquity. From Plato to Quintilian it had been maintained that the fundamental requirements for good speaking (or writing) were natural endowments (*natura*), a knowledge of art (*ars*), and constant practice (*exercitatio*); and these are among the general principles laid down in the *Metalogicon*.

Our author now carries his exposition one stage further by advocating in particular the study of grammar, which, as he points out, had been sadly neglected, in spite of the teaching of 'Donatus, Priscian, Isidore, our Bede',[3] and others. To their doctrines he makes brief reference; but into the study he brings new life and meaning, describing it as the foster-mother of literary study, and claiming for it the power of nourishing

---

[1] *Met.* 839 b.  [2] *Pol.* 618 b; cf. *ad Her.* I, i, 1.  [3] *Met.* 850 a.

infancy and of disciplining the mind. Its ultimate authority
he traces to nature; and in general its function is said to be that
of explaining what to avoid, and what to observe, in order to
attain a correct standard of writing. Among the faults to be
avoided, in the first place, was the use of corrupt diction or
barbarisms; and more than once our author quotes Caesar's
dictum in his *De Analogia*,[1] that 'as sailors shun a rock, so a rare
(*infrequens*) or unusual (*insolens*) word ought also to be avoided'.[2]
In matters of diction the ultimate authority he declares to be
Use or Custom; just as in legal affairs custom (*consuetudo*) is said
to be the best guide and interpreter. And he further reminds
his readers (here following Horace) that language is ever in a
state of flux; that words flourish, decay, and then come to life
again, if contemporary usage but wills it; and that in such usage
are vested judgment, authority and rule (*arbitrium et ius et norma*)
of a final and an absolute kind.[3] Equally serious, however, was
the use of solecisms, that is, defective expressions arising out of
faulty idioms or constructions; and these were also to be
studiously avoided. At the same time certain departures from
the normal mode of expression were said to be permissible when
properly employed, as, for instance, those unusual turns or
devices known as figures—metaphor, metonymy, synecdoche,
and the like. Such figures he describes, in the words of Isidore,
as 'vices used with propriety' (*vitia cum rationi*);[4] and their use
he justifies, either on the ground of necessity, that is, for the
sake of clearness, or again, as a means of adding beauty to
expression.[5] In verse more especially, he adds, such devices
give delight; and he recalls Augustine's description of them as
'the sweetest elements of poetry' (*carminibus suasissima condi-
menta*).[6] According to that same authority, however, they were
to be used with discretion; in ordinary speech they savoured
of ostentation, while in excess they were positively distasteful.
The correct employment of figures was thus held to be subject
to the strictest of laws, and their use in consequence was possible
only to the instructed. Moreover, some knowledge of those laws,

---

[1] See Gellius, *Noctes Atticae*, I, 10, 4.    [2] *Met.* 844 c; *Pol.* 748 c.
[3] Hor. *A.P.* 70-2.    [4] *Met.* 848 d; cf. Isid, *Etym.* I, 35, 7.
[5] *Ibid.* 845 b.    [6] *Ibid.* 849 a; cf. Aug. *de Ordine*, II, 4, 13.

it was added, was needed for a profitable reading of the Scriptures, seeing that figurative expressions abounded in the sacred text.

Of greater interest perhaps is our author's positive advice on the subject of good writing; for scattered throughout his works are numerous valuable precepts, many of which are drawn from Quintilian and others, though there are also important omissions. Thus characteristic of his teaching is his failure to emphasise the importance of sound subject-matter (*inventio*); or again, he refers but incidentally to the necessity for an orderly arrangement of ideas (*oeconomia*).[1] Both requirements were essential, according to ancient theory; and their omission at this stage is not without its significance. On the other hand his interest is practically confined to matters of style (*elocutio*); and here he recalls principles that are of definite and lasting value. He notes, for instance, that 'every language has its own idiom' (*ydiomata*),[2] its own mode of expression, and that he who writes in ignorance of this truth is like a magpie attempting human speech. Elsewhere he states, as Aristotle and Quintilian before him had stated, that 'the greatest virtue of speech is perspicuity and clearness of utterance';[3] and he calls attention to yet another ancient precept, namely, the need for an observance of *decorum* or propriety in expression. Thus in one place he asserts that 'the mode of utterance must be determined by the nature of the speaker, the quality of his hearers, the time and place of speaking, and the like';[4] or again, he states that 'he who adapts (*contemperat*) his words to the requirements of his theme and the occasion, observes the controlling rule (*modestissimam regulam*) of all eloquence'.[5] Apart from this he suggests as the equipment of a successful writer a rich vocabulary, fluency of speech, and ingenuity (*subtilitas*) of expression;[6] though in view of the characteristic verbosity of his age, he is careful to urge that such elements should be used with discretion. If discretion is wanting, he adds, all qualities run to excess, and the merits of ingenuity in particular are lost. And here he recalls the saying of the elder Seneca, that 'nothing is

[1] *Met.* 855 c.     [2] *Ibid.* 831 b.     [3] *Met.* 849 b.
[4] *Ibid.* 850 b.     [5] *Pol.* 664 a.     [6] *Met.* 865 a, b.

more distasteful than ingenuity where all is ingenious';[1] or again, the remark of the younger Seneca, that 'nothing is sharper than an ear of corn (*arista*), but then what is its use?'[2] Moreover, he points out that a flood of words is not everything. There are occasions, he states, when control must be rigidly exercised; and he quotes the saying of Sidonius Apollinaris, that 'It is no greater merit to have said what you know, than to be silent about things of which you know nothing'.[3] Again he urges that all irrelevancies of speech should be rigorously pruned, and such words alone be used as conduced to pleasure and profit, according to the Horatian formula. With younger writers, it is true, some indulgence was permissible in matters of style.[4] Just as their minds were to be nourished lest they became weak, so a certain prolixity and luxuriance might be condoned in their efforts to attain fluency and beauty of expression. But such defects were to be corrected later by constant filing; they were to form no part of the writing of maturity. For the rest, he advocates as a general guiding principle, widely current in antiquity, the need for the conceal-ment of all artistic devices. 'A display of art', he briefly explains,[5] 'is always mistrusted; success more readily attends the use of simple means.'

Such then was John of Salisbury's teaching on 'eloquence' or the art of good writing; and it represented something new in the history of English culture. Equally valuable, however, were his efforts to inculcate the value of literature, the third of the main objects he had in view; and indeed, nothing is more striking than the ardent enthusiasm with which he commends the literary legacy of the past to his readers. Of the limited sympathies of earlier ages, which saw in profane letters merely an aid to the understanding of the Scriptures or the defence of the Faith, there is little trace in his work. To him classical literature was a vast treasure-house of spiritual quality, the only source at which could be satisfied his intellectual. aspira-tions; and with him, it may be said, a new attitude towards

---

[1] *Controversiae*, I, pref. § 21.  [2] *Ep.* LXXXII, § 24.
[3] *Met.* 865 d; cf. Sid. Ap. *Ep.* VII, 9, 5.
[4] *Ibid.* 932 b; cf. Quintilian, *op. cit.* II, 4, 4.  [5] *Ibid.* 912 a.

literature was made manifest. For the written word, to begin
with, he has a regard amounting almost to veneration. It is for
him a preservative of the past, a means of perpetuating former
glories; and to this 'eternising' function of letters he refers
again and again. Thus 'to no purpose', he states,[1] 'are great
deeds done...unless they are made to shine forth in the clear
light of letters'; or again, 'the fame of Caesar is due to Virgil,
Varus and Lucan, more than to the vast treasures of which he
robbed many cities'.[2] But while this power of rescuing from
oblivion men and things worth remembering is for our author
one of the chief claims of literature, at the same time he is not
unmindful of other values which were calculated to touch his
readers even yet more closely. He himself had found solace and
companionship in the classics, had loved them as Cicero before
him had done; and in one place, speaking of the manifold
delights of literature, he recalls (in terms reminiscent of Cicero)
that from that source were derived 'comfort in sorrow, recreation amidst toil, joy in poverty, moderation (*modestia*) in prosperity'.[3] It is thus as the outcome of his own experience that
he commends literature on account of its pleasure-giving
element; though he is also aware of the Horatian doctrine,
according to which the poet aimed at improving (*prodesse*) his
readers as well as at giving delight (*delectare*).[4] Elsewhere
importance is attached by our author to the influence of
literature on human character, and to the guidance it gives in
matters of conduct. Thus in one place he states categorically
that all writings were useless except in so far as they helped in
the affairs of life (*afferunt aliquod adminiculum vitae*).[5] Moreover,
an ability to philosophise he describes as a fruit of the right use
of literature;[6] and 'this always is to be sought from reading',
he adds,[7] 'that he who reads may become better in himself'.
Altogether then it is clear that literature for him was primarily
a means of arriving at truth or wisdom and of conducing to the
betterment of the whole man. And this view he further supports
by a reference to Horace, who claimed to have derived more

[1] *Pol.* 385 c. Professor Mountford suggests here a reminiscence of Horace,
*Od.* IV, 9, 25.
[2] *Ibid.* 769 a.    [3] *Ibid.* 386 a.    [4] *A.P.* 333–4; cf. *Pol.* 405 a; *Met.* 865 d.
[5] *Met.* 825 b.    [6] *Pol.* 661 a.    [7] *Ibid.* 650 a.

profit from his reading of Homer than from the teaching of the Stoics.[1] He likewise recalls Cicero's praise of poets, historians, and the rest; how they censured vice—but did not teach it— by means of examples more effective than any precepts;[2] while not without its interest is his illustration of this aspect of literature, when he comments at some length on one of the classical writers. In the *Eunuch* of Terence, he explains, almost all of human life is depicted (*fere omnium vitam expressit*);[3] and by his interpretation of the doings of Gnatho, Thraso, and the rest, he shows the work to be an illuminating study of the actual world of men.[4]

Cherishing then these views with regard to the nature of literature in general, it is no wonder that he pursues his theme further, in proffering advice as to the proper use of this material. That the reading of great literature (*lectio auctorum*) was essential for intellectual and spiritual growth he is firmly convinced. Without it, he asserts, no man could be called educated (*litteratus*);[5] and he quotes in support the saying of the younger Seneca, that 'leisure without letters spells death and burial to a man while yet alive'.[6] With regard to the scope of a man's reading, to that he would set no limit. He recommended that all literature should be read; even though a cursory reading of some works would suffice, while others, though suitable for stronger intelligences, had but little to offer to simpler readers. On the other hand, the works most to be valued were those which went to the strengthening of character, or else helped in the formation of style;[7] and in reading such works he advised (here following Macrobius) that 'men should imitate the bees, which pass freely from flower to flower, turning all to honey'.[8] Then, too, he has advice of a more practical kind to offer, when he recalls with approval the methods adopted by Bernard of Chartres in his *praelectiones* for cultivating a proper appreciation of literary values.[9] Thus he requires that literature should be

---

[1] *Pol.* 656 d; cf. Hor. *Epist.* I, 2, 1–4.
[2] *Ibid.* 656 c; the reference is possibly to Cic. *De re publica* (see Webb's note *l.c.*): cf. also p. 32 *supra*.
[3] *Ibid.* 711 b.      [4] *Ibid.* 716 a–719 a.      [5] *Ibid.* 657 a.
[6] *Ibid.* 388 d; cf. Sen. *Ep.* LXXXII, 3.
[7] *Ibid.* 659 d.      [8] *Ibid.* 660 a.      [9] *Met.* 853 c ff.

read with a critical eye alive to the main details of literary effects; the appropriate treatment of the matter in hand, the value of effective arrangement, the effects of particular words, tropes or figures, and the graces which resulted from luxuriance or restraint in expression. Too meticulous a reading, however, he condemned as time-wasting and savouring of pedantry. There were, he points out, obscure and irrelevant passages in most writings; and he recalls Quintilian's somewhat caustic dictum that 'there are some things which it is a merit in a teacher of literature (*litterator*) not to know'.[1] Nor was he wanting in further injunctions concerning what he regarded as the best methods of understanding various kinds of writings. Thus, in general, he insists that 'words should be gently handled, and not tortured like captive slaves, till they yielded meanings which they never had';[2] a condemnation of the forced interpretations sometimes read into texts. Elsewhere, after pointing out unedifying elements in classical literature, he proceeds to recommend that such works should be read with discrimination; in such a way, that is, that the deference paid to antiquity should not override good sense (*auctoritas non praeiudicet rationi*).[3] At the same time he recognises the necessity for interpreting the Scriptures in the four-fold sense expounded by Cassian; so that into Biblical passages might be read historical, allegorical, tropological and anagogical meanings.[4] Yet such methods, he added, were not always applicable; they could not be applied, for instance, to philosophical or educational works, which were always to be understood in a literal sense. Then, too, in connexion with controversial writings he quotes the teaching of St Hilary, that the meaning of a passage was often best perceived in the light of the context and the nature of the cause defended (*ex causis dicendi*).[5] Thus a superficial reading of patristic writings, he points out, often led to interpretations that were wholly misleading. So that altogether for

---

[1] *Met.* 855 d; cf. Quintilian, *op. cit.* 1, 8, 21.
[2] *Ibid.* 891 d.                 [3] *Pol.* 660 c.
[4] *Ibid.* 666 b. These different senses are well defined in the verses quoted by Webb (note *l.c.*) : *Littera gesta docet, quid credas allegoria, Moralis quid agas, quo tendas anagogia.*
[5] *Met.* 849 d.

the understanding of literature generally, constant tact and discernment were required on the part of those who read. 'No slothful reader', he asserts, 'can carry away the golden apples of the Hesperides.'[1]

Thus far our author has been introducing his readers to classical literature, explaining in general terms what it has to offer, as well as the most profitable methods of turning it to account. This he follows up with some account of the achievements of ancient writers, so that now practically for the first time a general acquaintance with classical literature becomes possible for English readers. For this task he was well equipped; even though his knowledge of Greek was negligible, and for information concerning Greek authors he depended either on Latin translations or on remarks made by earlier Latin writers. In Latin literature, on the other hand, he was extraordinarily well-read, being familiar with practically the whole range of classical and post-classical developments, with writers, that is, of both poetry and prose, extending from Terence and Cicero to Ausonius and the Latin Fathers.[2] Some authors, no doubt, he knew only by name; but equally certain is it that of many he possessed a first-hand knowledge, as is shown by the innumerable quotations drawn from their pages; though, here again, some may have been taken from *florilegia* or else from grammatical treatises. Occasionally, it is true, his knowledge is found to be imperfect. He confuses the two Senecas, for instance, in assuming the *Controversiae* and the *Letters to Lucilius* to have come from one and the same pen.[3] Elsewhere he wrongly attributes the *Ad Herennium* to Cicero,[4] in accordance with the view current at the time. On the other hand his knowledge at times is astonishingly wide and accurate. He had access, for instance, to a more complete version of the *Satyricon* of Petronius than was available to scholars of the early Renascence;[5] while his use of Quintilian's *Institutio* shows that he

---

[1] *Pol.* 660 d.

[2] There were gaps of course. Cicero's *Brutus*, for instance, was unknown to the Middle Ages, and *de Oratore* and *Orator* were available only in mutilated texts.

[3] *Met.* 865 b.                    [4] *Ibid.* 851 a.

[5] Cf. his ref. to Trimalchio (*Sat.* § 49) in *Pol.* 736 a.

was acquainted with sections of that work which were wanting in almost all manuscripts before Poggio's discovery of the complete text in 1416.[1]

Of his various pronouncements on classical literature, many are clearly borrowed from earlier authorities, and therefore represent no great exercise of literary judgment on his part. He describes Virgil, for example (here following Macrobius) as 'the most successful imitator of Homeric perfection';[2] Socrates, again, as having been 'the first to direct philosophy to the correction and formation of moral character';[3] while elsewhere he states less happily, on the authority of Jerome, that 'whole tragedies of Euripides consist of foul abuse of women'.[4] It is upon Quintilian, however, that he draws mostly for judgments of this kind; as when, for example, he describes Lucan as 'the most weighty (*gravissimus*) of poets',[5] and calls attention to the rhetorical quality of his style. In more than one place, again, he praises Aristotle for his charm of utterance (*suavitas dicendi*), in which he is said to have approached most nearly to Plato; and for this our author was also indebted to Quintilian,[6] whose statement to that effect (based possibly on Aristotle's lost *Dialogues*) he quotes at length in his *Metalogicon*.[7] Then, too, there is his glowing eulogy of Cicero, whom he describes as the glory of Latin literature, one who might be compared or even preferred to all that 'insolent Greece' could boast (*quicquid insolenti Graeciae eleganter opponit aut praefert*).[8] This judgment was, however, based on a passage in the *Controversiae*[9] of the elder Seneca; and incidentally, it is not without its interest in literary history. The phrase *insolenti Graeciae* seems later on to have caught the fancy of Ben Jonson; and he makes effective use of the expression in his well-known eulogies of both Shakespeare and Bacon.[10] Isolated judgments of this kind, however, do not represent the whole of our author's borrowings. Some-

---

[1] Cf. *Met.* 859 a; see Webb's note, *l.c.*
[2] *Pol.* 728 b; cf. Macr. *De Somnium Scipionis*, I, 7, § 7.
[3] *Ibid.* 644 a; cf. Aug. *C.D.* VIII, 3.
[4] *Pol.* 755 a; cf. Jer. *Adversus Jovinianum*, II, 48.
[5] *Ibid.* 811 a; cf. Quintilian, *op. cit.* x, 1, 90.
[6] *Ibid.* 648 b; cf. Quintilian, *op. cit.* x, 1, 83.
[7] 859 b.      [8] *Pol.* 449 a.      [9] I, pref. § 6.
[10] Cf. Ben Jonson, *Underwoods*, xii; *Discoveries*, § 72.

times he weaves together fragments taken from various sources; and his pronouncements on Plato and Aristotle afford examples of this more constructive treatment. Concerning Plato he writes in enthusiastic vein, though he was probably acquainted with but an incomplete translation of *Timaeus*, together with some passages of the *Republic*. Relying on Apuleius, however, supported by Origen, Jerome and Augustine, he attempts a survey of Greek philosophy, in the course of which Plato comes in for special treatment. Thus he praises the vigour of Plato's genius, his incessant study, the beauty of his character, the charm and splendour of his eloquence; and, continuing, he adds that 'Plato by these qualities was raised aloft to such heights of philosophy, that seated as it were on the throne of Wisdom, he has seemed to command, by a certain pre-ordained authority, all philosophers who came both before and after'.[1] Nor was his account of Aristotle less stimulating in kind; though here, too, while familiar with Aristotle's *Organon* in translation, he looks for his main details to Quintilian, Aulus Gellius, Valerius Maximus and others. Thus Aristotle is said to have treated all branches of philosophy, and to have been the first to distinguish between esoteric and exoteric studies.[2] Gifted in speech, but more richly endowed in understanding, he is credited with special skill in argument; so that in logic, it was claimed, he had no equal. That his work was infallible (*sacrosanctus*) or free from error, was however denied;[3] in matters of theology, it was said, he often went wrong. Nevertheless, as to the real greatness of Aristotle our author has no sort of doubt; and this he makes plain in unmistakable terms.. 'The light of the world', he states, 'seemed to be extinguished when Plato died....But when Aristotle came, a man of surpassing genius, he shone forth as the morning star, with his manifold precepts of philosophy, ... dispersing the mists of vision, and restoring to men the sight of truth.'[4]

While borrowed estimates such as these were not without their value in acquainting readers with certain aspects of ancient literature, more significant were those occasional judgments which were due to John of Salisbury himself, and were thus

[1] *Pol.* 644 a.    [2] *Ibid.* 648 a.    [3] *Met.* 932 a.    [4] *Pol.* 647 e.

the outcome of his own critical faculty. Evidence of independent judgment, to begin with, is forthcoming from his comment on the theory that Plato in his writings had been influenced by Jeremiah and other Hebrew prophets.[1] He concedes that there were points of similarity in the works in question; that in *Timaeus*, moreover, the doctrine of the Trinity had seemed to be hinted at. But the main hypothesis he briefly dismisses as improbable on chronological grounds. It is with the younger Seneca, however, that he is for the most part concerned; and what he aims at here is a defence of that philosopher against the strictures of Quintilian, and the disparagement of those of his contemporaries who followed Quintilian in this matter. Of all the ancient philosophers Seneca was the most accessible and familiar to the Middle Ages. Endeared to men of letters by his human note and his spiritual sympathies, so closely akin to Christian sentiment, he appeared to be one of the outstanding figures of antiquity, despite the detractions of so weighty an authority as Quintilian; and our author in more than one place takes up the challenge, attempting a corrected estimate of Seneca's performance in the light of his own reading. The main charges brought against Seneca were those formulated in a passage of Quintilian's *Institutio*, which is quoted at length in the *Policraticus*, and is referred to again in the *Metalogicon*.[2] There Seneca is censured for his epigrammatic and sensational style, which was said not only to have impaired the effectiveness of his teaching, but also to have rendered him a dangerous influence in matters of style. This indeed to Quintilian had been the head and front of Seneca's offending; though he also suggests a lack of critical power in philosophical discussion. For the rest, Quintilian had freely recognised Seneca's genius and learning, as well as much that was edifying and even admirable in his work. To this attack our author replies by a confident appeal to the judicious reader, insisting meanwhile on the elegance of Seneca's moral teaching in the *Epistles* and elsewhere, the influence of which, he claims, was greater than that of any other philosopher.[3] That Quintilian was the most

---

[1] *Pol.* 645 d; cf. Aug. *C.D.* VIII, 11.
[2] *Ibid.* 763 a ff.; *Met.* 852 b; cf. *Inst.* x, 1, 125–31.     [3] *Pol.* 763 a, 764 a.

competent of judges in matters of philosophy he is disposed to deny, great as were that writer's merits both as scholar and teacher.[1] On the other hand he emphasises the universal character of Seneca's teaching, its applicability to all departments of life. He even finds virtue in his ornate style (*comaticum genus dicendi*), with its brief and sententious forms of expression. Indeed in grace and range Seneca was said to have been surpassed by few, if any; 'no one who loved virtue and eloquence', adds our author, 'could fail to find pleasure in him'.[2] Nor was this all that was said on Seneca's behalf; though a claim to veneration on the grounds that he had won the friendship of St Paul, and had been reckoned a saint by Jerome,[3] is no longer tenable; since it rests on nothing more than a pious forgery, on fourteen letters, dating from the fourth century, which were held to have represented a correspondence between St Paul and Seneca. More relevant is our author's reply to yet another charge brought against Seneca, namely, that he had disparaged the work of grammarians—an attitude, we are told, which had encouraged Cornificius in his scorn of all serious studies.[4] That Seneca had condemned those immersed in 'the minutiae of the literary craft'[5] is readily conceded. But the explanation given is that he was concerned with matters more important, with the teaching of virtue and virtuous living;[6] and that philosophy was thus his main pursuit. Such then were the main points in our author's defence of Seneca; and as a comment on views current at the time, it is not without its interest. Moreover, if devoid of criticism of an aesthetic kind, it has at least this further value, that in venturing to dispute the opinions of established authority concerning ancient literature, John of Salisbury gives evidence of an independence of mind and judgment far removed from the idolatry of later centuries.

Equally interesting in this respect, however, are his remarks on contemporary men of letters. For while he protests that reverence and authority should primarily be attached to the ancients, he is conscious of merit in the works of his own day;

[1] *Pol.* 764 c.   [2] *Met.* 852 b, c.   [3] *Pol.* 763 b.
[4] *Met.* 852 b.   [5] Seneca, *Ep.* LXXXVIII, 5.   [6] *Met.* 852 c, d.

and in connexion with these he supplies some valuable judgments. Significant, in the first place, are his views concerning
the age in general; that it was above all an age of detraction,
a carping and a critical age[1]—a description that is borne out
by the numerous satirical works that were then appearing. Or
again, there is his analysis of the main defects in the writings
of his day. These he describes as ignorance of the truth, a
deceitful and an impudent assertion of what was false, and a
turgid mode of expression.[2] On the other hand he recalls with
respect the achievements of contemporary scholars, including
Bernard of Chartres, Gilbert de la Porrée, William of Conches,
Robert Pullus and others.[3] Of the attempts of Bernard of
Chartres and his disciples to reconcile Plato and Aristotle,
however, he does not approve; he suggests that 'they had come
late and laboured in vain to reconcile in death men who in
their lifetime had not agreed'.[4] In like fashion he comments on
the philosophical efforts of his day, pointing out that philosophy
was treated mainly as a matter of mere words, and that well-
worn questions were the themes debated. 'In the labouring of
these questions', he states, 'the world had grown old, and more
time had been spent on them than Caesar had given to mastering
and ruling the world.'[5]

Most striking of all, however, are his remarks on the activities
of the *Cornificiani*, that group of charlatans, who, first of the
race of English Philistines, constituted a threat to all ideals of
culture. Their ignorance, he points out, was only equalled by
their arrogance and insolence. All forms of mental training
they openly derided, covering with obloquy those who studied
ancient poets and historians, and promising meanwhile short
cuts (*tramites compendiosi*) to both philosophy and eloquence.[6]
Such men, adds our author, were as lightly instructed as those
fabled beings of old who came forth poets ready-made, after
dreaming on Parnassus or having drunk of the waters of the
Castalian fountain.[7] At the same time, we are told, this new
school prided itself on its various innovations. In short, it was

---

[1] *Met.* 823 a.    [2] *Ibid.* 826 a.    [3] *Ibid.* 832 a ff., 853 d ff.
[4] *Ibid.* 875 d.    [5] *Pol.* 664 c.    [6] *Met.* 828 d.
[7] *Ibid.* 829 d; cf. Persius, *Sat.* prol. 1 ff.; Martial, *Epig.* IV, 14, 1; Ben
Jonson, *Discoveries*, § 130.

their boast that they had made all things new. Thus we learn that by them grammar was renovated, dialectic changed, rhetoric despised, and fresh methods were introduced into other branches of study.[1] Then, too, they gloried in a mode of expression and a jargon (*sartago loquendi*) all their own. No statement, for instance, was complete without a stereotyped reference to 'reason' (*ratio*) or to what was 'fitting' (*conveniens*); while the use of plain and concrete terms was strictly forbidden.[2] And since every argument was preceded by a technical description of the argument employed, it was, adds our author, as if no one could write in verse without first naming the verseform he was using. With them, in short, it seemed that 'to write in artistic fashion and to write about art was one and the same thing' (*ex arte et de arte agere idem erat*).[3] Such then, according to our author, were the extravagances which characterised both the thought and style of the *Cornificiani*; and the account is notable, not only for its shrewd analysis of a contemporary movement, but also for the sanity of its reply to what was in effect the first attack made by the 'moderns' on the literary traditions of antiquity.

The main contributions of John of Salisbury to literary theory and culture have now been mentioned, though some stray comments on poetic theory might perhaps here also be noted. Thus a few vague remarks on the poetic art occur, based mainly on Horace.[4] The poet, it is stated, should follow nature in manner, gesture, and even diction; in addition, he was to observe *decorum* in relation to age, place, season and the like. Elsewhere light is thrown on our author's conception of poetry by his acceptance of the convention (*ritus poeticus*) of allegorical interpretation; as when, for instance, he holds that Prudence, in the person of Minerva, was the constant companion of Homer's Ulysses, or again, that Virgil, under cover of fables, had expressed all the truths of philosophy.[5] Of interest, too, are his incidental references to dramatic theory, to those theories of tragedy and comedy, which, derived ultimately by fourth-century grammarians from some Hellenistic source,[6] were to

[1] *Met.* 829 d.        [2] *Ibid:* 830 a.
[3] *Ibid.* 867 a.        [4] *Ibid.* 847 b; cf. Hor. *A.P.* 102–3.
[5] *Pol.* 621 a, b.        [6] See pp. 31 ff. *supra.*

be current throughout the Middle Ages. In a well-known passage he meditates whether the drama of human life were a tragedy or a comedy.[1] That it was a drama of some kind he is firmly convinced; and commenting on a passage in the *Satyricon* of Petronius,[2] he holds that 'the whole world for the most part consists of players' (*fere totus mundus exerceat histrionem*).[3] But whether it was tragedy or comedy that was thus enacted, he explains, depended on the point of view. In tragedy, he implies, men are brought from high to low estate, in comedy from lowliness to greatness.[4] And since life mostly ends in sadness, he regards it as more closely akin to tragedy than to comedy; though the final judgment he leaves to the discretion of his readers. These then are the main comments on poetic theory made by our author; and the neglect of this particular aspect of ancient teaching is not without its significance. The truth was, as our author explains, that the status of poetics (*poetica*) was in dispute at the time. Some there were who regarded it as an independent 'art', according to the ancient tradition; while others held it to be merely a branch of either rhetoric or grammar, 'being so far related to both as to have precepts in common'.[5] Into this controversy, however, our author unfortunately refuses to enter. He merely contends that for practical purposes the study of poetry should be regarded as a branch of grammar, the parent study; since 'either *grammatica*', he explains, 'will continue to include *poetica*, or else *poetica* will be lost to liberal studies'.

In attempting some estimate of the critical achievement of John of Salisbury, importance, in the first place, must be attached to his insistence on the value of literature and a literary training, thus rendering timely service to his generation. In an age distracted by much confused thinking, when old prejudices against literature were still cherished, and new

---

[1] *Pol.* 488 d.       [2] § 80; cf. *Pol.* 488 c.

[3] *Pol.* 491 b; cf. also 489 b. From this comment by John of Salisbury is possibly derived the motto (*totus mundus agit histrionem*) which, according to tradition (see N. Drake, *Shakespeare and his Times*, II, 208), was inscribed under the figure of Hercules supporting the globe at Shakespeare's theatre, the Globe.

[4] *Pol.* 489 c, d.              [5] *Met.* 847 c. See also p. 110 *infra*.

enthusiasms for logic and the more practical studies of law and medicine had come to life, he argued for a return to that classical tradition which had played so great a part in the intellectual life of Greece and Rome. One of the great common-places of antiquity had been the power of Logos, of reason as it expresses itself in speech; and the cultivation of this power he propounds as the root principle of education. Nor does he fail to revive and quicken the tradition of literary study in England, even though his treatment is occasional, discursive, and lacking in system. For one thing, he was not limited, as Bede and Alcuin had been, to the teaching of fourth-century grammarians; he draws on Horace, Quintilian, Seneca and others, thus recapturing something of the ancient doctrine. Then, too, his approach to literature was not confined to Biblical and Christian writings. It embraced the literature of both classical and post-classical times; and the results are seen in his illuminating methods, in the body of sound theory he supplies, and in the introduction he affords to much that was valuable in the literature of the past. Not least significant was his abandonment of the arid and mechanical expositions of earlier grammarians. In their place he employs methods of a more reasoned and philosophical kind, methods involving the explanation of basic principles—the value of 'eloquence', the necessity of art, or the parts played by nature and art in literary creation—thus giving new life to the details of his teaching. And if that teaching is mostly of a derivative kind, being drawn almost wholly from earlier authorities, he never-theless presents it in rational and convincing form, while his good sense is seen in his choice of essential doctrines. One of his main objects was that of enabling men to write well knowingly; and he revives not a few of those guiding principles which had been operative and effective in classical antiquity.

Yet more stimulating was his teaching on literature itself, and this was perhaps his greatest service to his generation. What had formerly been regarded as so much material for grammarians and scholars was now shown to be a precious heritage for all men, a rich legacy handed down from an earlier civilisation; and for the proper understanding of such material he has some useful advice to offer, while he also introduces to his readers some of the outstanding writers of both Greece and Rome. His estimates, it is true, were often taken from previous authorities; but that does not detract wholly from their practical value. For the rest, he has judgments of his own to offer, wherein he shows himself capable of independent judgment, even where it ran counter to earlier authority; and his remarks on his contemporaries are eminently sane and judicious, free from bias, and based on standards of good sense. Of the aesthetic appreciation of literature, it is true, he gives but little evidence. Concerned for the most part with literature as a means of education, he concentrates chiefly on subject-matter, and thus fails to recognise the formal excellences of classical work, the merits of its structure, the varied qualities of its style —features which were to be appreciated at a later date. Nevertheless with him, it may fairly be claimed, literary criticism had entered on a new phase. Fresh life had been given to literary theorising, a beginning had been made with criticism of a judicial kind; and the way had thus been prepared for a further and a livelier development of critical activities.

Yet when all is said, it is neither as a literary theorist nor yet as a judicial critic that his best work on behalf of literature was done. More important than his achievement in either of these fields was his success in conveying to his readers his feeling for the past, and more particularly his sense of the value of the classical literature of antiquity. Now for the first time this pre-Christian literature was appreciated as so many human documents, living records of ancient wisdom, records too of human activities universal in their bearing. It was in short one of the most uncompromising statements since classical times of the value of literature. And in an age when theology was still the queen of studies and other-worldly interests prevailed, this revelation of human values in the literature of Greece and Rome was calculated to give new direction to contemporary thought. It not only suggested that such literature was intimately bound up with the life of men; it advocated as well a return to that ancient school of noble thought, and it came as a reminder that the proper study of mankind was man.

In fact, it represented the first challenge of Humanism on English soil, opening up fresh possibilities of thought and expression; and in this generous and illuminating appreciation of ancient literature lies the ultimate claim of John of Salisbury to recognition in the critical sphere. His work as a Christian Humanist was to be continued by sixteenth-century scholars. But none was to surpass him in breadth of outlook or in freedom from pedantry; indeed, in some respects he is more liberal and enlightened than were they all. It is therefore as the first great English Humanist that John of Salisbury figures in English critical history; and if nowadays his name is unfamiliar in the field of literary criticism, it is because justice has yet to be done to the merits of his achievement.

# CHAPTER V

## MEDIEVAL POETICS: GEOFFREY OF VINSAUF AND JOHN OF GARLAND

BY the end of the twelfth century the many-sided Renascence associated with that century had influenced in general the intellectual life of northern Europe; and in England, more particularly, literary activities and studies had entered on a new phase. That the movement of which John of Salisbury was the foremost English representative was both vital and widespread, ample evidence is forthcoming from many quarters. Indeed, everywhere was apparent a new sense of the value of the surviving fragments of ancient culture; and the results had been not merely a revival of classical learning, but also an awakening to the value of literature and literary processes, the formation of new ambitions where literature was concerned, as well as abundant literary activities which gave expression in Latin to the life and thought of the time. To begin with, it was now that medieval Latin literature reached its culmination; and to this triumph Englishmen had made no negligible contribution. Apart from the works of Angevin historians and satirists already mentioned, there had appeared a vast array of compositions both in verse and prose, full of classical reminiscences and written in a variety of metrical forms. Of the prose works, among the more notable were Geoffrey of Monmouth's *Historia Regum Britanniae*, which marked the emergence of Arthurian romance; the *De Naturis Rerum* of Alexander Neckam, a scientific treatise of a popular kind; and the miscellaneous but lively writings of Giraldus Cambrensis, which ranged over topography, history, politics and theology. Along with these there appeared an unbroken stream of poetry;[1] epigrams written in imitation of Martial by Godfrey of Winchester, occasional poems by Serlo and Laurence of Durham, and epics of which the most famous was Joseph of Exeter's *De Bello Trojano*. At the same time lyrical activities were also

[1] See F. J. E. Raby, *History of Secular Latin Poetry in the Middle Ages*, II, 89–142.

being revived; hymns were forthcoming from Becket and others, and contributions were made to Goliardic poetry. Moreover, by Neckam collections of fables were made from ancient sources; a new narrative form, based on a misconception of ancient poetry, appeared in the anonymous *comoedia* entitled *Baucis and Thraso*;[1] while earlier dramatic efforts now assumed the more elaborate form of Miracle plays. And in the meantime successful attempts were also being made to turn the vernacular to account, notably in Layamon's *Brut*, the *Ormulum* and *The Owl and the Nightingale*, works which marked the revival of literary English.

Equally interesting, however, were the occasional signs that were now appearing of a critical attitude being adopted in literary matters, so that more than one voice was being raised on behalf of classical ideals in literature. It was not without its significance, for instance, that William of Malmesbury (*d.* 1143) had advocated an advance on the methods of earlier annalists, recommending for that purpose the use of 'Roman salt' as a condiment (*exarata barbarice Romano sale condire*),[2] and suggesting that King Arthur was deserving of better treatment than that afforded by 'the mad fables of the Britons' (*de quo Britonum nugae hodie delirant*).[3] Elsewhere he claimed indulgence for Aldhelm's style in his *De Laudibus Virginitatis*, on the ground that it was the characteristic manner of those early English Latinists. He recognised in part its affectations and defects; but he also contended that style (*modus dictaminis*) necessarily varied with the national genius. He maintained that whereas the Greeks had cultivated a complicated style (*involute*), the Romans a judicious (*circumspecte*), and Gallic writers a sumptuous style (*splendide*), English writers for their part had written in ostentatious vein (*pompatice*).[4] Then, too, further evidence of new tastes and literary standards was forthcoming from the vivacious Giraldus Cambrensis (1147–1222), one of the most prolific writers in a prolific age. In one place, for instance, he gives expression to the new humanistic spirit, in

---

[1] See Raby, *op. cit.* II, 126: also p. 32 *supra*.
[2] *De Gestis Regum Angliae*, ed. Stubbs (Rolls Series), I, 2.
[3] *Ibid.* I, 11.                [4] *Ibid.* I, 31.

proclaiming his ardent love of letters, which, he states, had moulded his nature from early boyhood.[1] The business of writing, he concedes, necessarily involved labour; labour in the search for fitting material, labour in the due ordering of that material, labour also in devising fit expression; all of which were echoes of classical injunctions relating to *inventio, dispositio,* and *elocutio.* But to him, he explains, such toil had ever been pleasing, for he recognised the power of the written word. Spoken words, he maintained, soon vanished and were lost; but the written word remained, a lasting memorial to the glory or dishonour of the writer; and for such glory he longed, preferring fame in letters to the glamour of great riches. Nor is it here only that he betrays something of the ideals which animated his whole career. He is, for instance, loud in his praises of the studious life, drawing freely on the letters of Cicero, Seneca, and the younger Pliny for that purpose;[2] and elsewhere he reminds his readers that the greatest of rulers, Julius Caesar, Augustus and Charlemagne, had been the most devoted to literature.[3] For the rest, he constantly makes use of ancient writings, as indeed do most of his contemporaries; and of this his work *On the Instruction of a Prince* affords abundant examples.[4] He further recommends the assiduous study of Latin poets (*auctores*) and philosophers, to the neglect of which he ascribes the contemporary barbarisms in style and the prevailing ignorance of prosody.[5] In addition, he joins forces with John of Salisbury in emphasising the need for grammatical and rhetorical studies on the part of all who would speak *recte, lepide, et ornate.*[6] Yet what he advises is no slavish following of ancient devices. He recognises that words exist for the expression of human thought, that a new age gives rise to new modes of utterance (*novos mores nova sibi conformant tempora*);[7] and recalling Seneca's dictum that 'it is better to be dumb than to speak so as not to be understood' (*satius est mutum esse quam quod nemo intelligat palam proferre*), he therefore

[1] *Expugnatio Hibernica (Gir. Camb. Opera* (Rolls Series)), v, 211–14.
[2] *De Principis Instructione* (R.S.), VIII, lxiii.
[3] *Ibid.* vii.    [4] *Ibid.* xii.
[5] *Speculum Ecclesiae* (R.S.), IV, Proem 7 (f.n.).    [6] *Ibid.*
[7] *Expugn. Hib.* (R.S.), v, 208.

advocates the adoption of a plain and easy style, free from pedantry and embodying popular words and idioms—the style, in short, for which he strove in his writings for the less instructed readers of his day.

Incidental remarks of this kind were, however, not the only signs of increasing critical activities, for now appeared certain works definitely devoted to the study of literature, and representing a substantial and important contribution to literary theory. The main contributions by Englishmen were due to Geoffrey of Vinsauf and John of Garland; and their works were the outcome of a movement which was shared by both French and German contemporaries, and which, beginning in the twelfth century, reached its culmination in the first half of the century following. Nor were these writings concerned with the art of poetry alone. Some, for instance, dealt with prose, with the art of letter-writing (*ars dictaminis*); others, again, treated of contemporary oratory, that is, pulpit eloquence (*ars praedicandi*). Most significant of all, however, were the treatises on poetry, for they were destined to play a great part in the later literary development. Characterised by many faults and deficiencies, lacking too in system and vision alike, they are nevertheless possessed of considerable value historically, as embodying the main principles upon which the poetic craft of later generations was to be largely based.

The appearance of such works at this particular juncture is best explained in the light of the conditions prevailing in the twelfth and early thirteenth centuries. To the unprecedented output of poetry, both in Latin and the vernacular, which characterised the twelfth century in England, some reference has already been made. It was a movement which represented a new phase of literary activity, the awakening of new ambitions in literary culture; and incidentally it helped to foster the traditional teaching of Chartres, in giving fresh life and meaning to verse exercises in the schools. At the same time a new value was being attached to expression in verse. In accordance with the ancient precept that *metra iuvant animos paucis comprehendere multa*,[1] metrical form was held to be more elegant, more concise,

[1] Cf. Wiclif, *Sermones* (ed. Loserth), IV, 269.

more easily remembered than prose; and therefore the most effective means for the communication of all kinds of knowledge. Hence a 'craze' for versifying plainly visible in the twelfth century.[1] It was not merely that works on philosophy or science often assumed verse form; or that it had become a tradition since Angevin times that English historical writing should be in verse. Such works as summaries of Latin grammar in hexameter verse, metrical formularies for letter-writing, as well as charters in rhyme and sermons in rhythmical prose are also to be found; and it was now that the *Aurora*, the versified Bible of Peter de Riga, appeared, that vast poem of 15,000 lines consisting of a paraphrase of a large part of the historical Books of the Bible. In short, the use of verse became general in all fields of thought; and under these circumstances it is not strange to find that attempts were made to provide instruction in the poetic art by means of a number of school manuals. Already in the twelfth century Matthew of Vendôme had compiled his *Ars Versificatoria* (*c.* 1175), probably under the influence of Bernard Silvestris of Tours; and he was followed by certain writers in England and elsewhere. First came Geoffrey of Vinsauf with his *Poetria Nova* (1208–13), his *Documentum de modo et arte dictandi et versificandi*, and his *Summa de coloribus rhetoricis*; then Gervais de Melkley, whose *Ars Versificaria* (*c.* 1216) owed much to preceding theorists. The German Évrard followed, with his *Laborintus*, of uncertain date; and finally came John of Garland with his *Poetria* and his *Exempla vitae honestae*, about the middle of the thirteenth century. Thus was inaugurated the first extended exposition of the art of poetry; and as an attempt at teaching poetics where Bede had left off, the movement represented something new in literary studies.

It is with the contribution of Englishmen to these studies, however, that we are here particularly concerned; and some details must first be given relating to Geoffrey of Vinsauf and John of Garland, who, for the rest, may be regarded as representative of the whole movement. Of Geoffrey of Vinsauf, in the first place, but little is actually known, though some amount of conjecture has been based on historical allusions that occur

[1] See L. J. Paetow, *The Arts Course at Medieval Universities*, p. 34.

in his works.[1] Like many of his contemporaries he has been described as possessing a double fatherland, being English in origin and French by culture. Born about the middle of the twelfth century in Vinsauf, a town of Normandy, and subsequently educated at St Frideswide's, Oxford, he is known to have spent many years abroad in both France and Italy, was apparently sent on a Papal embassy by Richard I, whose death (1199) he laments in a familiar passage of the *Poetria Nova*,[2] and by *c.* 1210 he had completed that work, which contains, besides echoes of the third and fourth Crusades, a significant dedication to the then reigning Pope, Innocent III (*d.* 1216). Incidentally, he is sometimes identified with Gaufridus Anglicus, who wrote *Ars scribendi epistolas* (*c.* 1260); but this identification rests on insufficient grounds and is probably unfounded. Of Geoffrey's works already mentioned, the *Documentum* is mainly a prose version of the *Poetria Nova*, with much the same plan, the same doctrines and examples, though with certain differences; while the *Summa* represents a separate treatment of the 'colours' of rhetoric.

The main body of Geoffrey's teaching is thus contained in his *Poetria Nova*; and this technical manual in verse, which deals solely with narrative verse, had subsequently a great vogue, as is shown by the numerous manuscripts which survive, amounting to over forty all told.[3] Nor is its title without its interest, *Poetria* at this date being the recognised equivalent of the classical *Ars Poetica*[4] (i.e. a treatise on the art of poetry), though the use of the term in this sense is not easy to explain.[5] With regard to the general scheme and contents of *Poetria Nova*

[1] See E. Faral, *Les Arts Poétiques du XII*^e *et du XIII*^e *Siècle*, pp. 15–33, 194–327 for biography and texts.

[2] ll. 375 ff.

[3] Eighteen in England, ten in France, nine in Germany; see Faral, *op. cit.* pp. 27–8.

[4] Cf. *Documentum*, § 155, for "Horatius in *Poetria*" (i.e. Horace, *A.P.*) and elsewhere in thirteenth-century writings.

[5] Most probably *poetria* in this sense is a coinage or contamination of medieval Latinity. It can scarcely have been derived from Latin *poetria* (poetess). Later on in the form of 'poetrye' it came to stand for all imaginative literature in verse, though 'poesye' (Latin *poesis*) was also retained by later writers including Sidney, Bacon and Dryden. For Chaucer's use of both 'poetrye' and 'poesye' see p. 157 *infra*.

it is perhaps sufficient to say that in keeping with the current conception of poetry, it represents what is practically a treatise on rhetoric as applied to poetry. Thus, after a short introduction dealing with art in general and with the different ways of beginning a poem (ll. 1–202), it concentrates first on methods of amplifying and abbreviating expression (ll. 219–736), then on ornaments of style, tropes, rhetorical colours, and the like (ll. 737–1587), concluding finally with a variety of precepts more or less relevant to the subject (ll. 1588–2031). The teaching throughout is illustrated by examples drawn mainly from classical literature, though some are the product of the author himself. The work, however, nowhere rises above the level of a technical handbook. Limited in range and mechanical in treatment, its intrinsic value is but slight, while its style is frequently marred by indulgence in bombast and word-play.

Of John of Garland (c. 1180–1260) rather more is known,[1] though, like Geoffrey, he too was an Englishman who spent most of his life in France, where his activities were mainly directed to the task of salvaging Humanistic studies. He had studied first at Oxford under John of London; but his name was taken from the scene of his later labours in Paris—the 'clos de Garlande'—where he taught as a grammarian, producing many works (some yet unpublished) bearing on grammatical and kindred studies. Among those works were the two already mentioned as dealing with composition in verse, namely, Poetria[2] and Exempla honestae vitae.[3] The latter is a text-book treating of the use of the rhetorical figures. It supplies sixty-four illustrations of such devices, giving to each its appropriate name; but it represents nothing more than the conventional treatment of such matters found in other collections of a similar kind. The Poetria, however, is of greater significance; for it not only gives evidence of the current desire for instruction in

---

[1] See E. Faral, op. cit. pp. 40–6, for biography and works.

[2] Ed. G. Mari in Romanische Forschungen, XIII, pp. 883–965: a brief summary by E. Faral, op. cit. pp. 378–80. The concluding section (dictamen and ars rithmica) also appears separately in Mari's collection of eight tracts, I trattati medievali di ritmica latina, pp. 35–80, and is reproduced by E. Habel in Rom. Forsch. XXIX, 134 ff.

[3] Ed. E. Habel in Rom. Forsch. XXIX, pp. 131–54.

verse-writing, but it also enlarges in a sense on the earlier procedure. Thus, following the methods of previous theorists, such as Geoffrey of Vinsauf, it treats of the different ways of opening a poem, the methods of amplification, and the various ornaments of style; but in addition it devotes one section to the epistolary art (*dictamen*), and concludes with another on metrical matters (*ars rithmica*). The inclusion of the teaching on *dictamen* may be regarded as a concession to the needs of the time, though its presence is also due to a mistaken conception of the parts played by rhetoric in poetry and prose respectively. The metrical section, again, is conspicuous for its bewildering technical details; forty-four species of stanza-form are there defined and illustrated in meticulous fashion. Altogether the work bears signs of pedantic and ill-digested learning, with its many perversions of ancient rhetorical terms, its scraps of theory taken from various sources, and its confused and clumsy treatment of doctrines current at the time. To the study of poetry it added little or nothing. It lacked the directness of the *Poetria Nova*; and its interest is of a purely historical kind.

Such then were the contributions of Englishmen at this date; and despite their defects, from these two works—*Poetria Nova* and *Poetria*—with their common teaching, may be gathered some idea of current poetic doctrine. Not without its interest, in the first place, is the plea for the study of art put forward by Geoffrey of Vinsauf in opening his *Poetria Nova*.[1] The poet, he asserts, should take thought before entering on his task; his aim throughout should be to write well knowingly; and in a passage reminiscent of Horace's teaching he recalls not a few of the precepts which had animated ancient doctrine. Thus in building a house, he explains, plans are first devised; and in poetic composition, he adds, no less care is required. The theme, for instance, should be first digested, and a certain order arrived at; after which, it is stated, poetic craft (*poesis*) would invest the theme with words. Even so, however, further thought was also needed. It was the business of the poet to see that no part of his work was displeasing, that no 'shaggy locks' or 'tattered garments' disfigured his picture as

---

[1] ll. 43-75.

a whole. For if defects were present, the whole work, it was explained, would necessarily suffer; just as a little gall would embitter a jar of honey, or a single blemish impair the beauty of a human face. Unremitting care should therefore be exercised, if censure was to be avoided; to each section of a poem due attention should be given, and fitting qualities assigned to its beginning, its middle and its end. Here, then, by way of preamble, was a timely reminder of some of the lost secrets of the poetic art—the basic need for taking thought, the importance of effective arrangement, and the necessity in composition for viewing a work as a whole. Such formal considerations had hitherto escaped notice by theorists and writers alike. Thus medieval compositions were mostly lacking in the qualities of unity and proportion; a fact possibly due to the influence of oral traditions, according to which poems were recited episode by episode, instead of being written for readers capable of forming judgment with the whole works before them.[1] Yet Geoffrey's teaching in this matter was not entirely without its later influence. This particular passage of his work was quoted by Chaucer in his *Troilus and Criseyde*;[2] and in that poem, it is worth noting, the narrative moves in orderly artistic fashion to a significant issue.

After so suggestive an introduction, however, it is somewhat disappointing to find that the main body of theorising set forth by both Geoffrey and John of Garland deals primarily with formal and superficial considerations that have little to do with the essence of the poetic art. Useful precepts, it is true, are not entirely absent; but they are briefly and incidentally treated, whereas the chief place is given to a detailed treatment of such questions as, first, the different ways of opening a poem, secondly, the methods of dilating and abbreviating expression, and, thirdly, the proper use of ornaments of style. Nine-tenths (ll. 1–1840) of Geoffrey's work in fact, is taken up with discussions on these matters; and the doctrines thus enunciated form the really effective part of the teaching—that part which was to influence largely the methods of later medieval poets. For an explanation of this curious choice of matters regarded

[1] See Faral, *op. cit.* pp. 59–60.      [2] Bk. I, 1065 ff.

as essential, we must look to the confused ideas that prevailed concerning the nature of poetry,[1] and more particularly, to that rhetorical teaching which, along with grammar, had represented the sole guidance in matters of expression from post-classical times onwards. With the *differentiae* of poetry and prose but imperfectly apprehended, it was inevitable that rhetorical teaching should be applied to poetry, and that, in addition, the methods of earlier rhetorical treatises should be utilised for that purpose; and these were the factors that determined the character of the medieval *Poetics*, both in form and content, though also with considerable modification. Thus, whereas the post-classical treatment of rhetoric had embraced *inventio* (subject-matter), *dispositio* (arrangement of thought), and *elocutio* (style), the plan of medieval *Poetics* was in the main an adaptation of that system; *inventio* being discarded as of no practical importance, *dispositio* being limited to a treatment of the opening and conclusion of a poem, while *elocutio* dealt mainly with the use of amplification and ornaments of style. Nor was this rhetorical influence confined to the scheme of treatment. It determined also the nature of the poetic theory, its concern with stylistic detail, elaborate technique, and specious ornament; all of which were calculated to produce those artificial effects which from the time of the New Sophistic,[2] had distorted both poetry and prose, and were authoritatively set forth in Capella's *De Nuptiis* and other popular text-books. This then accounts for the misplaced emphasis on stylistic devices which from now on monopolised attention; and the fact is one of prime importance in the history of literary theory.

When we turn to consider more closely the details of this body of medieval theorising we note, first, the importance attached to the methods of beginning a poem.[3] Briefly stated, the teaching is as follows; a narrative may open in 'natural' order, that is, when events are related in the sequence in which they occurred; or again, it may open in 'artificial' fashion, as when a start is made, not with the actual beginning, but at some subsequent point, of the story, so that a plunge is made

---

[1] See p. 87 *supra.*
[2] See pp. 26–8 *supra.*
[3] Faral, *op. cit.* pp. 200–3, 265–8; Mari, *op. cit.* pp. 905 ff.

*in medias res.* Provided that the story had ready-made a beginning, a middle and an end, the 'natural' order was said to be
effective. Otherwise the 'artificial' order was recommended
as being the more elegant; though this arrangement, it was
added, for its proper effect, required to be prefaced by a proverb,
a wise generalisation (*sententia*), a short illustrative story (*exemplum*), or, according to John of Garland, by a prologue or
summary. The origin of this doctrine will be found in the
distinction drawn between *ordo naturalis* and *ordo artificialis*,
which had been a commonplace of post-classical rhetorical
theory, while it had also formed part of the teaching in *Ad
Herennium*.[1] Moreover, commentators on Virgil, from the fourth
century onwards, had noted how that poet in his *Aeneid*, so far
from beginning *ab ovo*, had placed 'later things first and first
things later', in accordance with Horace's precept;[2] and this
procedure was generally accepted as a confirmation of the
rhetorical theory in its application to poetry. By later theorists,
however, the doctrine was developed and systematised in
medieval fashion. No less than eight different ways of effecting
this 'artificial' opening were ultimately indicated; and the
additional use of proverbs and 'sentences', thus involved, was
advocated as a means of bringing out clearly the moral import
of a poem. The doctrine was one that became firmly established
among medieval poets; and the results are seen in the elaborate
artifices which mark the openings of many of the later poems,
those of Chaucer among the number.

Significant both in substance and method as this teaching
undoubtedly was (and Geoffrey briefly recommends the use of
proverbs and 'sentences' in concluding a poem), of yet greater
importance was the value attached to 'amplification' and
'abbreviation' in poetic composition.[3] For here begins what
is after all the main body of medieval theorising, those doctrines
concerned with the means of attaining that ornate and embellished expression in verse, in which was held to reside the
real essence of poetry. The reasons for the importance attached
to these two processes are briefly explained by Geoffrey.[4]

[1] I, 3, 9.   [2] Cf. *A.P.* 43–4, 147.
[3] Faral, *op. cit.* pp. 204–20, 271–84; Mari, *op. cit.* pp. 914 ff.
[4] Faral, *op. cit.* p. 314.

Among the main problems, we are told, which faced the poet in entering on his task was that of deciding whether his theme was to be treated in brief or elaborate fashion. If brevity were needed, then certain methods of 'abbreviation' were to be adopted, though care was to be taken lest excessive brevity should result in obscurity.[1] If however a more elaborate treatment were desirable, then other and more extensive prescriptions were commended. And to these matters considerable attention was given by theorists; though with 'abbreviation' they were less concerned, since conciseness was not in general regarded as a virtue of style. The process of 'amplification', on the other hand, was held to be of the first importance; and for the origin of the term we must once again look to the post-classical rhetorical tradition. Already in antiquity 'amplification' had been commended as a rational device for giving elevation to a subject. It had been accepted as an oratorical necessity, designed to render the communication of thought clearer and therefore more effective.[2] In post-classical times, however, its original function was misunderstood, and to the term was given an entirely new meaning. It became in fact little more than a mechanical means of extending and enlarging on a subject, of rendering the treatment more luxuriant, copious and grandiose, by means of figures and the like; and this decorative conception became one of the main doctrines of medieval poetic, as well as an ever-present feature of medieval poetry.

With 'amplification' thus interpreted to mean the process of giving amplitude to, or enlarging on, a theme, altogether some eight methods of obtaining this effect were in particular recommended. Of these methods the most important in practice were the interpolation of descriptive passages and the use of apostrophe, though the devices of personification, repetition, periphrasis and digression were also included under this head. To none, however, was greater value attached than to the use of 'description'; and this practice, in the first place, therefore calls for special consideration. As a poetic device its importance was first inculcated by Matthew of Vendôme,

---

[1] Cf. Hor. *A.P.* 25–6.    [2] Cf. Quintilian, *op. cit.* VIII, 4.

whose *Ars Versificatoria* (*c.* 1175) supplies what is perhaps the fullest exposition of its aims and methods. His teaching, characteristic of the School of Orleans, was doubtless supplemented by other theorists; and its effects are seen in the countless descriptions employed in twelfth-century poetry, which constitute in fact the most original feature of that poetry. While, however, the vogue for descriptive effects in poetry thus dates from the twelfth century, for its ultimate origin we must look to a yet earlier period, to the Sophistic theories current in the rhetoric of post-classical times. Among the devices most frequently used for purposes of inflation by post-classical writers was the use of a separable decorative 'description' (*ἔκφρασις*);[1] and this was doubtless the inspiration of the twelfth-century fashion. It is not without its significance, for instance, that Geoffrey recommends Sidonius Apollinaris (*c.* 430–484) as a model to be imitated in descriptive work;[2] and the importance thus assigned to descriptive passages in medieval poetry is indirectly a survival of post-classical rhetorical doctrine.

As for the actual teaching concerning this device of 'description', we must go to the work of Matthew of Vendôme already mentioned for an adequate idea of the underlying theory.[3] Geoffrey and John of Garland, on the other hand, provide merely examples of its working,[4] as if the doctrine were already sufficiently familiar in their day. It is noteworthy, in the first place, that Matthew demands that all descriptive passages should serve some definite and artistic purpose; though in later practice they were all too often mere excrescences in the narrative, irrelevant insertions tending to ostentation and display. Then, too, he insists that in general they should add to the beauty of a poem; and the 'descriptions' he has mainly in mind are those of feminine form, the seasons, a garden, and the like. In further developing his theory he was influenced by earlier methods prescribed for personal 'descriptions'. Thus both Cicero and Horace had outlined schemes for character-drawing, in which details of sex, age, rank, race, and the rest,

---

[1] Cf. C. S. Baldwin, *Med. Rhet. and Poetic*, p. 17.
[2] See Faral, *op. cit.* p. 273.
[3] *Ars Versificatoria*, i, 38–114 (Faral, *op. cit.* pp. 118–51).
[4] Faral, *op. cit.* pp. 214–7, 271–3; Mari, *op. cit.* p. 915.

were combined in accordance with the law of *decorum*;[1] and
Matthew to some extent adopts this procedure, as when, for
instance, he depicts a number of characters or types—a prelate,
a prince, a young man, an old woman—each with fixed and
conventional qualities. This, however, was not the chief method
recommended in practice. Of yet greater interest is the plan
implicit in the models he supplies; for this was the scheme that
was to be adopted in medieval writings generally, while traces
of it may be found in later literature. According to the *Ad
Herennium*,[2] two devices or figures were available for personal
description. One was *effictio* (χαρακτηρισμός) which supplied a
description of a man's outward appearance, the other, *notatio*
(ἠθοποιία) which described his moral qualities; and upon these
devices was based the normal formula for 'description'. Thus
a complete portrait was held to consist of two parts, one treating
of physical, the other of moral, qualities; though in practice the
moral aspect was often neglected. Physical attributes, on the
other hand, were invariably treated, and in considerable detail.
They moreover followed a fixed order, inspired in part by the
current idea that 'Nature...had framed man, beginning with
the head and ending with the feet',[3] partly also by the model
supplied by Sidonius Apollinaris[4] in his portrait of Theodoric,
which had conformed with the same idea. Hence a personal
'description' would normally begin with a reference to Nature;
and this was followed by details of face, body and clothing—
the face, hair, forehead, eyebrows, eyes, cheeks, nose, mouth,
teeth, neck, shoulders, arms, hands, chest, figure, stomach, legs,
feet—while hidden details were noted but left unspecified. Of
such 'descriptions' Geoffrey supplies a typical example in his
portrait of a beautiful woman;[5] and it is worthy of note that
Chaucer's sketch of the Duchess Blanche[6] represents a free
treatment of the normal details, arranged in due order and
including the references to Nature as well as to hidden beauties.
At the same time it should be added that such 'descriptions'

---

[1] Cf. *De Inventione*, I, 24–5; *A.P.* 114–27, 155–78.　　　[2] IV, 49–50, 63.
[3] Cf. Bernard, author of *De universitate mundi*, quoted by Faral, *op. cit.* p. 81.
[4] *Ep.* I, 2, 2; see Faral, *ibid.* p. 80.　　　[5] Faral, *op. cit.* pp. 214 ff.
[6] *Book of the Duchesse*, ll. 895–960; cf. J. M. Manly, *Chaucer and the
Rhetoricians* (Warton Lect. XVII), p. 11.

were not confined to personal portraits. Geoffrey, for instance, supplies pictures of two scenes, one a quiet season, the other a scene of sailors preparing for a voyage;[1] and it cannot be doubted that the twelfth-century doctrine of 'description' covered a wide field and embraced a host of subjects with which the extant theorists do not deal. This at least is suggested by the conventional descriptions of gardens, arms, furniture and the like, which appear in such abundance in later medieval poetry.

While however 'description' would thus appear to have been the main device for amplifying a given theme, other methods were also prescribed, and of these not the least important was the use of 'apostrophe', as is suggested by Geoffrey's lengthy treatment of that device.[2] And here, in the first place, we may note yet another instance of the confusion of terms. For whereas to the ancients the 'apostrophe' meant the procedure of turning from the judge to address an opponent in a law-suit,[3] at this later date it assumed the meaning of the figure known as *exclamatio*, that is, an impassioned or pathetic exclamation directed to some object, whether animate or inanimate.[4] In poetry an interpolation of this kind was calculated to emphasise an idea by pausing in the narrative; and in enlarging on the significance of that idea, it also heightened the emotional effect by a show of feeling on the part of the poet. The poet might, for instance, feign anger or joy or grief or wonder, occasioned by the situation described; and Geoffrey supplies examples of its working in apostrophes to certain individuals, to Nature, to Death and to God, while one again takes the form of the famous lament on the death of Richard I.[5] To the last-mentioned form special interest is attached; and this, not only on account of Chaucer's ironical reference to the passage.[6] Subsequently employed in isolation, this form of apostrophe ultimately gave rise to a new literary type, namely, the *Complaint*, a poetical form which was to be widely cultivated in later times.

---

[1] Faral, *op. cit.* p. 272.
[2] Faral, *op. cit.* pp. 205–11, 275; Mari, *op. cit.* p. 914.
[3] Quintilian, *op. cit.* IV, i, 63.     [4] *Ibid.* IX, ii, 27; cf. also *ad Her.* IV, 15.
[5] Faral, *op. cit.* pp. 208 ff.     [6] *Nun's Priest's Tale*, 527 ff.

The other devices prescribed for the amplifying of a theme may perhaps be more summarily treated, though all alike played their part in later literary history. There was, for instance, 'personification' (*conformatio*) or 'prosopopoeia', according to which inanimate things or abstractions were represented as possessing the power of speech.[1] Here, again, the idea was to enlarge on a situation by heightening the emotional and imaginative effects; and Geoffrey recalls more than one classical example of its use, such as that of Rome's lament on the death of Caesar in the *Pharsalia*, while he also adds illustrative examples of his own, including the lament of the Cross. Then there was the device of 'repetition' (*interpretatio*), the main object of which was that of emphasis.[2] It involved the presenting of one and the same idea in different ways, and its consequent elaboration by an accumulation of words and expressions. 'Periphrasis' (*circuitio*), on the other hand, aimed at amplifying by means of a roundabout method of expression.[3] As Geoffrey pointed out, it was specially effective in passages of praise or censure, or for avoiding direct reference to 'death' and the like; while it was also capable of adding dignity to style. Or again there was the device known as 'digression',[4] which had no counterpart in earlier rhetoric, but was a comprehensive term for all divergences from the main narrative. Thus it might involve an anticipation of a later scene, the use of a *sententia*, a simile, or an illustrative fable, all of which were calculated to dilate and expand a given theme. These, then, together with 'opposition' (*contrarium*),[5] that is, the trick of denying the contrary of an idea before affirming it, as well as 'comparison' (*similitudo*)[6] were the chief methods recommended for 'amplification'. All alike were designed as aids to a more copious and elaborate expression; but, mechanically applied in later literature, they were destined to lead, more often than not, to mere prolixity and pomp.

[1] Faral, *op. cit.* pp. 211–3, 275.
[2] Faral, *op. cit.* pp. 204, 277; Mari, *op. cit.* p. 916.
[3] Faral, *op. cit.* pp. 204, 273; Mari, *op. cit.* p. 915.
[4] Faral, *op. cit.* pp. 213–4, 274–5; Mari, p. 913.
[5] Faral, *op. cit.* pp. 217–8; Mari, *op. cit.* p. 915.
[6] Faral, *op. cit.* pp. 204–5, 274–5.

Concerning 'abbreviation', the contrary process, there is less to be said. For reasons already suggested, it received but slight attention from theorists, and in later literature it played no conspicuous part. Yet it formed a component part of twelfth-century theory; and both Geoffrey and John of Garland have something to say on the methods of attaining a requisite brevity in treating a given theme.[1] The first obvious rule was the avoidance of all those devices which conduced to an ampler treatment—the use of descriptive passages, the reiteration of ideas and the like. In addition, however, certain positive instructions were also given, requiring for the most part the use of figures. Thus absolute constructions were recommended; and so was the figure known as *significatio* (or *emphasis*), which required the use of pregnant expressions or words signifying more than was actually expressed. Another device was that of *occupatio* (or *occultatio*), which involved a refusal to describe or narrate, while referring briefly to a subject under cover of passing it over—a trick common in Chaucer. And among other figures recommended were *articulus* and *dissolutio*, by which conjunctions, the normal connectives of words or sentences, were omitted for effect; while the fusion of clauses was also prescribed.

So far the doctrines advanced have had to do with the means of enhancing literary effects in general. Now attention is given more particularly to style as such, to the artifices necessary for attaining a vivacious and ornate expression; and to these matters the greater part of the works of both Matthew of Vendôme and Geoffrey are devoted. Of style itself, an imperfect conception was held; and it is not surprising to find that this section with its pedantic divisions and subdivisions is complicated in the extreme. Classical doctrine had distinguished three main styles—high, middle and low—which were differentiated at first (as in *Ad Herennium*)[2] by their degrees of ornamentation, then later, by classical theorists, in accordance with their aesthetic effects. By this date, however, and in the eleventh century probably, a new and strange meaning was often given to these terms. The distinctions were said to rest on

---

[1] Faral, *op. cit.* pp. 218–20, 277–80.    [2] IV, 8.

the social dignity of the personages or subject-matter concerned; and Virgil's *Aeneid*, his *Georgics* and his *Bucolics* were
held to be representative of the three different styles.[1]

But while the earlier distinction between the three styles for
the most part persisted, the main interest was now concentrated
on the methods of attaining those styles. The 'high' style for
instance was employed in treating of lofty themes, and with it
were associated ten tropes, known as 'difficult ornaments'
(*ornatus difficilis*),[2] since they required the greater skill and
ingenuity. With the 'middle' and 'low' styles, on the other
hand, which treated of commonplace matters, went the more
mechanical devices, the so-called 'easy ornaments' (*ornatus
facilis*),[3] consisting of thirty-five figures of speech together with
some nineteen figures of thought, all drawn by Geoffrey from
*Ad Herennium*; and whereas the 'high' style might embody
figures as well as tropes, the 'middle' and 'low' styles were
limited to figures alone. In general, it may be said, both tropes
and figures represented departures from the normal usage in
speech. They were expressions which deviated from plain
straightforward statements for added effect, thus aiming at
something more than the mere necessities of communication.
Ostensibly the result of a more vivid or fanciful realisation of
a thing or an idea, they became at this date little more than
mere verbal artifices, though in practice they were distinguished
by certain differences both of nature and function. The broad
distinction between tropes and figures was that whereas the
former were devices, such as metaphor, in which human emotion has always found artistic expression, figures on the other
hand consisted of artificial and ingenious patterns of words and
thoughts, involving repetition, balance, changes of word-order
and the like. Then, too, certain differences marked the use of
the two categories of figures. Thus the figures of thought were
largely employed in the process of 'amplification', whereas the
figures of speech constituted for the most part the 'easy ornaments'; and it was the latter that were generally described

---

[1] Faral, *op. cit.* p. 312; Mari, *op. cit.* p. 920.
[2] Faral, *op. cit.* pp. 221–31, 285–93; Mari, *op. cit.* p. 898.
[3] Faral, *op. cit.* pp. 231–45, 293–303; Mari, *op. cit.* p. 901.

as 'colours of rhetoric',[1] though the term was also sometimes applied to figures as a whole. Chaucer, for instance, made use of both tropes and figures, the former being more frequent; and his Eagle in *The House of Fame*[2] was probably discriminating between these different usages when he prided himself on speaking 'simply...without any subtiltee...of figures of poetrye or colours'. All this theorising, however, led inevitably to a highly artificial and ornate form of expression. In short, the historical importance of these devices can scarcely be overrated; and an appreciation of this fact goes far to explain the formal features of much of the later verse.[3]

While however the characteristic and most influential of medieval poetic doctrines have now been outlined, not without their interest are those fragments of classical and post-classical theory interspersed throughout the treatises, even though their later influence was but slight. Concerning poetic expression, for instance, Geoffrey has many useful precepts to give, as when he emphasises the need for noble thought as a fundamental requirement for a lofty style. 'A mean thought richly decked', he explains,[4] 'is like [Horace's] picture, pleasing at a distance, but on careful inspection displeasing'; or again, 'words are but dead things if they rest not on sound thought'.[5] Elsewhere he insists on the need for perspicuity. 'To use obscure phrases', he states in characteristic fashion,[6] 'is like pouring water into a river, planting in dry soil, beating the air, or ploughing the sand.' He further recommends words in common use, quoting as the ideal the ancient dictum, 'to speak as the general, to think as the few' (*loquaris ut plures, sapias ut pauci*);[7] adding also a caveat against all vulgar expression, and urging the unvarying need for refinement (*facetus*) and taste (*facilis*). At the same time he recognises the virtue of novelty in poetic expression; and, following Horace, he approves of new word-formations, and of the freshness derived from ordinary words in a new setting.[8]

---

[1] Cf. Geoffrey's work, *de coloribus rhetoricis* (see Faral, *op. cit.* p. 231).
[2] ll. 855 ff.
[3] For list of these tropes and figures see Appendix, pp. 200–3 *infra*.
[4] Faral, *op. cit.* pp. 220, 284–5; cf. *A.P.* 361, *ut pictura poesis*.
[5] *Ibid.* p. 285.    [6] *Ibid.* p. 230.    [7] *Ibid.*    [8] *Ibid.* pp. 220–1, 311.

Nor is Geoffrey, in these borrowed fragments of theory, concerned with poetic diction alone. In his works are found remarks of value relating to style in general; though, in one respect at least, some reservation is necessary, as when he maintains that one art prescribes for both poetry (*metrum*) and prose (*prosa*), but in different degrees (*una ars ad utrumque facit, quamvis in dispari forma*),[1] since artistic laws were more rigidly applied in poetry than in prose. Among his more important principles is that of *decorum*, according to which an author's style should be adapted to the hearer and the occasion; and here, as elsewhere, custom (*mos*) should be the guide.[2] In addition, a writer's style should be uniformly sustained throughout; otherwise (and here Geoffrey misinterprets Horace's remarks on incoherent structure) by a mixture of styles a monstrous form of expression would result.[3] Or again, he emphasises the need for a judicious use of figurative expressions. They were to be sparingly employed and in ever-changing variety; since an untimely use rendered them worthless, and 'from flowers of varied scent', he added, 'came the sweetest fragrance'.[4] For the treatment of serious themes, he further explains, flowers of speech were necessary; whereas comic themes rejected elaborate expression and tolerated only plain (*plana*) words.[5] Then, too, following the practice of ancient theorists, he indicates certain common faults to be avoided by the writer, notably the use of hiatus, word-jingles, forced metaphors, and periods of excessive length.[6] As he explains, 'every device overdone becomes ineffective' (*omne quod est nimium res absque colore*);[7] and elsewhere, dilating on this same topic, he points out the defects to which each of the classified styles was liable, how the 'high' style overdone became turgid and inflated, the 'middle' style loose and formless, the 'low' style bloodless and arid, while brevity in excess readily became obscurity.[8] Nor was he wanting in hints of a more positive kind; as when, for instance, he suggests that indirect measures were often effective in satire, and that praise of a ludicrous kind

---

[1] Faral, *op. cit.* p. 254; see p. 87 *supra*.   [2] *Ibid.* pp. 230–1.
[3] *Ibid.* p. 315; cf. *A.P.* 21 ff.   [4] *Ibid.* pp. 234–5.
[5] *Ibid.* pp. 255–6.   [6] *Ibid.* p. 256.
[7] *Ibid.*   [8] *Ibid.* pp. 312–3; cf. *A.P.* 26 ff.

(*lauda sed ridiculose*) exposed the absurd;[1] or again, when he insists that both mind and ear should be brought to bear critically on literary work.[2] Likewise on the method of treating earlier well-worn themes he also has something to say. His advice (based on that of Horace) is to aim at an original version by avoiding arrogant openings, hackneyed details and irrelevant matters, while selecting at the same time fresh aspects of the story concerned, and observing *decorum* throughout in the characters depicted.[3]

Reminiscences of earlier theory of yet a different kind are also present in John of Garland's *Poetria*; and though intrinsically of no great value, consisting mainly of scraps of doctrine often misunderstood, they are nevertheless not devoid of historical interest. Of greatest significance perhaps are his references to the various forms of poetry. Thus he mentions the three kinds defined by Bede—the dramatic, the narrative and the mixed— and he also supplies a list of the various forms, classified on no clear basis, but including epithalamium, epitaph, bucolic, georgic, lyric, epode, secular hymn, satire, tragedy, comedy, elegiac, apologue and allegory.[4] On the subject-matter of the narrative *genre* he also makes some comments. He recalls the old Hellenistic distinction of *fabula*, *historia*, and *argumentum*; and defines *fabula* as a fictitious incredible story (*nec res veras nec verisimiles*), *historia* as a story of actual but distant events (*res gestae ab aetatis nostrae rebus remotae*), and *argumentum* as a story fictitious yet credible (*res ficta quae tamen fieri potuit*).[5] Nor are his references to tragedy and comedy without their interest; for here he supplies, with some differences, the post-classical conceptions current throughout the Middle Ages. Thus tragedy he defines as 'a poem written in the "grand" style (*gravi stilo*), which treats of shameful and wicked deeds (*pudibunda proferentur et scelerata*), and, beginning in joy (*gaudio*), ends in grief (*lacrimis*)'.[6] Comedy, on the other hand, he defines as 'a humorous poem beginning in sadness and ending in joy'.[7]

Such, then, was the main contribution of these medieval

---

[1] Faral, *op. cit.* p. 210.   [2] *Ibid.* p. 257.   [3] *Ibid.* pp. 309–11.
[4] Mari, *op. cit.* p. 926.   [5] *Ibid.*, see p. 33 *supra*.
[6] *Ibid.* pp. 918, 940.   [7] *Ibid.* p. 918.

*Poetics* to literary theory, and more particularly to the methods of cultivating an ornate and a highly coloured poetic style. It yet remains to notice, however, two more specialised aspects of literary study treated by John of Garland—one, concerned with metrical matters, the other, with *ars dictaminis*—both of which were representative studies at the time. Of the meticulous character of metrical studies at this date, the *Ars Rithmica*, with which John of Garland ends his *Poetria*,[1] affords a good example. There forty-four kinds of stanza forms are given with detailed analyses;[2] elsewhere the prosody of the line and other details are treated; and altogether the art of verse was being reduced to rigid, almost mathematical, form. Yet this intricate system of medieval Latin verse was not without its interest; for it marked a departure from both the quantitative measures of classical antiquity and the accentual unrhymed system of Old English verse; and its influence was destined to be lasting. The basis of *ars rithmica* was 'the harmonious equality of syllables contained within a fixed measure' (*rithmus est consonans paritas sillabarum sub certo numero comprehensarum*).[3] A variety of stanza-forms was developed, made up mainly of octosyllabic lines, but with no very elaborate rhyming arrangements; and by an easy transition these metrical devices passed subsequently into vernacular literature, thus giving rise to that syllabic system on which later English poetry was normally based.

Less far-reaching in its effects, though interesting historically, was John of Garland's contribution to *ars dictaminis*, which was also included in his *Poetria*, partly for reasons of convenience, partly on the ground that one art was held to legislate for both poetry and prose alike. In its earliest sense *dictamen* had stood for the art of composition in general. It embraced three kinds —composition in metrical verse (*metrica*), rhythmical verse (*rithmica*), and prose (*prosaica*)—but later the term was applied mainly to prose composition, and especially to the composition of letters and official documents which was taught in eleventh-century schools. From the first the teaching had consisted of

[1] See Mari, *I trattati*, pp. 35–80.
[2] For summary account see J. M. Berdan, *Early Tudor Poetry*, pp. 125–6.
[3] Mari, *I trattati*, p. 383.

an adaptation of earlier rhetoric, the primary function of which (that of persuasion in communal affairs) had long since been forgotten; and when in the twelfth century the new *ars dicta-minis* (or *ars dictare*) appeared, and became one of the chief studies throughout Western Europe, its main concern was with letter-writing and the drawing up of documents; while its principles were based on those of post-classical rhetoric. At Bologna and Orleans, in particular, the study flourished; and many manuals of epistolography were written to meet urgent needs arising out of the prevailing illiteracy and the lack of communications, though skill in *dictamen* also led to lucrative appointments. One example of such works was the *Ars scribendi epistolas* (*c.* 1260) of Gaufridus Anglicus; and together with John of Garland's contribution in his *Poetria*,[1] it witnessed to the vitality of this new phase of literary activity. Nor was the teaching of John of Garland on letter-writing without its special interest, inasmuch as it reflected doctrine then current throughout Western Europe. In general, definite rules were laid down, according to which the order and form of the various parts of a letter were fixed; and the system, which represented a modification of the divisions of an *oratio* as defined in *Ad Herennium*,[2] embodied a five-fold division calculated to ensure expression of a logical and persuasive kind. First came the 'salutation', which required a strict observance of etiquette in the form of address; this was followed by the 'exordium', consisting of a proverb or scriptural quotation, to win the reader's attention (*captatio benevolentiae*);[3] next came the 'narration', in which the special purpose of the letter was stated; then the 'petition', which developed the points made in the preceding sections; and finally the 'conclusion', which brought the communication to a seemly close. This, then, was the stereotyped technique advocated for both private and diplomatic letters during the twelfth and thirteenth centuries; and these precepts were generally accompanied, as in the *Poetria*, by examples of courtly correspondence as models for imitation.

---

[1] See p. 97, n. 2 *supra*.    [2] I. 3.

[3] The apology for lack of art which became a later poetic convention was probably a survival of '*captatio benevolentiae*'; see p. 177 *infra*.

In any attempt at estimating the value of this medieval theorising on poetry as a whole, the difficulties inherent in such theorising must first be taken into account. That such efforts should be based on earlier authorities was, in the first place, inevitable, since contemporary scholars were possessed of neither the poetic material nor the analytic faculty necessary for a first-hand inquiry. Authoritative teaching on poetry, however, was for the most part inaccessible, and what little was available was of a confused and indeterminate kind. For one thing, no clear conception of the ancient study of poetry (*poetica*) had as yet come down. As has been stated, already in the post-classical period poetry had ceased to be studied as an independent subject, and had subsequently formed no integral part of the normal educational scheme of the Liberal Arts. What treatment it had received was of an incidental and subordinate kind. It was regarded as belonging to the sphere of grammar or as a branch of rhetoric; in the thirteenth century there was a tendency to associate it with the study of logic;[1] and of this confusion of thought John of Salisbury and others give ample evidence. At the same time certain basic ideas concerning poetry had emerged out of the sporadic teaching of post-classical and later ages. These views were derived from earlier rhetorical theory, from treatises on grammar by Donatus, Diomedes and others, from the works of Martianus Capella and Isidore, as well as from the much admired poetic models of Ausonius and Sidonius Apollinaris. And, briefly summarised, they may be said to have embodied two main doctrines; first, that poetry consisted of metrical and rhythmical speech, secondly, that its expression was to be ornate and embellished with all the devices of rhetoric. It is true that vague references had occasionally been made to the nature and function of poetry, or again, to the classification of the various poetic 'kinds'. But all such references were of a rudimentary nature, reminiscent of post-classical doctrine, and therefore far removed from the illuminating philosophical treatment of classical Greece.

Such then was the mutilated and sterile conception of poetry

---

[1] See p. 135 *infra*.

handed down from post-classical times; and its influence had already been seen in the limited scope of Bede's teaching on poetry, confined as it was to principles of metric and verbal ornament. But these same matters continued to be the main concerns of medieval *Poetics*, which for the most part treat of poetry as a sort of versified rhetoric. That one of the chief components of poetry was held to be verse-form is shown by the detailed analyses supplied of a variety of metres; incidentally, too, by the description of certain of the treatises as *Ars Versificatoria* or *Ars Versificaria*; and equally notable was the importance attached to rhetorical ornament in poetry, as is shown by the extensive treatment of figures and tropes in all these works alike. For their material the authors had gone primarily to the sources already mentioned. Now, however, use was also made of two other works, drawn from classical antiquity; namely, Horace's *Ars Poetica*, for certain precepts and illustrations, the *Rhetorica ad Herennium*, for a concise and systematic treatment of stylistic ornament; and the effects of this additional material were considerable and far-reaching.

In view of the growing appreciation of the literary legacy of the ancients, it is not strange that certain elements of Horace's teaching were embodied in the new theorising on poetry. On the other hand, nothing in medieval theorising is more remarkable than the part played by the *Rhetorica ad Herennium* in the genesis of these *Poetics*; and its influence is a matter that calls for more than passing notice. An ancient text-book, of no great distinction in another field of study, becoming after many vicissitudes a main factor in the formation of medieval poetic theory—the story represents surely one of the curiosities of literary history. Originally a school rhetoric (*c.* 86 B.C.), embodying Hellenistic doctrine, and attributed by some authorities to one Cornificius, the *Ad Herennium* remained practically unnoticed during the Silver Age at Rome, was apparently brought to light by mere chance in northern Africa about A.D. 350;[1] after which, accepted by Jerome as one of Cicero's writings, it acquired considerable importance, and was utilised by Rufinus and Priscian in compiling their grammars.

---

[1] See p. 15 *supra*: also Atkins, *Lit. Crit. in Antiquity*, II, 16–18.

Throughout the sixth, seventh, and eighth centuries the work remained apparently unknown; and a reference to its existence by Servatus Lupus (*c.* 830) in one of his *Letters*[1] is the first evidence of renewed interest in the work. By the end of the tenth century, however, it had been frequently copied; and it soon became recognised as a useful manual on the art of writing in general, its exposition of figures and tropes being particularly valued. After this it was copied, translated, and adapted with ever-increasing zeal: and already in the twelfth century it had come to be regarded as an authoritative guide in matters of verse embellishment. Thus its teaching was now illustrated by collections of examples; a *Commentary* on the work was contributed by Theodoric of Chartres (d. *c.* 1150); John of Salisbury refers to it not infrequently; while the writers of *Poetics* drew freely on its pages for their views on figures, tropes, and the like. Nor did its influence cease with the thirteenth century. Linked from the first with Cicero's *De Inventione*, which was known as the *rhetorica prima* or *vetus,* it was familiarly described as the *rhetorica secunda* or *nova*; and throughout the Middle Ages it retained its authority in rhetorical and poetic matters. A clear witness to this is the unusually large number of manuscripts that survive, about a hundred all told; and although in the fifteenth century its claim to Ciceronian authorship was already in dispute, even as late as the sixteenth century works are found containing its doctrine, and representing it as pure Ciceronian theory. This, then, was the history of the work which more than any other gave colour to medieval poetic theory. Its influence, during the twelfth century and later, was due to several considerations; first, to the inherited conception of poetry as so much versified rhetoric, secondly, to the long-unchallenged association of the work with the name of Cicero, the unrivalled teacher of rhetoric, and, thirdly, to its convenient and summary treatment of stylistic ornament, which rendered it more suitable for school purposes than Cicero's greater and more philosophical writings, more especially as these were but imperfectly known.

In the light of this antecedent history it is therefore not

---

[1] *Ep.* I.

surprising that these *Poetics* of Geoffrey and John of Garland are possessed of disabilities which detract from their value as lasting contributions to literary theory. Their purpose, to begin with, was severely limited. Intended merely as hand-books for students engaged in verse exercises in the schools, they are devoid of that larger and more philosophical treatment calculated to throw light on the nature of poetry, its function, its subject-matter, its processes and its effects. Then, too, in the absence of an adequate conception of poetry itself, their range of treatment was also limited, being mainly confined to superficial and external details, to methods of achieving ingenuities of expression and verse-form; and to this end were prescribed rules based, not on psychological principles, but on the practice of selected twelfth-century verse writers, to whom poetry was little more than a modified rhetoric. Such elements of classical theory as filtered through (especially from Horace's pages) no doubt had their value. But they were often misunderstood or imperfectly apprehended; and to later generations they remained, for the most part, dead matter, whereas the vital part of the teaching lay in the instruction given in 'amplification', figures and the rest. Thus neither in doctrine nor in method was any permanent addition made to literary appreciation; and in organising the specious artifices of twelfth-century verse the authors of these manuals broke definitely with that classical tradition which had been tentatively fostered in monastic and cathedral schools.

At the same time, slight as was their intrinsic value, these works, and particularly those of Geoffrey, are of considerable interest in critical history. Within their limits they represent attempts to supply contemporary needs by introducing some amount of order into the prevailing literary confusion; and their complicated technique was moreover effectively presented for school purposes, with the aid of abundant illustrations and models. Still greater, however, was their historical significance; for now, for the first time since classical antiquity, systematic efforts were being made to treat of poetry as an art, with definite principles and rules, and with formal perfection as the ultimate ideal. Nor was the recognition given to the new rhythmical (or syllabic) verse system without its interest. From now on, this system (together with rhyme) was to establish itself as the normal poetic medium in both Latin and English; and it is noteworthy that at this early date the quantitative system of classical times had already been rejected in theory. Most important of all was, however, the influence of these manuals on later developments in the vernacular. Submitted at a time when French narrative verse needed some measure of formal refinement, and when the love-poetry inspired by the Troubadours called for polished expression in its play of ideas, these manuals supplied what seemed to be the requisite teaching. And in influencing this French poetry, which became later the model for all Western Europe, they gave direction to later vernacular efforts, and more especially to that courtly love-poetry, which became everywhere predominant, with its 'goodly' words, its 'reasonable' eloquence, its polite decorum and unending rhetorical subtleties. Traces of their influence are abundantly found in Chaucer and other English poets; and the tradition, it might be added, did not entirely cease with the sixteenth-century Renascence.

# CHAPTER VI

## CHECK AND COUNTER-CHECK TO LITERARY STUDIES: JOHN OF GARLAND, ROBERT GROSSETESTE, ROGER BACON, AND RICHARD OF BURY

IN the light of the activities already outlined, there can be no doubt of the reality of the twelfth-century Renascence or of its effects as seen in the literary interests evoked. Equally certain is it, however, that other intellectual forces were in the meantime gathering strength, forces which were to check for the time being the Humanistic movement, as well as those literary enthusiasms which had led to a broadening and a deepening of the stream of human culture. Already, as we have seen, the decline had been foreshadowed by certain hostile tendencies in the intellectual life of the time. Not without its significance, for instance, was the loss of educational zeal on the part of monastic reformers, and the fading of those aims to which learning in the past had owed so much. Then, too, patristic prejudices against pagan literature were still alive and active, and were being forcefully expressed, to the detriment of Humanistic studies. Most important of all, however, was the visible trend of contemporary studies in the direction of logic, which had called forth the vigorous protest of John of Salisbury on behalf of literature and literary studies, a protest in which he was supported by not a few of his contemporaries. Alexander Neckam, for one, had satirised the craze for disputation at Paris, while also deploring the decline of interest in literature;[1] and yet other pointed comments were made by Giraldus Cambrensis, when he lamented more than once the zeal with which the new subjects of Law and Medicine were being cultivated. The rapid rise during the twelfth century of Bologna and Salerno as the respective centres of those subjects of study had not been without its effects; and to those 'more lucrative studies', as Giraldus had pointed out, scholars had pressed in ever-increasing numbers.[2]

[1] *De Naturis Rerum* (R.S.), c. 173, p. 283,
[2] *Opera* (R.S.), ii, 348–9; iv, 7 (f.n.).

In the course of the thirteenth century, however, the new Logic and Scholasticism assumed full sway, and the Humanistic movement, despite its earlier vitality and promise, was arrested, at least for the time being. As at the later sixteenth-century Renascence, the root-cause of the change, ironically enough, was the recovery of a mass of new knowledge from antiquity; for with the opening up of communications with the East— the result of the Crusades, of intercourse with the Moors in Spain, and the travels of enterprising scholars—the main body of Aristotle's scientific and philosophical writings became now for the first time accessible to Western readers. For the most part those works had come down in Syriac and Arabic versions, accompanied by twelfth-century paraphrases and commentaries of the Arabic scholars, Avicenna (d. 1111) and Averroës (d. 1198); and they were subsequently translated into Latin by Michael Scot, Alfred the Englishman, and others. It was therefore an imperfect conception of Aristotelianism that was thus received; though with direct access to the original Greek rendered possible by the Latin conquest of Constantinople (1204), attempts were made to approach more nearly to the actual Aristotelian text. Yet in spite of defective transmission, these works of Aristotle were destined to transform intellectual life in the West. In the enthusiasm that followed, Aristotle became the accepted guide not only in logic but in natural science, metaphysics, and moral philosophy as well; and men's energies from now on were devoted to interpreting the new thought and to realising its implications in the fullest sense. Hence, for one thing, the fresh interest betrayed in scientific matters; and, what was more, the new direction given to theological studies. By the Arabic transmitters the anti-Christian element in Aristotle had been strongly emphasised, thus revealing a clash between the orthodox faith and the new learning. An outbreak of speculation followed, the main concern being that of reconciling Aristotelian philosophy with the doctrines of the Church; and for this task the dialectical methods of Abelard and twelfth-century Schoolmen were in general utilised. What had formerly been employed for the discussion of Universals became thus the main instrument of these wider inquiries; and Scholastic theology, as expounded by Albert the Great (d. 1280), Thomas Aquinas (d. 1274), Alexander of Hales (d. 1245), and others, now became the main preoccupation, to the neglect of earlier Humanistic and literary interests.

Nor was this the only cause of the sudden breakdown of Humanistic ideals at this particular date. Among the contributory factors must also be reckoned those new educational tendencies which now became insistent, and were successful in checking the revived classicism of the preceding age. With the founding of the University of Paris (1170), and the establishment of twelve similar institutions in the course of the thirteenth century, a new force, indifferent to the claims of literature, had appeared on the scene. At Paris, from the first, logic was strongly and permanently entrenched. It was to remain for centuries the nucleus of the Arts course in that University, thus giving tone and character to the medieval mind; while the other main subjects of study were philosophy and natural science, or at least such elements as could be assimilated from the pages of Aristotle. At the same time education in general now assumed a more practical and utilitarian form; and the results are seen in the importance assigned to Law and Medicine in the curriculum, as well as in the place given to *ars dictaminis*. Thus with the influx of these vocational interests the study of the Humanities was inevitably crowded out; and grammar, hitherto the most sedulously cultivated of the Seven Arts, now underwent a serious decline, becoming under the influence of Scholasticism a speculative science, with grammarians legislating by rules of logic. At Paris, moreover, merely the technical rules of language were being taught; and the *Doctrinale* (1199) of Alexander of Villedieu and *Graecismus* (1212) of Évrard of Béthune, with their barbarous Latinity, became the representative text-books of the new age. Nor was any place found for the serious study of classical literature, which was still being condemned by Jacques de Vitry (*d.* 1240) and others as a worthless subject of study and a danger to youth. From now on, the poets, historians, and orators of antiquity were practically excluded from the prescribed courses at the Universities, all that was read being excerpts designed to illustrate rules of grammar; and with these changes literary studies for the most part disappeared, and with them the high hopes of a liberal education that had been cherished in the century preceding.

Nevertheless, this discarding of classical literature and all that it stood for was not allowed to pass without some amount of protest; and John of Garland was among those who attempted to save Humanistic studies from the wreckage that threatened them. His general attitude is perhaps best represented in the *Morale Scholarium*[1] (1241), a work now ascribed to him, wherein a lament is made for the decline of the liberal Arts in the face of the more profitable studies then popular, and a warning is issued against the defects of the current text-books on grammar, notably the *Doctrinale* and *Graecismus*. The author, for instance, is loud in his praises of the ancient classics, and vigorously condemns all those who 'belittled Helicon'. Maintaining that profane poets were not without their value to the Church, since they often presented truth in attractive allegorical fashion, he is bold enough to suggest that the earlier studies should once again be re-established by law. As for the new grammars, he condemns them outright for their poor Latinity, their foolish pedantry and unwholesome doctrine; and this attack he reinforces by voluminous teaching of a more orthodox kind found elsewhere in his writings. Thus his *Compendium Grammaticae*, the *Clavis Compendii* (an abridgement of the foregoing), and the *Accentarium* all treat of grammar. His three *Dictionarii*, made up of collections of words for students, are otherwise notable as embodying the earliest known use of the word 'dictionary'; while of his work on Poetics something has already been said. His interests were therefore of a varied kind; and it is not without its significance that in his *Epithalamicum* he hints at the progress of learning, explaining how wisdom had swept westward from Jerusalem to Athens, from Athens to Rome, and from Rome to Paris. Yet his scholarship, it may be suspected, was not profound. His teaching at any rate in places is confused and pedantic, betraying but little of the enlightened

[1] See L. J. Paetow, *op. cit.* pp. 17–19.

enthusiasm of John of Salisbury; while in one place he ventures the opinion that the twelfth-century French poet, Alain de Lille, was *Virgilio major et Homero certior*.[1] His chief importance therefore lies in his championing of classical authors, and in his insistent pleading for a return to literary studies in a hostile age and environment. On the existing trend of contemporary studies he had but little effect, and his protest is thus mainly of historical interest nowadays. In one place he himself claims to have served as 'a whetstone, which (as Horace observes) sharpens but does not cut'; and this claim, it may be added, was not altogether unfounded.

Of more positive significance in its relation to literary studies was yet another intellectual movement that was forming at the time in thirteenth-century England. The movement, it is true, was not animated primarily by literary interests; but in recalling attention to some of the ancient writings, and in laying the foundations for a better understanding of those works, it constituted something of a reaction against the prevailing Scholasticism, and directed contemporary thought into channels which were ultimately not without their bearing on literary studies. To these activities several factors had contributed. With the coming of the Dominicans and Franciscans in the third decade of the century, also with the swift growth of intellectual life, particularly at Oxford, and the emergence of a dynamic personality in Robert Grosseteste, Bishop of Lincoln, a new atmosphere had been generated, which not only gave rise to fresh ideals in the spheres of religion and learning, but also gave access to new modes of thought and sources of information. At the head of the movement stood Grosseteste (1175–1253), a great progressive force in both Church and State, whose influence extended to all branches of intellectual activity.[2] It has latterly been usual to emphasise his political and ecclesiastical services to the neglect of his achievements as scholar and scientist. To his contemporaries, however, he was conspicuous also as a pioneer in literary and scientific pursuits, one whose enthusiasm communicated itself to the group of scholars

---

[1] *De Triumphis Ecclesiae*, p. 74, quoted by Sandys, *op. cit.* 1, 554.
[2] See *Roger Bacon, Commemoration Essays*, ed. A. G. Little, pp. 33–54.

gathered around him, including Adam Marsh, John of Basingstoke, Nicholas the Greek, and the more famous Roger Bacon; and his work in these fields was accomplished, first by his lectures at Oxford, and subsequently by his writings and his tireless organising ability in educational matters. With his contributions to theology and philosophy, mathematics and natural science, we are here not concerned. What however is important is their underlying aim and motive; for it was none other than a critical revision of those scientific and philosophical doctrines which had gone to the building up of Scholastic theology. His main contention was that the logical and speculative impulse which had inspired the work of earlier writers was now exhausted for lack of matter, and that the search for truth should proceed on surer foundations than the mere syllogistic method and the positive knowledge then available. In matters of religious doctrine the accepted guide was the corrupt Paris text of the Vulgate, or the *Sentences* of Peter Lombard, a compilation of passages drawn from Scripture and the early Fathers. Nor were the main sources of philosophical and scientific knowledge any more reliable, consisting as they did of imperfect translations of Aristotle. What was therefore needed in the interests of sound learning was recourse to more accurate versions of the Bible and Aristotle; and for this an acquaintance with the languages of the originals—Greek, Hebrew and Arabic—was said to be essential, together with a knowledge of grammar and more accurate methods of translation.

This then was the new direction given at this date to contemporary studies which Grosseteste did much to foster. For a direct statement of his aims, it is true, we should seek in vain in his pages: but his animating ideas, and notably his views on translation, may be adequately gathered from remarks made in his various writings, as, for instance, in the Introduction and Commentary to his translations of "Dionysius the Areopagite", where Roger Bacon's teaching is plainly foreshadowed.[1] Apart from this, he did much to promote the revival of Greek studies in England, summoning Greek scholars from abroad, and arranging for Greek manuscripts to be brought from Athens,

[1] See p. 129 *infra*.

Constantinople and elsewhere. In the actual work of translation he also played a part; but even yet more valuable were his efforts at organising the work of collaborators. Thus, for the first time, Greek learning, and more particularly Aristotle's teaching, were being interpreted and assimilated by English scholars; and the process marked an advance in the fields of philosophy and science. But it represented also something more than this; for in this insistence on the importance of ancient teaching and of a right understanding of what the ancients had written, contemporary studies as a whole had been brought nearer to reality and truth. A new spirit, in short, had been devised for an approach to ancient writings, and a new method inaugurated, which was essential not only to a grasp of philosophical and scientific truth, but ultimately to an appreciation of literature and literary values as well.

For a more definite expression of the reaction to Scholasticism and the partial revival of literary interests which followed we must, however, turn to the works of Roger Bacon (*c.* 1214–92),[1] without doubt one of the great intellects of the Middle Ages, an Englishman whose fame has undergone strange vicissitudes, and whose place in the history of thought has yet to be adequately appreciated. The main facts of his career are now tolerably clear. After studying at Oxford (1230–5), where he came under Grosseteste's influence, he proceeded to Paris and there became master of the learning of the day. About 1247 his outlook and activities underwent radical change. Having entered the Franciscan order on his return to England (*c.* 1250), he forthwith discarded the traditional methods and objects of study, and, convinced of the inadequacy of Scholastic logic as an instrument of truth, he devoted himself from now on to independent thinking in matters of theology, and to the amassing of positive knowledge in the field of science. This resulted in conflict with the leaders of contemporary thought; and his tirades against authority led subsequently to his removal to the headquarters of his Order at Paris, where he was kept

---

[1] See E. Charles, *Roger Bacon* (1861), Sandys, *op. cit.* I, 589–97; also *Cambridge History of English Literature,* I, 205–10, and *Roger Bacon, Commemoration Essays,* ed. A. G. Little (1914).

in close confinement until 1266. In that year, however, so great was his repute for learning that he was asked by Clement IV, the reigning Pope, for a review of contemporary studies, by way of suggesting remedies for the prevailing evils of the time. Within fifteen months he had completed, under conditions of hardship, his three great works, the *Opus Majus*,[1] the *Opus Minus*,[2] and the *Opus Tertium*[2] (1267), which were followed by his *Compendium Studii Philosophiae*[2] (1272); and in these volumes were embodied Bacon's views on the whole field of learning. Taking all knowledge for his province, and betraying a vast range of scholarship and interests, he discoursed freely on theology, philosophy, mathematics and other sciences, pointing out defects of method, suggesting lines of treatment of a more promising kind, while also indulging in prophecies concerning the possibilities of science and its value when applied to human needs. After this, his main effort for the advancement of learning, he fell once more under ecclesiastical suspicion. In 1277 an attack on prevailing heresies was instituted by Pope Gregory X; and Bacon's contempt for authority, his free-thinking, and his practice of 'magical' sciences, led ultimately to his conviction. He was confined to the cloister for the rest of his days (1277–92); and his life-work was ended with the appearance of his *Compendium Studii Theologiae* in 1292.

From this account it becomes clear that Bacon's primary interests were not concerned with literature as such. They were bound up rather with the search for truth, with efforts to consolidate the foundations of learning, and to improve the methods of theological, philosophical and scientific studies generally. Thus he anticipates his later namesake, Francis Bacon, in his analysis of the general causes or stumbling-blocks (*offendicula*) which had hindered the progress of true learning.[3] He defines them as undue reliance on earlier authority, the tyranny of established custom, feeble submission to popular opinion, together with the pretentious ignorance of scholars.

---

[1] Ed. J. H. Bridges, 2 vols. 1897, tr. R. B. Burke (Univ. of Pennsylvania Press), 2 vols. 1928.
[2] *Bacon, Opera Inedita*, ed. J. S. Brewer (Rolls Series), 1859.
[3] *Opus Majus*, I, 2–3.

And of these the most baneful influence is said to have been the blind following of authority; for 'authority', he states, 'may compel belief, but cannot enlighten the understanding'. On the other hand the three sources of knowledge he describes as authority, reasoning and experience. But the only authority he recognises is that which comes from God; reasoning or logic he decries as an imperfect means of arriving at truth; and in the last resort experience is for him the only test. While, however, such doctrines as these represented a revolt against the whole system of Scholasticism, a plea also for freedom of thought, equally significant is his positive teaching concerning the aims and methods which were to characterise the new learning. Taking as his starting-point the existence of a supreme body of wisdom to be found in the Scriptures, he makes it his main object to expound that wisdom, calling to his aid all branches of learning. First among his requirements was thus an accurate text of the Bible. But since truth therein, he added, was often implied rather than explicitly stated, some acquaintance with other studies was also needed for an elucidation of its meaning. Thus philosophy he regarded as a limited revelation of that truth which in its entirety had been committed to patriarchs and prophets; science, again, as a knowledge of the laws of nature through which some conception of the Creator might be obtained. Both studies, he maintained, were to be applied to the interpretation of Biblical truth. And both for that purpose were to be established on scholarly foundations; the philosophy of Aristotle on a more accurate knowledge of his texts, the various sciences on a first-hand acquaintance with the facts of experience. This then, in brief, was the essence of his reforms in the field of learning. His ultimate aim was to arrive at a mistress-knowledge, theology, to which philosophy and the sciences were to be ancillary; though in science it was that his most lasting results were obtained, notably in the value he attached to experimental methods, in his researches into mathematics, physics, and the like, and in the visions he cherished of future scientific advance.

In view of these facts it would therefore seem futile to look for any treatment of literary matters in these encyclopaedic works of Roger Bacon. In the working out of his scheme, however, he touches incidentally on certain aspects of literature; and his remarks are not without their interest. In the first place it must be conceded that his treatment is confined almost wholly to 'the literature of knowledge' as opposed to 'the literature of power'. In other words his aim throughout is utilitarian, the establishment of sound learning; the appreciation and encouragement of 'belles lettres' formed no real part of his task. At the same time in directing men's attention anew to ancient writings and in suggesting fresh methods of approach, he opened up the path to a more genuine appreciation of ancient literature; and for him it may be claimed (as for other English Franciscans) that he maintained and developed the earlier traditions of the school of Chartres. Thus he is at one with the earlier Humanists in commending ancient writings to his readers, as in general the main sources of wisdom, of theological and philosophical truth. Equally significant, however, is his repeated caveat against a slavish following of the ancients. 'Aristotle himself', he states,[1] 'did not know everything; he did what was possible in his age'; and elsewhere he points out that whereas Aristotle had planted the tree of science, he had nevertheless not produced all its branches or fruits. The truth was, he explains,[2] that the ancients were fallible because they were human; also because they were the ancients, and thus representative of a more youthful age.[3] Reverence was therefore due to them, but not blind worship; they were to be contradicted and corrected wherever necessary.

Illuminating as was this attitude towards ancient writings at this date, yet more fundamental in kind was Bacon's insistence on the need for a correct reading of those ancient authorities. The main hindrances, it has been stated, were, first, the corrupt state of what passed for the Biblical text, and, secondly, the inaccurate translations of Aristotle's works then current; and on both textual criticism and the process of translation Bacon has something of value to say. Concerning the defects of

---

[1] *Op. Majus*, 1, 10.                          [2] *Ibid.* 1, 9.
[3] Cf. Francis Bacon's use of the same argument—*Antiquitas saeculi iuventus mundi* (*Advancement of Learning*, ed. W. A. Wright, p. 38).

the Paris Vulgate, Bacon, in the first place, is explicit and outspoken. He calls attention to the manifold corruptions introduced by contemporary theologians, booksellers, scribes, and self-styled 'correctors'. Their unfounded and capricious readings, he states,[1] had led to the mutilation of the sacred text, the utterances of which had been treated with a licence which would not have been permitted in connexion with the works of secular writers. What he therefore advocates is a return to Jerome's text of the Vulgate, with the help of those versions which had come down from the time of Gregory and Isidore, all of which were said to be free from other than scribal errors.[2] And in support he quotes the rule laid down by Augustine, that 'when Latin MSS. disagree, reference should be made to the many and the oldest of those MSS. (*ad antiquos et plures*), since ancient texts are to be preferred to the [more] modern, the many to the few'.[3] Elsewhere Bacon recommends an examination of those earlier manuscripts which were to be found in various monasteries in their original condition;[4] and if doubt still remained as to any particular reading, then recourse was to be had to those Greek and Hebrew texts on which Jerome's version had been originally based. Thus did Bacon suggest principles which were to facilitate the correct reading of ancient texts. The oldest manuscripts were to be regarded as the most authoritative; there was to be a careful collation of ancient and more modern readings; and the methods thus outlined form the basis of the textual criticism of the present day.

Equally suggestive, however, were his remarks on the methods of translation—ideas, as we have seen, inspired by his master, Grosseteste. On the inadequacy of the current translations of Aristotle he dilates in more than one place. The works of Michael Scot, Alfred the Englishman, William the Fleming and others he condemns, for instance, as mere travesties of the originals.[5] The study of such works he held to be sheer waste of time; and in view of the error thus inculcated in connexion with Aristotle's teaching, he wished that all such perversions

---

[1] *Op. Min.* (R.S.), p. 330.     [2] *Ibid.* p. 335.
[3] *Ibid.* p. 331; cf. Aug. *Contra Faustum*, xxxii, 16.
[4] *Op. Maj.* (Bridges), iii, 95.     [5] *Comp. Stud. Phil.* (R.S.), viii, 471.

could be committed to the flames.[1] At the same time he is alive
to the necessity for translations as such. He contended that all
that was great in ancient thought had first made its appearance
in Hebrew, Greek, or Arabic form; whereas the Latins themselves had produced no great text of a theological or philosophical kind.[2] Hence the need for the transference of this
learning into a more familiar Latin dress, if the wisdom of
antiquity was to be made accessible. That something would be
lost in the process, of this he is also aware. It was only in the
original language, he stated, that the essential truth and beauty
of ancient thought could be fully appreciated; 'just as wine',
he added, 'is purer when drawn from the original cask'.[3] But
while translations for this reason could not displace original
documents, they nevertheless had their value in a scheme of
culture; and Bacon shows himself to be conscious of the difficulties inherent in the task of translation. Thus he quotes
Jerome to the effect that one language cannot adequately be
represented by another. 'That which sounds well in one
language', wrote Jerome, 'becomes harsh (*absurdum*) and ludicrous in another; Homer turned into Latin is made ridiculous
and devoid of all eloquence.'[4] And Bacon goes on to explain
why this is so; because, firstly, the idioms of one language cannot
with absolute fidelity be reproduced in another, and, secondly,
because of the difficulty of finding equivalents in Latin for
scientific terms originally expressed in a different tongue, Greek
or Arabic, for instance.[5] In such cases, Bacon adds, the translator was wont either to preserve the original terminology,
which was intelligible only to those who knew the language, or
else to attempt some sort of new coinage, which was understood
by himself alone. He therefore urges on all translators two
main requirements: first, that they should be well versed in the
languages concerned, so as to appreciate fine shades of meaning,
and, secondly, that they should have some knowledge of the
subject-matter treated, to minimise the risk of absurd misinter-
pretations.[6] These injunctions he repeats on more than one

---

[1] *Comp. Stud. Phil.* (R. S.), VIII, 469.
[2] *Ibid.* VIII, 465.          [3] *Ibid.*
[4] *Op. Tert.* (R. S.), XXV, 90; cf. Jerome, *De Optimo genere interpretandi*, II, 381.
[5] *Comp. Stud. Phil.* (R. S.), VIII, 466.
[6] *Op. Maj.* (Bridges), III, 33; *Op. Tert.* (R. S.), X, 33.

occasion; and in thus placing on a sounder foundation the work of translation, he prepared the way for a more effective use of the writings of antiquity.

In yet one other way did Bacon strive for a truer apprehension of what the ancients had written, and that was in emphasising anew, as the earlier Humanists had done, the need for the study of grammar. In a sense this demand followed naturally from the new value attached to a knowledge of languages, which he had described as 'the first gate that led to the acquisition of wisdom' (*notitia linguarum est prima porta sapientiae*).[1] But whereas the Humanists of the preceding generation had Latin grammar chiefly in mind, Bacon now extends the field, and insists on the need for a grammatical knowledge of all the learned languages, notably Greek, Hebrew and Arabic. With the study of the vernaculars—*Anglicum* and *Gallicum*—he is not seriously concerned, though in one place he hints at the advantages, both commercial and political, to be derived from a study of languages generally.[2] It is in the languages of antiquity, however, that he is mainly interested; and a knowledge of grammar he held to be more necessary for his generation than the study of logic, inasmuch as it led to a more accurate reading of ancient works, thus opening men's eyes to the full light of antiquity, while also correcting those false etymologies, those obscure and barbarous forms, then so prevalent. Nor does he confine his efforts to pleading the cause of grammar. His intention was to write a series of manuals dealing with Greek, Hebrew and Arabic grammar, though apparently he achieved only a treatment of Greek. His *Greek Grammar*, however, survives in a fairly complete form; while his teaching on the subject is also referred to elsewhere in his writings.[3] That work in the main is a treatise on the comparative grammar of Greek and Latin, embodying also a treatment of Greek idioms, accidence, prosody and the rest.[4] In view of the limited supply of Greek literature then available, the manual gives ample evidence of Bacon's keen intellect and wide reading; and it is otherwise notable as

[1] *Op. Tert.* (R. S.), xxviii, 102.      [2] *Op. Maj.* (Bridges), iii, 96.
[3] Cf. *Op. Tert.* (R. S.), lx, 236–8; *Comp. Stud. Phil.* (R. S.), vii, 451–519.
[4] See *Roger Bacon, Commemoration Essays*, ed. A. G. Little, pp. 115–51, for a fuller treatment.

being one of the first attempts before the later Renascence to foster an acquaintance with Greek in England.

So far, then, it may be claimed that Bacon, in his efforts to bring about a revival of sound learning, was indirectly instrumental also in advancing the cause of literary study, by preparing the way for a truer understanding of the writings of antiquity. This in itself was preliminary work of an essential kind. It provided the necessary foundation for further critical activity, for ultimately an aesthetic appreciation of ancient literature; and it constituted his main contribution to literary culture. At the same time evidence is not wanting that he also shared in some measure in Humanistic sympathies and aims; and this is seen not only in his wide acquaintance with classical literature, but also in scattered reminiscences of linguistic and literary theory, in occasional pronouncements on formal matters, and in critical judgments on contemporary activities. To begin with, the power of 'the word'—traditional in classical antiquity—had been a familiar theme of earlier Humanists; and Bacon's remarks on the nature of language are not without their interest, embodying as they do not only current doctrine, but also some speculations of his own. Recalling, for instance, the opinions of Aristotle, Boethius, Augustine and others, he declares in one place that ' the first writers (*auctores linguarum*) had invented languages', or that the diversity of tongues was due to Divine intervention at the tower of Babel.[1] Elsewhere, however, he shrewdly suggests that differences of language were the result of geographical factors;[2] and he points to the various idioms of Picardian, Gallic and Provençal, all of which were described as varieties of Latin, differentiated by differences of locality.[3] Concerning the innate power of words he has also something to say; and here again his remarks are a blend of fancy and truth. Words, he describes as ' the highest product of the rational soul (*opus animae rationalis praecipuum*), elements capable of affording the greatest delight'.[4] They are said to have special force when they are 'the outcome of profound thought, great longing, fixed intention, and strong faith'; for then the soul

---

[1] *Op. Tert.* (R.S.), xxviii, 102.     [2] *Ibid.* xxxvii, 120.
[3] *Ibid.* xxv, 90.     [4] *Ibid.* xxvi, 96.

gives to expression something of its own quality and virtue. Almost all miracles, he adds, had been performed by means of words. Moreover, words were said to have given to the prophets of old their power of utterance; and from the same source, we are told, came also the occult effects of charms and incantations. Nor does he fail to refer to those mystical properties of words which formed part of traditional theory. In the Bible, for instance, the manifold power of words was said to be further enhanced by that use of figurative speech in which a spiritual meaning was ascribed to every word over and above its literal sense, and allegorical, tropological and anagogical interpretations were read into any and every text.

Of the artistic treatment of words and those various devices by which words had been raised to a higher power in classical antiquity, he has less to say. He is too immersed in his task of establishing a sound body of learning to care much for fine shades of literary expression or mere formal excellences. Yet he is not altogether devoid of that sense of form which the earlier Humanists had imbibed in part from their classical studies. In one place indeed he shows clearly his understanding of the part played by both subject-matter and style in literary composition, when he states that ' Wisdom without eloquence is like a sharp sword in the hands of one palsied, whereas eloquence without wisdom is like a sharp sword in a madman's grasp '.[1] Moreover he explains, in accordance with ancient theory, that the three functions of a writer (or orator) are to reveal the truth, to delight his readers (or hearers), and to persuade their minds; and that, corresponding to these functions, three styles are possible, namely, the plain (*humilis*), the middle (*mediocris*), and the grand (*grandis*).[2] For himself, he adds, he eschews all verbal ornaments, all rhetorical devices, and adopts a plain or simple style. This he regards as in keeping with his main objective; and for truth unadorned he claims an appeal of its own. This, however, does not mean that he neglects entirely all formal considerations. On the contrary he is aware that good writing is an art, and incidentally he refers to some of its underlying principles—principles reminiscent largely of ancient teaching.

[1] *Op. Tert.* (R. S.), I, 4.　　　[2] Cf. Cic. *De Oratore*, II, 128.

Thus he requires in the first place sound subject-matter; then, too, a judicious selection of that material. In addition, style, he adds, should be appropriate to the subject treated. Brevity of treatment should also be aimed at, since verbosity hindered the apprehension of a theme, besides making a work distasteful. Perspicuity, again, is said to be essential, even though to be brief and at the same time clear was not at all easy.[1] In general he commends the advice of Aristotle that it was necessary 'to speak as the common people do, but to think as the wise'; and elsewhere he recommends variety of expression, quoting Seneca to the effect that 'nothing is pleasing unless refreshed by variety of effect'.[2]

Beyond elementary matters such as these, Bacon does not go far in his injunctions concerning literary composition; though he has some glimmerings of higher ranges of literary art, and this would appear from occasional references in his writings. Thus in one place he expresses a wish that he could induce his readers to seek out the works of Cicero, Seneca and other classical writers, 'in which shine the beauty and dignity of wisdom';[3] and here he is surely speaking as one of the Humanists. But he has glimpses too of yet loftier reaches in the realms of art. He held that 'poetic material (*argumentum poeticum*), of moral or theological import, should necessarily be clothed in metrical or rhythmical beauty', and 'adorned also with all the colours of rhetoric';[4] and this he asserts on more than one authority. First he quotes the example of Holy Writ, and recalls in its pages the presence of metrical and rhythmical passages, which were so written, he explains, to entice the reader to Divine wisdom by their musical qualities, and to bring him near to the mysteries of God.[5] This he supports by the teaching of Avicenna and Alfarabi of Bagdad (d. 950), according to which, poetic material should be rendered *sublime* and *decorum* by means of metre and rhythm, so as to inflame the reader with a love of virtue and a hatred of what was evil.[6] And such use of metre and rhythm, together with an observance of *decorum*

---

[1] *Op. Tert.* (R.S.), XVI, 57.
[2] *Comp. Stud. Theol.* (Rashdall), Pref.                    [3] *Ibid.*
[4] *Op. Tert.* (R.S.), LXIV, 266.          [5] *Ibid.*          [6] *Ibid.*

in matters of time, place and person, he further states to have been part of Aristotle's doctrine in his *Poetics*[1]—an interesting reference at this particular date. To the Middle Ages Aristotle's *Rhetoric* and *Poetics* were practically unknown; all that was available in the matter of texts being Alfarabi's Glosses on the *Rhetoric* and the paraphrase of the *Poetics* due to Averroës. Neither, however, furnished an adequate version of the original Greek. Indeed, Averroës's paraphrase, which had come through the distorting medium of two oriental translations— being based on an Arabic text (tenth century), which rested in its turn on an earlier Syrian translation—presented but a garbled version of the ancient Greek treatise; and to this fact Bacon incidentally bears witness when he states that Hermann l'Allemand, a scholar at the court of Frederic II, had not ventured to translate either the *Rhetoric* or the *Poetics* on account of the defective nature of the versions then available.[2] At the same time it is perhaps worth noting that Bacon at this date had already recognised the importance of these works of Aristotle. He regarded them, it would seem, as an extension of Aristotle's teaching on logic, and as inculcating a form of reasoning different from that of the demonstrative kind expounded in the *Organon*.[3] In other words, their teaching was held to represent a more effective means of bringing about persuasion in philosophy and theology; so that for Bacon both poetic and rhetoric were little more than a higher form of logic. It was a conception of poetry that was shared not only by other Scholastic philosophers, but also by scholars of the later Renascence as well;[4] and it was obviously the outcome of an imperfect reading of Aristotle. Yet even this vague recognition of the importance of Aristotle's *Poetics* has its interest, in view of the fuller revelation of its value which was to be made at the sixteenth-century Renascence.

Such then are the sporadic comments on literary theory found in Bacon's writings, and they are supplemented by occasional judgments of a limited kind, based mainly, as would

[1] *Op. Tert.* (R. S.), LXIV, 266, LXXV, 306.
[2] *Comp. Stud. Phil.* (R. S.), 473; *Op. Maj.* (Bridges), III, 59.
[3] *Op. Maj.* (Bridges), IV, ch. 2.
See J. E. Spingarn, *Literary Criticism in the Renaissance*, pp. 24–7.

be expected, on subject-matter rather than on artistic qualities. Thus Seneca, for instance, is praised for his ethical teaching, his belief in progress, and his respect for reason; while Ovid, on the other hand, is condemned as frivolous, his 'fables and follies' being described as full of vain superstitions and corrupt morality, and therefore of little use for edification.[1] Then, too, the incoherence and irrelevance of contemporary expositors of Aristotle are censured. They are said to busy themselves with superfluous questions and worthless trifles to the neglect of his essential teaching, which, it was suggested, would be more effectively presented by means of compendia or abridgements, bringing out clearly the main objects of the various studies.[2] Elsewhere Bacon has some comments to make on artistic matters, though poets (as well as philosophers) he is wont to regard as but 'broken lights' of truth. Thus he criticises in spirited fashion the poetry of the Latin hymns then current, which he describes as artificial, devoid of simplicity and emotional value, the work moreover of men altogether ignorant of prosody.[3] More significant still is his judgment on the affected eloquence of his day, as represented in contemporary preaching. There, he maintains, vanity and bad taste reigned supreme. Most preachers are said to make use of a futile and pedantic art, in which subtle distinctions were made after the manner of Porphyrius, vain consonances of words being sought, while periods were made to end in symmetrical fashion and in a regular return of the same sounds.[4] Such meticulous and precious utterance, he added, was devoid of all genuine artistic merit, all persuasive quality. It was mere childish display, a pretentious eloquence, which degraded the sacred themes thus treated; and the only remedy was a study of the ancients, and more especially of Aristotle's two treatises, his *Rhetoric* and the *Poetics*.

From what has so far been said of Bacon's varied activities, and more particularly of his occasional references to literary matters, some idea may now be formed of his attitude to literary culture, and of the part he played in furthering literary studies.

---

[1] *Op. Tert.* (R.S.), xv, 55.          [2] *Ibid.* v, 18–20.
[3] *Ibid.* LXXIV, 302.          [4] *Ibid.* LXXV, 304; cf. also Wiclif, p. 149 *infra*.

In the first place to suggest that his influence was great in the sphere of literature would be grossly to exaggerate. He nowhere betrays any great insight into literary problems or standards; while the critical faculty with which he was richly endowed was applied in the main to other fields of study. Yet his contribution to literary studies at this date was by no means negligible. In his efforts to establish learning on a sounder basis, he was instrumental in calling attention anew to the priceless legacy of ancient writings, and in preparing the way for a more fruitful approach to those writings. Here then lay his most substantial contribution to critical thought where literature was concerned; and, preparatory work though it was, its historical significance is considerable. In an age when Scholasticism was wrecking the hopes of earlier Humanists, his teaching tended to revive twelfth-century enthusiasms, by giving to them new direction and scope. But it did also more than this. In providing the key for the unlocking of ancient treasures it anticipated the findings of later textual critics, and revealed for the first time the necessary foundation on which an aesthetic criticism of literature was ultimately to be based.

Apart from this he has but little to offer that is of permanent critical value. Some reminiscences of ancient literary theory occur, as well as an occasional literary judgment; though he is but remotely interested in formal details, in the graces of style or the art of poetry. Yet here again he is not without his teaching for the ages that followed. He is for instance the first English scholar to suggest the value of Aristotle's *Poetics*, however vague and imperfect his knowledge of that work may have been. He also hints at Aristotle's limitations and fallibility, as well as at the need for regarding all knowledge as progressive.[1] And whereas the *Poetics* was to be rediscovered and more fully appreciated two centuries later, the wisdom of his teaching with regard to the lack of finality in Aristotelian doctrine passed unheeded for the most part, thus accounting for the idolatry displayed by literary theorists in the seventeenth century and later. A similar neglect was, however, the treatment meted out to his works in general. Few direct allusions to his writings are

---

[1] *Op. Maj.* (Bridges), I, 6; II, 14; cf. also John of Garland, p. 122 *supra*.

found before the Renascence; and then he was best known as charlatan and sorcerer, while also figuring as a legendary character in *Friar Bacon and Friar Bungay*. Some there were who more accurately assessed his value; and his later namesake, Francis Bacon, probably owed not a little to the seminal ideas he had scattered so prodigally. It has in short been claimed for him that 'he pointed out the line of intellectual advance which the world was to follow two centuries after his death'; and in the history of letters he is no negligible figure, but one who, in inaugurating a new approach to ancient literature, prepared the way for a wider and keener vision in literary matters.

There yet remains to mention the work of Richard of Bury (1281–1345), who, in the generation following, contributed to the revival of literary interests by his *Philobiblon*,[1] a Latin tract which embodied much of the earlier Humanistic teaching. An Oxford scholar and bibliophile, he served first as tutor to the future king, Edward III, later as envoy (1330 and 1333) to the Pope at Avignon; and subsequently being appointed to the see of Durham, he bequeathed at his death his valuable library to Durham (later Trinity) College, Oxford. His *Philobiblon*, of which some thirty-five manuscripts have come down, was completed at the close of its author's life; though it has also been attributed to Robert Holkot, one of Richard's chaplains, but on inconclusive evidence. As one of the most attractive of medieval treatises it offers advice on the making, collecting, and preserving of books, provides a vivid picture of copyists, scribes, correctors, illuminators, *stationarii* and *librarii*; and while embodying not a few of the views on literature then current, it also conveys to its readers something of its author's genuine love of letters.

Not least valuable is the light thrown on contemporary views concerning literature and literary studies, most of which are inspired by the writings of John of Salisbury and other Humanists; though echoes of Italian thought seem also present, ideas suggestive of Boccaccio's later *De Genealogia Deorum* (*c.* 1360), which may possibly have been communicated to Richard by Petrarch during their meeting at Avignon in 1330.

[1] Tr. by E. C. Thomas, *The Love of Books* (King's Classics), 1902.

Thus our author extols the works of the ancients, maintaining with the old grammarian, Phocas, that all fields of learning had been explored by them, so that all that was left for later writers was to summarise their teaching (*multa loqui breviter*).[1] At the same time he laments, as John of Salisbury before him had done, the shallowness of contemporary studies, with young fledglings repeating aimlessly the rules of Priscian and Donatus, or chattering in futile fashion about Aristotle's *Categories* and *Peri Hermenias* (*De Interpretatione*); [2] and as the indispensable key to ancient literature he recommends the study of grammar.[3] Elsewhere he takes up the earlier attack on utilitarian legal studies as hindering the more liberal pursuit of the humanities; [4] while he also urges the need for an acquaintance with Greek and Hebrew, if the Bible and Latin writings were to be understood.[5] Earlier ideas thrown out concerning intellectual progress are also expounded.[6] He traces, for instance, the growth of learning from Babylon to Paris and Britain, and maintains that by gradual accretions knowledge had grown. Even Aristotle, he adds, was not independent of predecessors. He was said to have pruned and supplemented earlier teaching, and to have held that even those who erred helped in the search for truth. And a similar sense of historical development is revealed in our author's comments on literary affairs. Virgil is said to have been indebted to Homer, Theocritus and Lucretius; and Rome in general to have been 'watered by the streams of Greece'. In addition he has something to say in defence of literature and poetry; and his apology, couched in the terminology of the time, is one of the earliest attempts of the kind in England. In the first place he claims for literature (i.e. books of the Liberal Arts) the dignity of a *scientia*, inasmuch as it represented a body of knowledge, a fixed 'science' based on universal principles, whereas law on the other hand was but a variable *facultas* resting on mere practice or custom.[7] Then, too, he replies to detractors who had assailed 'the fables of the poets' as lacking in truth.[8] He points out, for instance, that the study of even

---

[1] c. IX.  [2] *Ibid.*  [3] c. XII.  [4] c. XI.  [5] c. X.
[6] *Ibid.*; cf. also John of Garland and Roger Bacon, pp. 122, 137 *supra*.
[7] c. XI; cf. John of Salisbury, *Met.* I, 11; IV, 8.  [8] c. XIII.

unseemly fiction might help in forming an effective style; while an edifying story, under the veil of allegory, might reveal truths of nature or history [1] In short, he maintains that 'if a man found profit in poetry, as Virgil claimed to have done in Ennius, he will have done well'; and in support of his position he quotes the familiar dictum of Horace concerning the function of poetry. Therefore, he adds, the study of poetry should be encouraged; more especially as saintly writers had often made use of poetic utterances, and some knowledge of poetry was thus needed for an understanding of their works.

The outstanding feature of the work, however, is the tribute therein paid to literature in general; and this our author does with an eloquence and a fervour reminiscent of John of Salisbury. He praises books, first of all, as the most effective and delightful of teachers. 'Truth', he explains,[2] 'that triumphs over all, seems to endure more usefully, and to bear fruit more abundantly, in books. The voice's utterance perishes with the sound; truth latent in the mind is hidden wisdom, a treasure unseen. But truth that shines forth in books will manifest itself to all our senses, to the sight when read, to the hearing when heard, to the touch when transcribed, bound and corrected.' 'Then, too,' he exclaims,[3] 'what delightful teaching there is in books. They are masters who instruct without rod or ferule. If you draw near to them they are not asleep; if you inquire of them they do not hold back; they do not chide when you make mistakes; nor do they laugh if you are ignorant.' Then resorting in medieval fashion to figurative language, he proceeds to describe them as 'wells of living water', 'golden pots in which manna is stored', 'the ark of Noah', 'the ladder of Jacob', and 'the scrip of David from which smooth stones are taken for the slaying of Goliath'. Nor does this exhaust his panegyric; for, rising to a higher note, he declares books to be 'ambassadors to our friends and messengers to the world; in prosperity a joy, a comfort in time of trouble; a means whereby things present are perpetuated and things past recalled; by which also faith is established, vice reproved, and the contem-

---

[1] Cf. Boccaccio's teaching, pp. 171 *infra*: also C. G. Osgood, *Boccaccio on Poetry*, pp. 48, 164.       [2] c. 1.              [3] *Ibid.*

plative life fostered'. 'Thus', he continues, 'we are enabled to survey the world and time, viewing the things that are and the things that are not, as it were in the mirror of eternity'; and, finally, 'with their aid we soar to the First Cause, the Creator of all, to lose ourselves in love unending.'[1]

In view of this tribute none can mistake the author's position in the sphere of letters, which is that of one of a select minority who, in the age of Scholasticism, saw clearly the possibilities of literature and learning, and strove to communicate their enthusiasms to others. Much of his thought is doubtless borrowed, notably from John of Salisbury and Roger Bacon among English predecessors. Original and personal, however, is his profound love of letters, as well as the ardent expression of that love, which treats of books as living things, endowed with the faculty of communicating both life and thought. And in his treatment not least valuable is the importance he attaches to poetry and the reading of poetry, for which he provides a defence in anticipation of Boccaccio. That defence has limitations characteristic of the age; it is based on non-aesthetic, allegorical grounds. But the attempt in itself is significant, as pointing to a widening of Humanistic sympathies. It is, in short, as one, and not the least, of the medieval Humanists that Richard of Bury figures in literary history. He carries on the movement which began in the twelfth century and culminated in the later Revival of Learning.

[1] c. xv.

# CHAPTER VII

## NATIVE LITERARY PROBLEMS: *THE OWL AND THE NIGHTINGALE*, WICLIF, CHAUCER

SO far the contributions to literary theorising have been those of Latinists, Englishmen writing with Latin as their literary medium, and discussing literary matters from various standpoints, but always with the cultivation of a medieval Latin literature in mind. With the fourteenth century a marked change came over the form and nature of these discussions. Not only was English used as the means of expression, but problems of the vernacular literature also began to engage the attention; and from now on, critical activities entered on a new phase, in which sporadic attempts were made, directly or indirectly, to deal with native literary matters—the application of medieval poetic to vernacular literature, the possibilities of the vernacular as a means of expression, or the appreciation of various poetic achievements. To this change many political and social causes contributed, factors resulting in a fusion of the various elements of English life into a national unity. It was significant, to begin with, that English by the fourteenth century had become the official medium of instruction in schools, while in 1362 a statute was passed permitting the use of English in the law courts. Meanwhile a national consciousness was slowly emerging; the voice of the people was making itself heard; new conceptions of personal and religious liberty were in process of forming; and with the break-up of the old literary commonwealth of the Middle Ages, Latin now ceased to be the only vehicle of deeper thought, while expression in the vernacular acquired a new dignity and importance. One interesting phase of this wider national movement was the revival of alliterative verse (1350–1400), which represented an attempt to recapture something of the Old English spirit, with its vigorous measure and its archaic diction. Attempts were also being made to develop a literary prose; notable contributions to English poetry were forthcoming from Chaucer, Langland and others; and in the interest thus aroused in native literary matters, it was inevitable that some attention should be paid to literary theory and judgment. Thus from Wiclif, Chaucer and others came critical comments of various kinds; and these native interests remained uppermost in the incidental remarks of fifteenth-century writers.

Meanwhile this change of direction in critical activities had been anticipated a century previously in the poem, *The Owl and the Nightingale*[1] (*c.* 1210), which in the form of a debate had discussed the relative values of certain forms of contemporary poetry. The poem, written by an author unknown—possibly one Nicholas of Guildford, referred to in the poem—is a work of considerable historical and artistic value. In it are reflected most of the intellectual interests of the age; the revival of dialectic as a means of arriving at truth, the fondness for allegory, animal fables and *débats*, the enthusiasm for recent legal developments as seen in the procedure of the law courts cunningly counterfeited, or again, the arrival of the Troubadour love-lyrics, which came as something new to contemporary minds. Nor is its treatment of these elements less noteworthy. Weaving together his variegated material into an artistic whole, the poet has given new life to the old *conflictus* by his well-designed structure, the realism and humour of his characterisation, his picturesque imagery and skill in dialogue, his use of the familiar style, and the art with which he handles the octosyllabic couplet; so that altogether the poem represents one of the outstanding performances in medieval English literature.

Of special interest, however, is the element of literary criticism embodied in the poem, consisting of a discussion on what must have been a pertinent question at the time, namely, the relative values of the old traditional didactic themes and the new love themes of the Troubadours as subject-matter for poetry. The debate, it is true, is treated in allegorical fashion, and is further veiled by being conducted on the lines of a contemporary law case. Nevertheless the main motive emerges clear and unmistakable. The dispute from the first is definitely stated to be primarily concerned with the singing of the two birds (*hure ʒ*

---

[1] Ed. J. W. H. Atkins, with Intro., trans. and notes (1922).

*hure of oþere songe*);[1] and though personalities and other side-issues subsequently enter in the heat of the argument, it is the subject-matter of their respective songs that remains throughout the main bone of contention. Allegorically interpreted, this can have only one meaning. The poem is in effect a criticism of the poetic values of those didactic and love themes, of which the two birds by tradition were regarded as representative.

Concerning religious and didactic poetry, in the first place; it is claimed that its virtue lay chiefly in its moral teaching, which directed men's minds to spiritual ends, by means of exhortations to repentance, by visions of things to come, and by expositions of hidden truths and their symbolical meanings.[2] Lacking in artistic grace, monotonous and harsh in treatment,[3] such poetry, it was added, offered delight to but few with its warnings, its terrors and laments. On the other hand the main function of love-poetry was said to be that of giving pleasure and of diffusing happiness among men.[4] Inspired by sheer joy in living and with its expression enhanced by skilful technique,[5] an uplifting effect was incidentally claimed for this type of poetry, inasmuch as all courtly songs were said to be 'a preparation for the harmonies of heaven'.[6] Thus far the two types of poetry were distinguished by their moralistic and hedonistic aims respectively—the two-fold function ascribed to poetry from the earliest classical times. And although, in accordance with the debate convention, no explicit judgment is given, yet the preference of the writer seems instinctively to incline to the more joyous love-poetry,[7] thus challenging the traditional form and claiming for the new poetry due recognition.

At the same time certain objections to the new school are also discussed. The main charge is that the conventional love themes were often immoral in kind, celebrating the amours of wives in accordance with the doctrine of the Courts of love, thus conducing to looseness of living.[8] The justification for such themes, on the other hand, was said to be found in those unhappy marriages where a jealous husband (*le jaloux*) tyran-

---

[1] l. 11.
[2] ll. 869, 927, 1213.
[3] ll. 40, 310 ff.
[4] ll. 433 ff., 986.
[5] ll. 48, 757 ff.
[6] ll. 717–18.
[7] ll. 1649 ff.
[8] ll. 1045 ff.

nised over his unfortunate wife (*la mal mariée*)[1]—a situation
which aroused the sympathy of the poet, though mere wanton-
ness in wives was not thereby condoned. But, apart from this,
it was contended that love in itself was no unworthy theme of
poetry, since all human love was by nature pure unless
corrupted.[2] Moreover, sins of the flesh were not the most
heinous; there was authority for stating that spiritual pride was
the most deadly of sins.[3] And, in addition, such love-poetry
was said to have positive ethical value; it might convey moral
truths of a valuable kind, such as the virtue of fidelity or the
transitoriness of earthly passion.[4]

This then is the defence of love-poetry submitted by an
English writer of the early thirteenth century. The arguments
advanced, it is true, are mainly ethical in kind; but not without
its interest is the expression, however inadequate, of the aesthetic
possibilities of such poetry and its pleasure-giving qualities.
Then, too, a certain freshness of mind and independence of
judgment are shown in the criticism of the artificial code which
prescribed the limited themes of the Courts of love. The full
potentialities of the romance of love as a subject for poetry later
generations were to reveal; though Euripides long ago had held
that 'Love was a prime source and inspiration of poetry'. It
is, however, as the first critical inquiry of its kind in English
that the discussion in *The Owl and the Nightingale* calls for
attention. Coloured inevitably by the ethical preoccupations
of the age, though not wholly devoid of aesthetic insight, it
nevertheless reflects that spirit of criticism which for the first
time at this date was challenging old traditions in literature
and life.

While however *The Owl and the Nightingale* thus represents
the first venture in vernacular criticism, such activities per-
ceptibly developed in the course of the fourteenth century,
when matters of special contemporary interest were discussed
in works of various forms, including an anonymous *Treatise on
Miracle Plays*, remarks on the art of preaching and prose composition by Wiclif, and Chaucer's parody, *Sir Thopas*, on the
popular romances. Not without its interest, in the first place,

[1] ll. 1075 ff.    [2] ll. 1378 ff.    [3] ll. 1395 ff.    [4] ll. 1347, 1450.

is the discussion that dealt with those vernacular Miracle plays which represented one of the chief literary products of the time, and marked the beginnings of the English drama. Already popular in the thirteenth century, such plays in the century following were removed from the precincts of the Church, and, passing under the control of municipalities (Chester, York, Coventry and the rest), they became subject to abuses of which Grosseteste, William of Waddington and Robert Manning had from time to time complained; and in the *Treatise against Miracle Plays*[1]—a sermon preserved in the library of the British Museum (Add. 24.202)—the attack assumes something like systematic form. The work opens with the general statement that the representation of Christ's miracles on the stage was a desecration of sacred subjects; after which arguments in support of the practice are assembled and confuted. It is argued, to begin with, that such plays were really a form of worship, that they were calculated to lead to a better way of life, and that not infrequently they moved men to tears and directed their thoughts to religious ends. Moreover they were said to supply an elevating form of necessary recreation; and since sacred pictures were everywhere accepted, no objection should therefore be raised to the more effective dramatic treatment of sacred themes. To these claims our author replies, maintaining that such plays were designed not for the worship of God but for the pleasure of men; and, so far from converting men to a better way of life, they more often resulted in leading men astray. Moreover the emotions they excited were said to be false, being due to mere play-acting and not to a consciousness of sin; while as a means of recreation they were described as worthless, since the fruit of good works was not forthcoming in their patrons. Sacred pictures, on the other hand, were defended when they conveyed plain truth in simple fashion, and were not the occasion of idolatry; but Miracle plays stood condemned on account of the sensual delight they afforded, thus conducing to wickedness rather than to godliness. After this, his main indictment, our author concludes

[1] See T. Wright and J. O. Halliwell, *Reliquiae Antiquae*, II, 42 ff.; A. S. Cook, *Literary Middle English Reader*, pp. 278–86.

with arguments drawn from the Scriptures. He describes such plays as a breach of the third Commandment, a light and unworthy treatment of holy things; and, further dilating on the social evils resulting, he calls attention to the reckless spending and the indulgence in gluttony on the part of those who were wont to witness these spectacles.

It is clear at once that as a contribution to literary criticism in its truest sense this tract has but little intrinsic value. In the claims advanced and the opposing arguments alike, moral and religious considerations are all that matter; and the treatise is merely yet another of those attacks on stage-plays which had appeared from the time of Tertullian onwards, and were to be represented even in Elizabethan days. The truth was that old prejudices died hard, and as yet there existed no sense of aesthetic values. That the plays were capable of emotional effects and of giving delight greater than could be obtained from books, this much was conceded. But such pleasure was suspect on moral grounds; and not least significant was the weight attached to the social evils bound up with these performances. At the same time the attack is not without its interest historically. In form it is reminiscent of earlier dialectical methods, in its marshalling of the various pros and cons; while its arguments are mainly those of previous writers. Its chief interest, however, lies in the light it throws on the contemporary attitude to stage-plays; and as the first pronouncement on the English drama it is not without its significance in critical history.

Of more lasting importance was the movement of the latter half of the fourteenth century which aimed at rendering English prose a more effective instrument of expression. Hitherto vernacular prose had been used mainly for practical purposes, being employed in documents, sermons, and writings of limited appeal; and as such it had been for the most part naïve, formless and crude, but little removed from colloquial discourse, or else coloured by false rhetoric and by devices of regular verse. With the resurgence of the national spirit, attempts were now made to devise a more efficient prose, the immediate occasion being the desire to furnish Englishmen with religious teaching in their own tongue, to present them above all with a Bible in English, and to render accessible in the vernacular the standard works of the time bearing on secular knowledge. To these tasks both Wiclif (*c.* 1320–84) and Trevisa (1326–1412) contributed, the former by his *Sermones* and the 'Wiclifite' Bible, the latter by his translations of the works of Bartholomaeus Anglicus and Higden; and some interesting views on translation, on preaching, and on the art of prose generally, were therefore forthcoming at this date.

Concerning the processes of translation Trevisa, in the first place, has something to say. In the Dialogue between a lord and a clerk (i.e. Lord Berkeley and Trevisa himself) which forms the Preface to his translation of the *Polychronicon* (1387), the use of the vernacular for purposes of translation is vigorously defended. At the same time the traditional use of verse in translations is also discussed; and the preference is given to the medium of prose, since 'comynlich prose is more clere than ryme, more esy and more pleyn to knowe and understonde'. Other questions are raised by Wiclif and his fellow-workers, Nicholas Hereford and John Purvis.[1] The medieval conception of translation had in general been that of paraphrase; but special care it was felt was needed in translating the Bible. And here the translators betray some difference of opinion. Hereford stood for a literal translation of the Latin version; whereas Purvis, in the Prologue to his revision of the 'Wiclifite' Bible, insists on the need for a free and idiomatic rendering, for a translation 'aftir the sentence (i.e. meaning) and not oneli aftir the wordes, so that the sentence be as opin, either openere, in English as in Latyn', without however going 'fer fro the lettre'.[2]

Yet more significant were the remarks made on the writing of prose. That the need for a more effective prose was felt by others was suggested by the remarks of Thomas Usk in his *Testament of Love* (1387),[3] when he lamented the prevailing fondness for 'quaint Knitting colours' to the neglect of the thought, and declared his intention of writing plainly so as to be understood. But it was the forceful personality of Wiclif

---

[1] See G. P. Krapp, *The Rise of English Literary Prose*, pp. 224 ff.
[2] Wyclif, *Selections*, ed. H. E. Winn, p. 27.
[3] *Chaucerian and other Pieces*, ed. W. W. Skeat, p. 1.

which gave direction and impetus to the movement, by his deliberate choice of English as a means of exposition and persuasion; and in his Latin *Sermones*,[1] collected probably in retirement during the last five years of his life, he set forth his ideas on the art of preaching, and, indirectly, of prose writing in general. As his starting-point he complains of the defects of the prevailing methods of preaching; the frequent resort to the *pomposam eloquenciam*[2] of the grammarians, the indulgence in logical subtleties and points of natural history, or again, the use made of 'gests, poems, and fables', together with rhythmical ornament of various kinds.[3] All such rhetorical devices, he maintained, obscured the essential teaching. And it was therefore necessary above all that expression should, first, be adapted to the needs of the hearers (or readers), and, secondly, that simplicity and plainness of utterance should be the prime essentials. To these basic requirements he again and again reverts.[4]

On these matters he enlarges further when he replies to current arguments advanced in defence of the more pretentious style. There was first the contention that learned preachers had necessarily to be ornate in expression in order to be distinguished from uncultured brethren. This plea Wiclif summarily dismisses as mere vain-glory.[5] Or again it was held that style should be in accord with subject-matter; and as theological themes were the most exalted of all, to them should be given the most elevated expression. This was said to result from the use of rhetorical and rhythmical ornament (*color rethoricus et colligancia rithmica*); and in this way, it was maintained, eloquence became part of wisdom. These arguments, however, Wiclif stoutly opposes. He denies that wisdom consists in beauty of words, and that for its utterance a meretricious style was needed. Such laboured ingenuities he describes as a corruption of divine teaching; and what was therefore required was sincerity of speech, the expression of plain truths simply and aptly (*nude et apte*).[6] Nor is he able to accept the further argument that because certain Books of the Bible were metrical

---

[1] Ed. Loserth, 4 vols. (1887–90).

[2] *Sermones*, I, 209.

[3] *Ibid.* II, 18; IV, 265. See p. 136 *supra*.

[4] *Ibid.* I, 35, 107; II, 79, etc.

[5] *Ibid.* IV, 266–7.

[6] *Ibid.* IV, 267–8.

in form, therefore exhortations in prose should make use of the same device. In songs and prophecies, he conceded, metrical devices were effective; but in prose exposition such ornaments were a hindrance, since they distracted the attention of hearers, attached greater importance to manner than to matter, and provided after all merely a tickling delight *(titillans delectacio).*[1] The truth was, added Wiclif, that the most effective means to a given end were the means that should be employed; and instruction in religious matters, he held, was best attained by plain and direct speaking *(plana locucio),* and by discarding the method of 'heroical' declamation *(declamacio eroyca).*[2]

Thus did Wiclif submit to his generation his conception of the art of preaching; and his teaching represents an important contribution, not only to homiletics, but to critical theory as well. He is dealing, it is true, with spoken, as opposed to written, language; but his basic principles are applicable to all forms of prose composition; and they constitute an epoch-making departure in the development of English prose theory. Now for the first time a direct attack was being made on the false rhetoric cherished throughout the Middle Ages; though Bacon before him had censured the affected eloquence of his day.[3] That system, originally inspired by the New Sophistic of post-classical times,[4] had embodied much that ran counter to classical tradition and good taste; and Wiclif, with characteristic energy, challenges the whole position. In so doing he was doubtless animated by the promptings of his own native genius. But probably he drew inspiration also from Augustine's *De Doctrina Christiana,* that most illuminating of post-classical works on rhetoric, written some ten centuries previously, to which he makes frequent reference, and in which an attempt had been made to counter Sophistic in its earlier stages by adapting the teaching of Cicero.[5] Faced with the same problem Wiclif puts forward the same fundamental doctrines, shorn however of their details and their systematic form. And in his insistence on the need for plain and simple utterance in accordance with both speaker and hearer, as well as on the avoidance of all

[1] *Sermones,* IV, 269–70.   [2] *Ibid.* IV, 271.   [3] See p. 136 *supra.*
[4] See p. 26 *supra.*   [5] See p. 14 *supra.*

artificial emotional devices whether rhetorical or rhythmical,
he was essentially at one with Aristotle in his opposition to
Gorgianic prose, when the latter declared clearness and propriety to be the two fundamental virtues of good speaking and
writing.[1] In this way did Wiclif unconsciously revive in England
certain elements of the teaching of classical antiquity of permanent value. Incidentally he also distinguished between the
principles of composition in poetry and prose, a service no less
valuable at this particular date. Notable as was his achievement, however, his immediate influence was but slight. Opposition to Lollardry in the years that followed militated against
the formation of a school of popular eloquence on the lines
suggested. Yet he had accomplished work of lasting importance; he had revealed the secret of all good prose, and the
foundations on which later masters of English were to build.

It is in Chaucer, however, that the critical spirit of the
fourteenth century becomes most clearly apparent; and with
him vernacular criticism assumes its most notable form. Of
direct and explicit literary criticism, it is true, he supplies no
trace. Yet his work is suffused throughout by the critical temper,
which is visible not only in his attitude to contemporary life,
with its foibles, its hypocrisies, its superstitions and the like, but
also, and more constructively, in his reasoned artistic treatment
of his borrowed material, and in his numerous experiments
in verse-form and expression. Nor was this critical tendency
without effect on his development as a poet; for he is seen to
advance from the cramping technique of medieval poetic, with
its rhetorical artifice, its conventional mechanical processes,
its elaborate descriptions, apostrophes, and *exempla*, to creative
methods of a freer kind, in which scope was given to the
dictates of genius, wherein imagination, a sense of fitness, and
a knowledge of human nature, all played their part.[2] Of the
conscious critical effort involved in this development no definite
statement is made by the poet himself; but in him as creative
artist a potential literary critic was ever at work. All that
emerges of a critical nature from his writings are occasional

[1] Aristotle, *Rhetoric*, iii, ii, 1.
[2] See Manly, *op. cit.*

oblique judgments on current literature and literary methods, as well as stray fragments of theory drawn from earlier authorities.

His most substantial contribution to literary criticism will be found in his *Tale of Sir Thopas*, a burlesque romance, intended most probably as a satire on the degenerate rhyming romances of the day. This, the traditional view, has however been challenged of late, and attempts have been made to interpret the satire as ridiculing primarily, not defective romances, but rather the stupidity and gaucherie of contemporary Flemings.[1] That a bourgeois colouring, reminiscent of Flemish life and character, runs throughout the narrative must obviously be conceded. Yet this colouring would seem to have been the means, and not the motive, of the actual satire; an incidental effect, that is, which lights up the main purpose. What at any rate seems certain is that to a popular audience, such as Chaucer was presumably addressing, the current metrical romances, with which all were familiar, would more readily occur than the manners of Flemish burghers, whose contacts with English life were of a limited kind. And in the light of Chaucer's artistic tact, this fact is not without its importance; it suggests that the more familiar motive is likely to be the more probable. Moreover the traditional interpretation derives support from the glaring defects of the metrical romances then in vogue, which cannot have failed to appeal to Chaucer's rich vein of humour. By this date something of the glamour and freshness of the old romances had been lost. Written originally for travelling minstrels, they had formerly appealed to popular audiences by their simplicity and directness. By the fourteenth century, however, these saving graces had vanished in an accumulation of hackneyed and redundant details; and with the passing of the oral tradition, and the emergence of a new taste for compositions of a more reflective and elaborate kind, the ancient stories were freely adapted, as in *Sir Gawain and the Green Knight*, or else transformed into romantic tales, such as Chaucer's

---

[1] For discussions of this problem see L. Winstanley's ed. of *Tale of Sir Thopas*, Intro. lxv–lxxvii, J. M. Manly's contribution to *Essays and Studies by members of the Eng. Assoc.* (XIII), pp. 52–73, and W. W. Lawrence, *Satire on Sir Thopas* (*P.M.L.A.* 50, pp. 81 ff.).

*Troilus and Criseyde.* Meanwhile the romances had been abandoned to rude rhymers of the highway, whose productions were little more than travesties of the old heroic stories; and these compositions it was that most probably formed the subject of Chaucer's satire. That his attack was directed, not against romances as such, but against current absurdities, need scarcely be urged. Elsewhere in his works the spirit of the old romances persists; and in the eighteenth century Richard Hurd had already recognised that fact.[1]

Not without its interest, to begin with, is the parody form adopted by Chaucer in his *Tale of Sir Thopas.* By the Greeks that device had long ago been employed as the most natural means of pronouncing literary judgment, while in the hands of Plato it had become something of a fine art. And it is worth noting in passing that in this, the first attempt at judicial criticism in English, Chaucer unconsciously follows the ancient practice; though his treatment may also have been suggested by Geoffrey of Vinsauf, when he recommended praise of a ludicrous kind for exposing the absurd.[2] As the theme of his narrative Chaucer relates the adventures of a peerless warrior who, bound on a knightly quest, fell in love with an elf-queen, and when challenged by Sir Olifaunt, giant guardian of the realm of Fairye, proceeded to arm himself for combat—at which interesting point the narrative abruptly breaks off. Here then is material out of which romances were made; and Chaucer's criticism emerges from his treatment of the theme. By infinitely subtle touches he hints at the defects which marked the romances of his day; the excessive fondness for strange marvels and long tedious descriptions, the stock epithets and phrases, the inevitable comparisons and catalogues, the rhyming tags and doggerel verse, and above all the poverty of the action, which was often lost in a maze of digressions and descriptions. And that such features were characteristic of the contemporary romances is seen from a comparison with those collected by Robert Thornton[3] (early fifteenth century), and notably in such narratives as *Sir Eglamour, Sir Isumbras,* and *Torrent of Portugal.*

---

[1] *Letters on Chivalry and Romance,* XI.
[2] Faral, *op. cit.* p. 210, see pp. 110-1 *supra.*
[3] See *Thornton Romances,* ed. J. O. Halliwell, Camden Society, 1844.

Nor is the skill with which Chaucer imparts his judgment less remarkable than the critical insight he displays. By holding up a mirror to the romances in question he contrives that the reader should form his own estimate; and such suggested criticism is more effective than any formal statement could have been. Then, too, his purpose is partly concealed by his disarming air of naïvety, and by the restraint he exercises throughout, so that the narrative never descends to the level of gross farce or caricature. Yet his points are made, and with greater force, as the imitation proceeds, with its subtly veiled hints and occasional touches of manifest absurdity. Such touches are specially found in those places where a bourgeois element[1] is worked into the romance, and where bathos or the art of sinking[2] is otherwise employed with telling effect. Altogether the work is an excellent example of Chaucer's humour at its best; while the parody affords a lasting judgment on certain contemporary literary abuses. Like *The Owl and the Nightingale* it is literary criticism of an oblique kind, that represents a contribution to literature itself.

But while *Sir Thopas* constitutes Chaucer's most coherent effort of a critical kind, further covert criticism is also present here and there in his works, supplying running judgments on other literary problems of his day, such as are found later in the creative literature of Elizabethan times. Many of these pronouncements of Chaucer are of the nature of dramatic utterances, and therefore not necessarily representative of the poet's own views. But when read in the light of his actual poetic development, it can scarcely be doubted that they are significant comments, in keeping with the poet's sympathies and practice alike. Nothing, for instance, is more pronounced in Chaucer's technical development than his gradual emancipation from the devices prescribed by earlier medieval authorities.[3] He never quite freed himself, it is true, from the traditional teaching. Yet his later work reveals plainly a simpler and more natural style, a mode of expression dictated rather by artistic requirements than by conventional rules; and it is thus not

---

[1] Cf. ll. 14, 52, 144, 161, 204.
[2] Cf. ll. 18, 33, 45, 55, 121.
[3] See Manly, *op. cit.*

strange to find in his works occasional hints of his views on these matters of literary technique.

Of his attitude in general to the apparatus of medieval poetic, something, in the first place, may be gathered from his reference to Geoffrey of Vinsauf in the *Nun's Priest's Tale*.[1] Here he recalls the formal and inflated 'Complaint' against Friday (the day on which Richard I was slain) supplied by 'Gaufred, dere mayster soverayn', in his *Poetria Nova*;[2] and then laments his own inability to rise to similar heights of pathos on behalf of the hapless Chauntecleer. From its context in a mock-heroic poem the passage is obviously an ironical tribute to that earlier theorist; and Chaucer is here plainly ridiculing the mechanical use of such devices by his usual method of burlesque or parody. In other places he presents his views in more particular fashion, as when he suggests the need for a more realistic style in narrative than was possible under the prevailing conventions; and this demand for plain and natural utterance, which constituted his main doctrine, he makes persistently and in various forms. Thus readers are reminded more than once that 'wordes mote be cosin to the dede',[3] that diction and style should be in keeping with both character and subject-matter; and in support of this doctrine (drawn probably from Boethius[4]) reference is made to the teaching of Plato and to Biblical practice. More frequently, however, the methods employed are of an indirect kind, though their significance is still tolerably clear. When the Eagle in *The House of Fame*,[5] for instance, at the end of his learned scientific discourse, prides himself on the skill with which he had avoided all 'subtiltee' and 'prolixitee' of speech—including philosophical terms, figures of poetry and colours of rhetoric—it is significant that his performance meets with the hearty approval of the poet. And if it be argued that here the poet had spoken under obvious duress, there is also the later advice of the common-sense Host to the Clerk that he should avoid all these same devices, and speak in such a way as to be understood.[6] Then, too, there are the apologies for

---

[1] ll. 527 ff.    [2] ll. 375 ff.; see Faral, *op. cit.* p. 208.
[3] *Prol.* 742; *Manc. T.* 104.
[4] Cf. Chaucer's trans. of *de Consolatione Philosophiae*, III, pr. xii, 220.
[5] II, 345 ff.    [6] *Clerk's Prol.* 16 ff.

this plain and natural utterance which Chaucer sees fit to make in deference to established standards. The poet, for example, asks for indulgence for his realistic style on grounds that are incontestable. He claims that it was due, not to coarse breeding (*vileinye*), but to his desire to attain truth to Nature;[1] and whereas the apology of the Franklin is couched in less direct but more humorous terms, yet the intention of the poet seems none the less clear. It is the plain (*burel*) man speaking, ignorant of 'rethorik', and boasting that he has not slept on mount Parnassus, knows nothing of Cicero's teaching, that the only colours he is aware of are those of flowers, of dyes and paintings;[2] and Chaucer is here surely condoning the liberties in expression taken by the Franklin. There can thus be little doubt of Chaucer's advocacy of a simpler and more realistic style in narrative, one free from the shackles of medieval 'rhetoric' or poetic. And further evidence of the same intention might incidentally be gathered from his remarks on contemporary preaching, when he satirises the tricks of the Pardoner's professional manner, in his use of the 'high' (*hauteyn*) style, well seasoned with *exempla* and with Latin words to colour (*saffron*) his expression.[3] In thus voicing his conviction that to write plainly for plain men was, broadly speaking, the main aim of the narrative poet, Chaucer was making his most valuable contribution to literary theory; and in so doing he was joining hands with Bacon and Wiclif, who had also called men to sounder principles of composition, away from the false glamour of medieval 'rhetoric'.

But while this demand for a more natural utterance may be said to represent Chaucer's main literary doctrine, other places in his works (though fragmentary in kind) are of critical interest, as throwing further light on his views concerning literature and the literary art. That he shared the Humanistic enthusiasm for ancient literature is everywhere apparent. To him ancient writings were 'old fields from which came new corn year by year';[4] they were also 'the keye of remembraunce', recalling

---

[1] *Prol.* 735 ff.  [2] *Franklin's Prol.* 46 ff.
[3] *Pard. Prol.* 1–2, 16–17, 108–9; also *Clerk's Prol.* 16–18.
[4] *Parlement of Foules,* 21.

old events, doctrines and stories.[1] Of aesthetic evaluation, however, there is less evidence, in view of the undiscriminating catalogues in which Dares and Dictys appear along with Homer and Latin classical poets.[2] Not without its significance, however, is the distinction he draws between the ancient classics and later vernacular literature, conceding apparently to the former the greater seriousness and value. This he does by dignifying as 'poesye' or 'poetrye'[3] the works of the ancients alone (together with Dante and Petrarch[4]), while reserving the native terms 'making' and 'makers'[5] for vernacular efforts. Into questions of the nature of poetry he does not enter, though he has constantly in mind as its two-fold function, that of affording instruction (*sentence, doctrine*) and also delight (*solas, mirthe, disport, game*),[6] in accordance with Horatian doctrine. But while recognising at least the aesthetic side of poetry, it is its didactic aim to which in practice he attaches the greater weight, owing doubtless to current ideas and also to the teaching of medieval poetic. According to medieval doctrine special importance was given to the *conclusioun*, or main purpose, of a poem; and Chaucer in one place definitely states that 'th'ende is every tales strengthe'.[7] Hence the significance of the moral and didactic endings of many of his tales,[8] and his final apology for his 'endytinges of worldly vanitees' and for 'the tales of Caunterbury... that sounen into sinne'.[9]

Equally interesting, however, are the occasional hints he gives of some of the principles that governed his poetic processes. Most significant of all is his recognition of the need for reasoned form in art, the absence of which had constituted the main defect of medieval literature generally. Plato long ago had emphasised the need for taking thought in all artistic creation, pointing out that no true artist, whether painter or builder or poet, ever worked at random.[10] And much the same

---

[1] *Legend of G.W. Prol.* 15 ff.    [2] Cf. *H.F.* III, 376 ff.
[3] *T. and C.* v, 1790, 1855; *H.F.* III, 388 ff.
[4] *Monk's T.* 470; *Clerk's T.* 31.    [5] *Leg. of G.W. Prol.* 74, 403, 473.
[6] *Prol.* 800; *Sir Thop.* 3; *T. and C.* II, 256; cf. also *Prol. to Melib.* 17.
[7] *T. and C.* v, 260.
[8] *T. and C.* v, 1849; *Leg. of G.W.* IX, 162; *Clerk's T.* 1086 ff.; *Monk's T.* I, *passim.*
[9] *Parson's T.* 1080 ff.    [10] *Gorgias*, 501–3.

teaching, surprisingly enough, had been repeated by Geoffrey
of Vinsauf in the passage beginning

> Si quis habet fundare domum, non currit ad actum
> Impetuosa manus; intrinseca linea cordis
> Praemetitur opus.[1]

The almost literal translation of this passage in *Troilus and
Criseyde*[2] (i.e. *Ne renneth nought...with rakel hond, but he wol...
send his hertes lyne out fro withinne*) shows Chaucer's acquaintance
with the principle involved; and that the teaching was represented in his practice can scarcely be doubted. Then, too, he
throws light by the way on the doctrine which governed his
treatment of subject-matter, when he points out the transformation (or *forme*) of the old story represented in *Troilus and
Criseyde*.[3] The proper handling of classical material had been
commonly dealt with in medieval *Poetics*. In spite of the
deference paid to ancient authority, a variation of theme was
definitely recommended, by which fresh aspects of the story
concerned would be made to emerge;[4] and Chaucer here reveals
his adherence to this sound principle of presenting old and
familiar matters in new and unfamiliar guise. Concerning
the development (*ordo*) of his narratives, on the other hand,
he has nothing to say, though in practice he would seem
to have followed the advice that in tale-telling *primum est
continuare*; and this is suggested by his frequently expressed
intention of 'shortly for to telle' or 'to leten other thing
collateral'[5] (i.e. to omit irrelevant details). Elsewhere he
notes the virtue of brevity in style. Apart from the greater ease
of memorising thoughts concisely expressed,[6] 'greet effect', he
explains, 'men wryte in place lyte'.[7] Then, too, there are the
Parson's contemptuous remarks concerning alliterative verse
and doggerel rhyme[8]—possibly Chaucer's own estimates, of the
former as provincial, of the latter as degenerate. Or again,
there is his reference to the part played by 'delivery' in oratory,
when the speech of the knight at Cambinskan's court is praised,

---

[1] Faral, *op. cit.* pp. 198–9; see also pp. 98–9 *supra.*
[2] I, 1065–9. Professor Charlton notes Browning, *A Grammarian's Funeral,*
ll. 69 ff.     [3] v, 1854.     [4] Faral, *op. cit.* pp. 309–10.
[5] Cf. *Kn. T.* 142; *T. and C.* I, 262.     [6] Cf. *R. of R.* 2349–50.
[7] *T. and C.* v, 1629.     [8] *Parson's Prol.* 42 ff.

not only for its correctness but also because 'accordant to his wordes was his chere'.[1]

In yet another field does Chaucer reveal something of his technique, when Pandarus prescribes for Troilus the proper method of letter-writing.[2] Throughout the Middle Ages the study of *ars dictaminis* had received much attention; but the resultant teaching had been mainly of a mechanical and stereo-typed kind.[3] Here Chaucer suggests epistolary methods of a more liberal nature; and in few places are his artistic instincts more clearly seen. Thus he recommends that an appropriate tone, free from rancour, should be adopted throughout, and that too professional (*scrivenish*) a manner should also be avoided. The writer's feelings, on the other hand, should be incidentally revealed; and if a pretty phrase were used it should not be elaborated or repeated, lest it lose its effect.[4] Then, too, the polite *decorum* characteristic of courtly love (*loves termes*) should be everywhere observed; and above all there should be a pervading sense of unity, a freedom from discordant elements. Otherwise, it was added, the result would be as absurd as the picture of a fish with ass's feet and a monkey's head—a mon-strous and ludicrous effusion, as Horace long ago had main-tained in similar terms.[5] And in this plea for restraint, *decorum*, the expression of personal feeling and unity of effect, Chaucer breaks away once more from earlier formulae and prescriptions, and enunciates principles based on sound psychological grounds.

It yet remains to mention what is perhaps, historically, his most interesting contribution to critical theory, namely, the conception of tragedy he sets forth, partly by way of definition in the Prologue to *The Monk's Tale*, partly also by implication in the Monk's tales themselves, which illustrate and complete that statement; and what he here presents is the idea of that literary form, prevalent during the Middle Ages, and interesting alike in its genesis and its later bearings. Thus it is learnt that tragedy was to him essentially a story of the fall of an exalted personage from prosperity to misery;[6] and that such disaster

---

[1] *Sq. T.* 95–6; cf. Faral, *op. cit.* pp. 259–60.
[2] *T. and C.* II, 1023 ff.       [3] See p. 113 *supra*.
[4] Cf. Faral, *op. cit.* p. 256.
[5] Cf. Hor. *A.P.* 1–5.       [6] *Monk's T.* Prol. 85 ff.

was due mainly to the machinations of Fortune, though moral considerations might also enter.[1] To this he adds that while tragedies had formerly been written mostly in hexameter verse, other metres as well as prose had also been employed;[2] and this latter statement, while obviously a misrepresentation, has yet this significance, that it illustrates the prevailing idea of tragedy as a species of narrative (distinct from dramatic) poetry,[3] and the absence of any real conception of ancient dramatic art.

In defining tragedy, in the first place, as the story of the fall of an exalted personage, Chaucer was adopting a conception which, probably a Hellenistic modification of Aristotelian doctrine to begin with, was subsequently endorsed by post-classical authorities,[4] and then accepted by the Middle Ages as the authentic teaching of antiquity on the subject. With this doctrine John of Salisbury had already shown his acquaintance;[5] and while it formed the inspiration of Boccaccio's *De Casibus Virorum Illustrium* (*c.* 1363) and its many imitations, it also goes to explain Chaucer's somewhat free description of *Troilus and Criseyde* as a 'tragedie',[6] since therein was related the 'double sorwe'[7] of Troilus. But while this 'reversal in the fortunes of heroic characters' constituted the whole substance of Hellenistic and post-classical definitions, in medieval times a qualification was added, ascribing the 'reversal' to the workings of Fortune, and in a lesser degree to moral factors; and in this addition lay the characteristic medieval note. Already in decadent Rome the goddess Fortuna had been regarded as a capricious and ruthless deity, gifted with occult power over the lives of men; and as the goddess of Chance she persisted throughout the medieval period, a mutable and incalculable force, no mere literary fiction but a living power, which exercised a profound influence on contemporary thought.[8] To her were consequently

---

[1] *Monk's T. passim.*　　　　　　[2] *Ibid.* Prol. 90 ff.
[3] Cf. *ditee* (story) applied to tragedy in the *Glose*, probably due to Trivet, in Chaucer's trans. of Boethius *de Cons. Phil.* II, pr. ii, 79. See also pp. 31–2 *supra.*　　　　[4] See p. 32 *supra.*　　　　[5] See p. 87 *supra.*
[6] *T. and C.* v, 1786.　　　　　　[7] *Ibid.* I, I.
[8] See H. R. Patch, *The Goddess Fortuna in Mediaeval Literature* (1927), pp. 34–87.

attributed the various evils which befell mankind, and particularly those unforeseen disasters which overwhelmed men of high estate, according to the accepted idea of tragedy. At the same time her existence and powers had also been challenged by the Christian Fathers and others, from the days of Augustine onwards. The existence of a righteous God and an ordered universe compelled belief in the workings of a moral code; and the 'reversals' were therefore also explained as the natural results of breaches of the moral law. Both doctrines are represented in Chaucer's conception of tragedy, and are drawn from different sources. For the part played by Fortune, there was the outstanding authority of Boethius, who, in his disquisition on Fortune in his *De Consolatione* (translated by Chaucer), had maintained that ' the cryinges of tragedies' bewailed none other than ' the dedes of Fortune';[1] and as for the moral considerations implied, they were mainly due to Christian teaching. Boccaccio, for instance, had already attributed to sins committed the downfall of Fortune's victims—an explanation readily accepted by Chaucer with his predilection for moral and didactic endings. That Chaucer's conception of tragedy was neither fixed nor completely thought out, seems therefore probable. But this much may be said, that he at least modified the idea that the tragic 'fall' was due solely to the caprice of a heartless and irrational Fortune. That deity is described in *Troilus and Criseyde* as the mistress of Destiny (*executrice of wierdes*), who, 'under God', was the controller (*hierdes*) of events and their mysterious (*wrye*) causes.[2] Yet at the end Troilus himself confesses that his downfall had been due to his own wrong-doing (*a-gilt and doon amis*).[3] Similarly in *The Monk's Tale* frequent references are made to the influence of Fortune; though at the same time various disasters are also ascribed to sins of pride, misgovernment and the rest. And this conception of the tragedy of Fortune, as a non-dramatic form of literature with an indeterminate tragic ἁμαρτία, was handed down to Renascence times to be ultimately transformed by Aristotle's teaching and Shakespeare's dramatic genius.

Not altogether negligible therefore is Chaucer's contribution

[1] II, pr. II, 75–6.    [2] III, 617–20.    [3] V, 1684.

to this first phase of critical activities in England, indirect and casual as that contribution undoubtedly was. Sound in his artistic judgment on a declining form of contemporary literature, the romance, he is yet more illuminating in his challenge of the orthodox poetic theory with its 'rhetorical' rules, and in his inculcation of a more natural form of utterance and of an art based on psychological grounds. His conception of the function of poetry is Horatian in kind; and he is also alive to the need for reasoned form in art. By occasional hints he throws further light on certain elements of literary technique; while his conception of tragedy marks a definite stage in the evolution of that literary form. Lacking in both system and range his critical contribution may be; but it is wanting neither in historical interest nor in suggestiveness. His remarks form a running commentary on his actual practice; and the comments of a great artist on his craft are always of value.

# CHAPTER VIII

## NATIVE LITERARY PROBLEMS (continued):
## CAXTON, HAWES, SKELTON

URING the fifteenth and early sixteenth centuries critical activities, still tentative and sporadic, assumed yet a new form, in spite of the marked decline in literary achievement, and the distraction of wars, both at home and abroad, for the best part of the fifteenth century. As before, matters connected with the vernacular literature still occupied the attention; but in the meantime fresh problems had arisen, new influences were at work, and with the appearance of a considerable body of English poetry, attempts at literary judgment of a sort were for the first time forthcoming. Not without its significance, in the first place, was the recognition accorded to the discovery of the century preceding, namely, that for Englishmen English was the natural medium of expression. From now on, Latin ceased to be generally employed for literary purposes; and though Gower for one had viewed the change with some amount of suspicion, the cultivation of the vernacular became one of the main concerns of later writers. Meanwhile certain important changes were taking place in the development of the English language itself, which were not without their bearing on literary matters. By the end of the fifteenth century, owing to natural causes, final -*e* had ceased to have syllabic value; there was a general clipping of inflexional endings; and a host of new words had been introduced, a continuation of the process already visible in Chaucer's day. At the same time these changes were now accompanied by a more conscious and deliberate movement for the enriching of the vocabulary and the elevating of poetic style. Inspired by enthusiasm for the vernacular and guided by earlier teaching, efforts were now made to create a new and more ornate poetic diction; and this 'aureate' language became the subject of comment by more than one writer. Then, too, the influence of Boccaccio's teaching in *De Genealogia Deorum* (*c.* 1360) was being increasingly felt; and in consequence not only was fresh impetus given to allegorical poetry, which from now on became the characteristic form, but attempts were also made by Hawes and Skelton to present to their readers theories of poetry on the lines of Boccaccio. In addition, with the growing interest in vernacular verse some amount of comment on earlier achievement became inevitable. The accepted masters were Gower, Chaucer, and Lydgate, who were regarded as heralds of the new generation; and from later poets came a host of tributes which, while lacking in serious judgment, are yet of interest as throwing light on contemporary standards and taste.

For the key to the understanding of the new trend in critical activities we must look in the first place to the revived influence of medieval 'rhetoric' or poetic at this stage. In the preceding century efforts had been made by Chaucer and Wiclif to inculcate a more natural expression, both in verse and prose, than had been possible under the prescriptions of the conventional code. Now, however, with genius silent, the earlier protests against false artifice ceased; and the normal encyclopaedic teaching, still active in Universities and schools, is found re-asserting itself. Rhetoric is studied with increasing zeal and medieval 'rhetoric' or poetic, with its teaching adapted to vernacular needs, becomes once more the main guide in literary matters. Not without its significance, to begin with, is the fact that this 'rhetorical' bias is by no means limited to activities in the vernacular. It may be traced, for instance, in the early fifteenth-century *Tractatus de modo inueniendi ornata uerba*, attributed to either John de Blakeney or John de Norwich;[1] or again, in the fifteenth-century Latin formularies or collections of letters, sermons and the like, where it is the fruit of an imperfect apprehension of that Italian Humanism which had begun to make its influence felt on English life and letters. The truth is that attempts were now being made to write in Latin as the much-admired Italian scholars were supposed to write. The result was the cultivation of an ornamental and flowery style, tortuous, obscure, bombastic, overloaded with imagery and classical allusion, and with special attention paid to unusual

[1] See R. Weiss, *Humanism in England during the Fifteenth Century*, p. 11 note.

diction and to a *florida verborum venustas*;[1] and of this new tendency the *Letters* of John Whethamstede, abbot of St Albans (d. 1465), afford illuminating evidence.[2] With regard to the vernacular, a similar tendency also becomes visible, encouraged no doubt by the teaching of Boccaccio, who, while maintaining that poetry transcended mere rhetoric,[3] had yet recognised the part played in poetic creation by rhetorical ornament (*figuras dictionum, orationum colores*),[4] and had further recommended recourse to the schools to learn 'what licence ancient authority had granted to poets in such matters'.[5] Then, too, the influence of Lydgate (*c.* 1370–1450) must also have counted for something; for, according to tradition, that prolific poet is said to have established a school of rhetoric and poetry at Bury St Edmunds, so that both by precept and example he inculcated the importance of rhetorical studies for poets. And on his own and the following generations his influence was considerable, since, writing under the patronage of Humphrey, Duke of Gloucester, the Maecenas of the age, he was generally regarded as the most elevated and stylish of poets. But whatever may have been the causes, it cannot be doubted that there emerged at this juncture a new enthusiasm for the study of rhetoric,[6] and for its application to contemporary needs; and more than one writer attempts to reproduce for the first time in English something of the earlier doctrines.[7]

Of these efforts a notable example is found in the allegorical poem, *The Court of Sapience* (formerly attributed to Lydgate on doubtful grounds[8]), in which the poet is led into the hall of Wisdom to be instructed in the Seven Liberal Arts, and a summary account is given of Dame Rethoryke and her

[1] See E. F. Jacob, *Florida Verborum Venustas* (Bulletin of J. Rylands Lib., vol. XVII, no. 2).

[2] See W. F. Schirmer, *Der Englische Frühhumanismus*, pp. 88 ff.; R. Weiss, *op. cit.* pp. 28 ff.

[3] *De Gen. Deorum*, 14, 7.      [4] *Ibid.* 14, 12.

[5] *Ibid.*; see Osgood, *op. cit.* p. 61.

[6] Cf. Traversanus, *Nova Rhetorica* (1478) written at Cambridge, published by Caxton 1479.

[7] E.g. the short passage on rhetoric in Caxton's *Mirrour of the World* (1481), E.E.T.S. 1912.

[8] See H. N. MacCracken, *Minor Poems of Lydgate*, E.E.T.S. 1910, XXXV; and *Court of Sapience*, ed. Spindler, Intro.

work.[1] From the first it is clear that the conception of rhetoric set forth is that of Rhetorica in Capella's *De Nuptiis*,[2] or again, of Rhetoric in the *Anticlaudianus* of Alanus de Insulis. Thus Dame Rethoryke is described as the mistress of ornate and grandiloquent speech; her 'beau parlaunce', her words 'depuryd and enlumynyd' are said to ravish every heart; and her utterance is claimed to be free from all discordant elements (*cacemphaton*). Moreover she is said to instruct in 'the craft of endytyng' by indicating the vices to be avoided and the 'colours' to be employed; and while for an ampler treatment she refers to earlier authorities, notably Geoffrey of Vinsauf[3] and the author of *Rhetorica ad Herennium*,[4] she herself is said to be well skilled in 'prose and metyrs' of all kinds. Yet more elaborate is the treatment of the subject which appears in Hawes's *Pastime of Pleasure* (*c.* 1506),[5] a moral allegory, inspired in part by *The Court of Sapience*, which has for its theme the experiences of Graund Amour in his preparation for the active life. After due preliminaries he is instructed in the Seven Liberal Arts, and then he meets La Bel Pucell (the true aim of life), to whom he is finally wedded after many knightly adventures. Of outstanding importance in the training of the hero is the part assigned to Rhetoric, the account of which forms a considerable part of the work.[6] And here again Dame Rhetoric is represented on traditional lines, as an imposing figure, garlanded with laurel and surrounded with fumes of incense. She begins by explaining the origin of rhetoric as having been founded for the governance of man, and in order to purify his speech; after which she treats of its five divisions—*inventio, dispositio, elocutio, pronuntiatio, memoria*—assigning to *elocutio* (style) the main consideration. With the teaching of rhetoric in the classical sense, however, she has no concern. Her interests throughout are limited to poetic composition; and it becomes clear that rhetoric to her is little more than medieval poetic, having as its main object the cultivation of an ornate and grandiose style.

---

[1] Sts. 271–6; see D. L. Clark, *Rhetoric and Poetry in the Renaissance* (1922), pp. 47–50.          [2] See p. 27 *supra*.

[3] The reference is to *Tria Sunt*, the first words of G.'s *Documentum* (see Faral, *op. cit.* p. 265).          [4] I.e. 'Tullius'.

[5] Ed. W. E. Mead, E.E.T.S. 1927.          [6] I.e. 108 stanzas.

With the effects of this movement on contemporary literature we are not immediately concerned, though the results are everywhere apparent in the devices taken over from earlier rhetorical treatises and adapted to vernacular uses. Figures, for instance, were freely employed by fifteenth-century poets; as were also all sorts of ingenuities (*'colours'*) in the way of verbal and stanza arrangements—words arranged in anagram or woven into quaint patterns (crosses, diamonds), words repeated throughout a poem, final words supplying the initial words of the following lines, besides retrograde verses and macaronic verses (with Latin tags)[1]—forming altogether a most complicated and artificial poetic technique. While, however, these artifices were now adopted without further comment, one special problem presented itself with some urgency at this date, namely, that of fitting the vernacular for poetic purposes. That poetry required a heightened form of expression had been inculcated by the traditional 'rhetorical' teaching, and more particularly by the part played by *amplificatio* in medieval poetic. Moreover, Chaucer, it was recognised, had already done much to give literary value to the vernacular; and the matter now received attention from more than one writer, while in practice efforts were everywhere made to beautify expression.

Of the deficiencies of the vernacular for literary purposes Caxton, for instance, speaks in the Preface to his translation of *Eneydos*[2] (1490), when he states that the language was rapidly changing, that the English of his childhood differed greatly from that in current use, and that what had been intelligible a generation before was then read only with difficulty because of its crude and obscure expressions. A little later Skelton also complained that the language of his day was useless for poetic purposes. In *Phyllyp Sparow* (before 1508) he stated, in characteristic terms, that English was 'rusty' and 'cankered', rude and hard to polish; and that when he tried to write ornately he knew not where to turn for fitting terms. Moreover, Gower's English, he added, was then out-of-date, and was reckoned of no value; while men were wont to 'barke' even at Chaucer's

---

[1] For an interesting account see J. M. Berdan, *op. cit.* pp. 130 ff.
[2] Ed. Culley and Furnivall, E.E.T.S. 1890.

English, though much commended in former days.[1] In the light of these pronouncements the condition of the vernacular becomes plain. Some conscious effort was needed to extend the vocabulary, and to give colour to expression; and guidance was forthcoming from medieval 'rhetoric' or poetic, in which, it should be noted, a similar problem had been dealt with in connexion with medieval Latin verse. There rules had been laid down for finding suitable rhyming words; and among the devices recommended were the use of compound words (*compositio*), the use of foreign terms (*aliene dictionis introductio*), or again, the use of intelligible new formations (*nove dictionis fictio*) in keeping with the nature of the subject.[2] Such devices, it was urged, not only supplied rhyming needs; they were also a means of adding vigour to expression, and of attaining that much sought-after medieval quality, refinement (*subtilitas*) of style. Nor was this teaching without support from later authorities; for Boccaccio had called attention to the beauty residing in foreign words, had recommended for poetic purposes 'such alien terms as were permissible beyond common and homely use', and had further quoted Petrarch's dictum that 'in narrative, above all, poets maintain majesty of style and corresponding dignity'.[3] It is therefore not strange to find that writers at this date should have adopted similar methods for enriching the native poetic vocabulary, making use of new compounds, coinages, Romance and Latin formations; and this, it should be noted, over and above the schemes and tropes of medieval poetic, as represented in the 'hauteyn' style derided by Chaucer. And with Lydgate the use of this artificial and often obscure diction began, to become a marked feature of later poetry. Such diction was subsequently known as 'aureate' language; and not without its significance in this connexion was the term *vox aurata* which had been attributed to the Rhetorica of Capella *De Nuptiis*.[4] The expression 'aureate terms' apparently first appears in Lyndsay's *Testament of Papyngo*,[5]

---

[1] ll. 774 ff. (Dyce, 1, 75).
[2] G. Mari, *I trattati med. de rit. lat.* pp. 484 ff.; see also J. M. Berdan, *op. cit.* pp. 136 ff.    [3] *De Genealogia Deorum*, 14, 12; see Osgood, *op. cit.* p. 61.
[4] See pp. 27–8 *supra*.
[5] l. 15; see E. Tilgner, *Die Aureate Terms als Stilelement bei Lydgate*, p. 12.

though 'aureate' itself was a common enough epithet with Lydgate and others.

Concerning the value of these attempts to achieve a more ornate diction, contemporary views were not lacking. In one of those open letters which constitute his *Prefaces* Caxton, for instance, joins hands with Wiclif and Chaucer, and questions the superiority of the 'depured rethoryk' over the 'langage rude' of everyday life. Censured, on the one hand, for using terms which could not be 'understande of comyn peple', and urged, on the other hand, by 'honest and grete clerkes' to make use of the most 'curyous termes' he could find, he confesses himself to be 'abasshed' by the problem, and finally resolves by way of compromise to make use of an English 'not ouer rude ne curyous, but in suche termes as shall be understanden'.[1] By Hawes, on the other hand, the new aureate diction was welcomed enthusiastically and without reserve. Indeed, his *Pastime of Pleasure*, in which incidentally he explains the nature and aims of the new experiment, is everywhere redolent of its 'lusty rethoryke', its 'dewe aromatyke'. The function of elocution (or style) in poetry, he maintains, is 'to exorne the mater ryght well facundyously'

> In fewe wordes, swete and sentencyous,
> Depaynted with golde hard in construccyon,
> To the artyke eres swete and dylycyous
> The golden rethoryke is good refeccyon,
> And to the reder ryght consolacyon.[2]

Thus, in general, he implies, does this gilded diction provide refreshment for the poet and pleasure for the reader. Then, by a flight of audacious fancy, he explains its further merit in ridding expression of rude and homely terms, while supplying words more glamorous, drawn from various sources.

> As we do golde frome coper puryfy,
> So that elocucyon doth ryght well claryfy
> The dulcet speche frome the langage rude,
> Tellynge the tale in termes eloquent
> The barbary tongue it doth ferre exclude,

---

[1] Preface to *Translation of Eneydos* (E.E.T.S. 1890).
[2] *Pastime of Pleasure*, ed. Mead, c. XI, ll. 911–5.

> Electynge wordes whiche are expedyent
> In latyn or in englysshe after the entent,
> Encensynge out the aromatyke fume
> Our langage rude to exyle and consume.[1]

He even insists that such processes were essential:

> For thoughe a mater be neuer so good,
> Yf it be tolde with tongue of barbary,
> In rude maner without the discrete mode,
> It is dystourbaunce to a hole company.[2]

And elsewhere, with yet another simile drawn from unnatural
natural history, he claims for this diction an illuminating effect.
Carbuncles, he states, shine in the darkest night;

> And so these poetes with theyr golden streames
> Deuoyde our rudenes with grete fyry lemes:
> Theyr centencyous verses are refulgent,
> Encensynge out the odour redolent.[3]

Judgment of a more sedate kind came from John Metham
of Norwich (late fifteenth century), who, in the Envoy to
his metrical romance *Amoryus and Cleopes*, praises Lvdgate's
'retoryk', and more especially his

> Halff chongyd Latyne with conceytys off poetry
> And craffty imagynacionys off thyngys fantastyk,[4]

thus suggesting, so it would seem, that fresh colour was provided by these Latinised terms, associated as they were with
old poetic fancies. Nor were Skelton's later comments without
their interest. He pays conventional tribute for instance to
the 'aureate' style in which Lydgate, he recognises, had
been supreme. Yet he notes also its main defects, namely, that
it was often difficult to see the poet's meaning, and that it
lacked the clearness of Chaucer's style. Elsewhere he asserts
that the examples of Juvenal and Martial had justified his plain
speech in his *Satires*.[5] But his concluding remarks on Lydgate
are perhaps most representative of current views on the subject.
He states that 'some men fynde a faute, and say he wryteth to

---

[1] *P. of P.* ed. Mead, c. xi, ll. 916–24.
[2] *Ibid.* c. xii, ll. 1198–1201.          [3] *Ibid.* c. xi, ll. 1131–4.
[4] John Metham's Works; ed. H. Craig (E.E.T.S. 1906), St. 317; see also
E. Tilgner, *op. cit.* pp. 13–14.          [5] *Poems*, ed. Dyce, i, 130.

haute';[1] and with this condemnation of the obscurity and *subtilitas* of the aureate style most modern readers would cordially agree.

In the meantime even more significant perhaps were the efforts being made at formulating views on the nature of poetry itself. Hitherto poetry had been tacitly accepted as little more than metrical speech of a highly embellished kind,[2] a branch of rhetoric, grammar, or even logic,[3] or again, an exercise capable. of affording both pleasure and instruction, yet otherwise calling for no profound or philosophical treatment. Now, at this date, reflexions on its essential qualities were inspired by Boccaccio's *De Genealogia Deorum*; and the effects are seen, not only in the new direction given to fifteenth-century poetry in England, but also in the attempts now made, for the first time by English writers, to propound views on poetry of a larger and more generous kind. In that work Boccaccio's primary object had been to collect and interpret the myths of classical poetry, and thus to reveal the vitality and splendour of that ancient literature. This he does in Books I–XIII by pointing to the truths underlying those myths when interpreted allegorically; and then he concludes with his famous defence of poetry (Books XIV and XV), in which are set forth his views on the nature of poetry, based largely on the pronouncements of post-classical and patristic authorities. The method he adopts is to arraign in picturesque fashion the various contemporary detractors of poetry (worldly jurists, false philosophers, and the like),[4] and to enumerate all the objections raised against poetry from the time of Plato onwards,[5] which he then proceeds to confute.

Of the highest significance, in the first place, is the claim Boccaccio makes that poetry is something more than mere versified rhetoric, thus breaking definitely with the earlier medieval tradition. That technique had a place in poetry he subsequently conceded; but poetry to him is essentially a *scientia*, that is, in medieval terminology, a body of knowledge containing truths of a permanent kind, as distinct from a

---

[1] *Phyllyp Sparow*, 817–18.
[2] Cf. Dante: "fictio rethorica musice composita" (*De Vulgari Eloquentia*, II, ch. IV: trans. Dent 1904, p. 77).     [3] See p. 135 *supra*.
[4] *De Gen. Deorum*, XIV, 4 and 5.     [5] *Ibid.* 5.

*facultas,* such as law, which represented knowledge based on mere practice, and thus variable and unstable in character.[1] With the importance of subject-matter re-established, Boccaccio further points out that the truths of poetry, the *gaia scienza,* were veiled in fictions which, interpreted allegorically, revealed the moral teaching of the poet.[2] Thus he writes that 'whatever is composed as under a veil and thus exquisitely wrought, is poetry, and poetry alone';[3] and in this conception of allegory as 'the warp and woof' of poetry lay his main doctrine, which furnished the line of defence for a century or more. That obscurity of utterance occasionally resulted he held to be no defect; for poets were said to have veiled their truths for various reasons, to conceal them from the irreverent, or to render those truths more precious when finally discovered; and in any case, effort was necessary for the understanding of poetry.[4] Apart from this, however, he puts forward other notable ideas concerning poetry, as when, for instance, he insists on its dignity as 'a thing inspired',[5] and on its processes divine in their origin and sublime in their effects, impelling the soul to utterance and to new and strange creations. Then, too, he points out the essential differences between poetry and rhetoric:[6] while he also distinguishes poetry from both philosophy and history.[7] Yet more valuable perhaps than his actual doctrines is the enthusiasm with which he endeavours to give to poetry a new status in contemporary intellectual life. That the study of the Liberal Arts, of Medicine and Law, had led to the neglect of poetry he vigorously maintains; and he is at pains to restore it once more to its rightful place of honour. To the secular charges brought against poetry—its unreality, its immorality, its futility and the like—he therefore replies;[8] and he

---

[1] *De Gen. Deorum,* XIV, 4.         [2] *Ibid.* 7, *et passim.*

[3] *Ibid.* 7, *ad fin.*; see Osgood, *op. cit.* p. 42.

[4] *De Gen. Deorum,* XIV, 12; cf. also Petrarch's definition of the poetic function: Officium [poetae] est fingere, id est, componere atque ornare et veritatem rerum vel mortalium vel naturalium vel quarumlibet aliarum artificiosis adumbrare coloribus, velo amoenae fictionis obnubere, quo remoto veritas elucescat, eo gratior inventu quo difficilior sit quaesitu (*Ep. Sen.* XII, 2).

[5] *Ibid.* XIV, 7; i.e. fervor quidam exquisite inveniendi atque dicendi.

[6] *Ibid.* 7, *ad fin.* and 12.      [7] *Ibid.* 17 and 19.      [8] *Ibid.* 13.

boldly refuses to think that Plato would have excluded poets from his commonwealth.[1] Moreover he points out that poets were able to confer immortality on men,[2] that the Bible itself was full of fine poetry;[3] and he also recalls to his readers the testimony of Jerome, Augustine and others regarding the virtues of poetry, mentioning also the use made by St Paul of that ancient art.[4] Altogether he is convinced that poetry could become a humanising factor in society; and it is as an agent of regeneration in the life of the community that he commends to his generation its ardent pursuit. Much of his doctrine was to be superseded later by Aristotelian teaching; but the influence of his work was to be considerable for two centuries or more; and it had already become visible in attempts made by English writers to expound theories of poetry on similar lines.

The first attempts in English to discuss the nature of poetry appeared in the two poems, Hawes's *Pastime of Pleasure* and Skelton's *Replycacion agaynst certayne yong scolers abjured of late* (*c.* 1528). Medieval manuals of an earlier date had confined their treatment to matters of technique, to superficial and external details; and now, under Boccaccio's influence, efforts were made to explain something of the essence of poetry itself, its function and its processes. The results, it is true, are for the most part but faint, and often distorted, echoes of Boccaccio's teaching; but they have at least historical interest as representing an approach to poetry from a new and more intimate angle, thus marking a development in the critical tradition. With Hawes, it is clear, the rhetorical conception of poetry is still present, despite the distinction drawn by Boccaccio between poetry and rhetoric. It is significant, for instance, that Dame Rhetoric in *The Pastime* is responsible for instruction in poetry; while the subject is treated under the rhetorical heads of *inventio, dispositio,* and the rest. Then, too, certain fragments of earlier medieval doctrine are also introduced. There is, for instance, the preliminary advice already quoted by Chaucer concerning the need for taking thought:[5]

---

[1] *De Gen. Deorum*, XIV, 19.    [2] *Ibid.* 4.    [3] *Ibid.* 16.
[4] *Ibid.* 18.    [5] Faral, *op. cit.* pp. 198–9; see p. 158 *supra*.

> It is euer the grounde of sapyence,
> Before that thou accomplysshe outwardly,
> For to reuolue understandynge and prepence
> All in thy selfe full often inwardly
> The begynnynge and the myddle certaynly
> Wyth the ende, or thou put it in vre,
> And werke with councell that thou mayst be sure.[1]

Or again, the poet is urged to 'conclude full closely',[2] and to make an effective ending, so as to render his teaching clear.

At the same time an advance in the treatment becomes visible, notably in the deference paid to the ancients as guides in literary matters, and in the importance attached to subject-matter and the ideas conveyed. As Boccaccio had done, Hawes incidentally inveighs against the detractors of poetry, men 'rude and dull of wytt', who railed against matters which they did not understand, and held

> That nought do poetes but depaynt and lye,
> Deceyvyng...by tongues of flatery.[3]

He likewise follows Boccaccio in his praise of ancient poets, commending their efforts to 'dysnull vyce and the vycyous to blame', while singing of great deeds by which they had won enduring fame.[4] Moreover he hails them as 'the springes of famous poetry', on the ground that

> Our connynge frome you so procedeth,
> For you therof were fyrst orygynall grounde,
> And vpon youre scrypture our scyence ensueth,
> Your splendent verses our lyghtnes renueth.[5]

—an ample recognition of the authority of the ancients. It is therefore ostensibly as a follower of the ancients that Hawes submits his theory of poetry. But when he proceeds further it is Boccaccio whom he follows, rather than the ancients. The poet's function, he explains, was to present truth obscured by a veil of beautiful fiction, while poetry was none other than truth set forth in allegorical fashion. Thus he explains that

---

[1] *P. of P.* ed. Mead, c. xi, ll. 1100–6.
[2] *Ibid.* c. xi, l. 1114; see p. 157 *supra*.
[3] *Ibid.* c. ix, ll. 811–2.
[4] *Ibid.* c. viii, ll. 776 ff.
[5] *Ibid.* ll. 786–9.

It was the guyse in olde antyquyte
Of famous poetes ryght ymagynatyfe
Fables to fayne by good auctoryte:
They were so wyse and so inuentyfe
Theyr obscure reason, fayre and sugratyfe,
Pronounced trouthe vnder cloudy fygures.[1]

and upon these main features Hawes dilates at some length. First came the pleasing fictions, 'tales newe from daye to daye' conjured up by the 'ymagynacyon'; then the moral teaching conveyed by those fictions, for 'no fable was fayned without reason'. Equally important, however, would seem to have been the need for obscurity or subtlety of expression. The moral teaching, he reiterates, was to be 'cloked full subtyly' by means of 'mysty figures', 'covert lykenesse', and 'colours tenebrous'; and this element of obscurity (or *subtilitas*), condoned by Boccaccio and others, thus became with Hawes a characteristic feature of poetry—a point not without its bearing on contemporary productions. Furthermore, the moral teaching of poetry is illustrated by several examples; and, finally, Hawes concludes by recommending the study of poetry as an elevating and profitable pursuit.

Yet another break-away from the earlier conception of poetry as mere versified rhetoric is seen in Skelton's *Replycacion*, in which the poet joins with Sir Thomas More in fighting the heresy of his day, while censuring in particular two young scholars, Thomas Bilney and Thomas Arthur, who had 'abjured of late'. In the course of the argument Skelton maintains his right as a poet to treat of theological and other serious matters; and the result is a defence of poetry, based on grounds which differed from those of Hawes, though they also had formed part of Boccaccio's doctrine. In an earlier work, *The Book of Good Aduysement*, Skelton would seem to have dealt with the nature and function of poetry;[2] and here he presents a summary of his conclusions. Replying to the charge that 'poetry maye nat flye so hye' as to deal with theology, philosophy and the like, he reminds his readers that David in the *Psalms* had dealt

---

[1] *P. of P.* ed. Mead, c. VIII, ll. 715–20.
[2] See W. Nelson, *John Skelton*, p. 217.

with the greatest of all themes, and had been described by Jerome as the prophet of prophets, and the poet of poets, greater than Horace or Catullus or the 'rest of the ancients.[1] Moreover, for all poets he claimed divine inspiration, here following Boccaccio's theory that 'all poetry proceeded from the bosom of God'.[2] In all 'laureate creacion', Skelton explains, there is at work a mysterious energy of heavenly inspiration, kindled by an indwelling God who directs the poet's pen and causes him to write, 'somtyme for affection, somtyme for sadde (serious) direction, somtyme for correction'. In other words, the poet is but the mouthpiece of the Divine Will, guiding and reproving men for their good; and here for the first time the doctrine of poetic inspiration was being expounded in English.

Apart from this the period has little to show in the way of literary theorising, though the post-classical doctrine of tragedy, accepted (and modified) by Chaucer, is occasionally recalled, accompanied by the corresponding post-classical conception of comedy. Thus Lydgate, referring to tragedy in his *Troy Book* (1412–30) states that

> It begynneth in prosperite
> And endeth euer in aduersite,
> And it also doth þe conquest trete
> Of riche kynges and of lordys grete.

to which he adds that

> A comedie hath in his gynnyng
> A prime face, a maner compleynyng,
> And afterward endeth in gladness.[3]

Hawes's recognition of the theory is moreover suggested by his description of Chaucer's *Legend of Good Women* as consisting of tragedies;[4] and the same doctrine is repeated in Henryson's *Testament of Cresseid*,[5] though throughout the sixteenth century the idea persisted, being doubtless fostered by the popularity of Lydgate's translation of Boccaccio's *De Casibus*. For the rest, Hawes's reference to music is not without its interest. He

---

[1] *Replycacion*, 379–93.    [2] *De Gen. Deorum*, xiv, 7.
[3] *Troy Book*, ed. Bergen (E.E.T.S. 1906), pp. 168–9; see also MacCracken, *op. cit.* p. 73.    [4] *P. of P.* ed. Mead, c. xiv, l. 1326.
[5] *Poems of Robert Henryson*, ed. G. G. Smith, iii, 3.

defines it as concord and also peace, bringing into unity all discordant elements and 'deuoydyng' evil;[1] and his statement is one of the comparatively rare references to the sister arts in medieval literature.

It yet remains to mention the various efforts made at literary appreciation during this period. Consisting as they did of the earliest judgments passed on native poets, they represent a notable extension of critical activities, the tentative beginnings of practical criticism; and despite their manifold shortcomings they have definite value for later ages. For the most part, it is true, they are of the nature of sporadic and more or less stereotyped statements, tributes paid by poets to acknowledged masters, and accompanied by some amount of self-depreciation; and as such they represent little more than a fifteenth-century convention, designed to win the good-will of the reader, after the fashion of the epistolary device, *captatio benevolentiae*,[2] of which to all appearances they are in some sort a survival. At the same time they are something more than mere formal compliments; for suggestive and significant comments are occasionally found in their remarks. Moreover, they undoubtedly throw valuable light on contemporary literary tastes and standards; they give evidence of aesthetic interests which had hitherto been singularly lacking; while incidentally they point to the new status of vernacular literature at this stage, and the increased regard in which it was held.

Among the main contributors to these running judgments were Lydgate, Caxton, Hawes and Skelton; and noteworthy in the first place is the limited range of their appreciations. To much of what was valuable in the earlier native literature no single reference is made. The old romances, the works of Langland and the West Midland poet, the contemporary ballads and lyrics, all alike escape their notice. And significant in this connexion is Hawes's condemnation of light fables and 'balads of fervent amyte' as time-wasting 'gestes and tryfles without fruytfulnes'.[3] It thus becomes evident that the sole

---

[1] *P. of P.* ed. Mead, c. xvi, ll. 1542 ff.
[2] Cf. *ars dictaminis*; see p. 113 *supra*.
[3] *P. of P.* ed. Mead, c. xiv, ll. 1390 ff.

interest throughout is concentrated on the reigning school of poets, on Gower, Chaucer and Lydgate as heralds of a new order of poetry. Then in forming their estimates of the various poetic achievements it is likewise clear that each writer had primarily in mind certain standards or tests which, naturally enough, were based on current poetic doctrine. First and foremost came the value attached to elevated and gilded diction, in accordance with the revived 'rhetorical' tradition. With this went the demand for moral teaching, which was to be concealed under a veil of pleasing fiction. And thirdly, stress was laid on the *subtilitas* of the treatment, on the skill with which truth was pronounced 'under cloudy figures'. With these as the main criteria of poetic value judgments were accordingly pronounced, and appreciation in general was limited to that extent.

Of Gower, to begin with, but little is said. Conventional homage is paid to him as one who first adorned the vernacular. He is also praised for his moral teaching, his 'sentencyous dewe'; but, as Skelton noted, though his matter was worth gold, his diction and style were no longer acceptable, judged by current standards.[1] Chaucer, on the other hand, received considerable attention; and Lydgate set the fashion, in acknowledging him as his master, of describing him as the first 'to enlumine our langage with flowres of Rethorike'.[2] Throughout the fifteenth century this remained his chief claim to fame. With his 'colours purperate of rethoryke' he is said to have freed English which had hitherto been 'rude and boistous'; elsewhere he is hailed as 'the fader and founder of ornate eloquence';[3] and to Dunbar he is still 'the rose of rethoris all'.[4] Hawes alone stresses his moral tendencies; though others found in him some amount of 'fruitful sentence'. 'His depured stremes', wrote Hawes,[5] 'kyndled hertes with the fyry leames of morall vertue'; and to that writer the allegorical *House of Fame* and the 'swete and prouffytable' *Legend of Good Women* ranked higher as poetry than the 'tales of Caunterbury', some of which were 'vertuous', and others merely 'glade and mery'. It was

---

[1] *Phyllyp Sparow*, 817 ff.
[2] *Serpent of Division*, ed. MacCracken, p. 65.
[3] Anon. *Book of Curtesye* (E.E.T.S. 1868), st. 48.
[4] *Golden Targe*, 253.          [5] *P. of P.* ed. Mead, c. xiv, ll. 1320 ff.

Lydgate, however, who came in for the greatest praise, and at the close of the fifteenth century he is generally accepted as the great exemplar in poetry. By one writer he is extolled for 'his colours freshe on every side', for 'his sadnesse (weight) of sentence';[1] and after death, it is worth noting, he is represented as singing among the nine Muses before Jove himself, and is hailed as one of the immortals whose fame was universal. Hawes also recognises in him the peerless poet, excelling all others and unrivalled in fame. He praises the poet's 'elocucyon', his 'depured rethoryke';[2] he also stresses his moral teaching, pointing out how in the *Fall of Princes* men were taught to despise the world, so full of mutability, or again, in the *History of Troy* that 'woman was the confusyon'; and further, the same writer notes with admiration the *subtilitas* of Lydgate's treatment, how 'under colours he cloked craftely' his various teachings. It only remained for Skelton to concede the loftiness of Lydgate's expression, while shrewdly expressing a doubt as to the merits of that aureate style, on the ground that 'it was diffuse to finde the sentence (meaning)' of the poet's utterance.[3]

Yet these running judgments were by no means limited to points of 'rethorik', moral teaching and the like. Occasional comments appear which betray a juster appreciation of literary values; and concerning Chaucer in particular some interesting remarks are made,[4] which suggest that the age was not wholly blind to some at least of his merits, despite the glamour of the prevailing aureate diction. Already during Chaucer's lifetime Thomas Usk had commended his 'manlyche speche', his good sense, and his manner free from futile artifice;[5] and these qualities were noted by more than one of the later writers. Thus Caxton, 'abasshed' by the 'curious' terms then in circulation, praises him unreservedly for using 'no voyd words', for 'eschewyng prolyxte', and 'casting away the chaf of superfluyte';[6] and in so doing he implies the virtues of an

---

[1] *Book of Curtesye* (E.E.T.S. 1868), pp. 36–40.
[2] *P. of P.* ed. Mead, c. xiv, ll. 1352 ff.    [3] *Phyllyp Sparow*, 810 ff.
[4] See C. F. E. Spurgeon, *Five Hundred Years of Chaucer Criticism and Allusion*, Part i, to which I am indebted.
[5] *Testament of Love*, Bk. iii, c. iv (*Chaucerian and other Pieces,* ed. W. W. Skeat).
[6] *Prohemye to Cant. T.*

English that was plain. Elsewhere in the anonymous *Book of Curtesye* (printed by Caxton, 1477–8) Chaucer receives yet more discerning and sympathetic treatment. There his works are said to be

> ful of plesaunce,
> Clere in sentence, in langage excellent.
> Briefly to wryte, suche was his suffysance.
> Whateuer to wryte he toke in his entente,
> His langage was so fayr and pertynente
> It semeth vnto mannys heerynge,
> Not only the worde but verely the thing.
>
> .  .  .  .  .  .  .  .  .  .  .
>
> Sentence or langage or both fynde ye shalle
> Ful delectable; for that good fader mente
> Of al his purpose and his hole entente
> How to plese in euery audyence,
> And in our tunge was welle of eloquence.[1]

Here, then, is evidence that some of Chaucer's qualities were being appreciated, notably his simplicity and directness, his natural and life-like mode of expression, his language adapted to his theme, yet 'ful of plesaunce'; and not least significant was the claim advanced on behalf of the poet that his constant aim had been to afford delight, as opposed to the didactic conception of the poetic function which then held the field. Beyond these details contemporary criticism failed to penetrate, though enthusiastic tributes of a less reasoned kind came from various quarters. Hoccleve, for one, maintained that Chaucer belonged to the great tradition, rivalling Cicero in eloquence, Aristotle in philosophy and Virgil in poetry.[2] Lydgate, again, saw in him a true poet, one who had drunk of the well of Parnassus, and was for later comers 'the gronde of wel seying'. He further noted Chaucer's kindly tolerance and indulgence to young writers, in that 'hym liste not pinche nor gruche at euery blot'; and added finally that none was 'worþi his ynkhorn for to holde'.[3]

Such then were the sporadic comments made on Chaucer during the fifteenth century, and it is obvious that as yet the

---

[1] Sts. 49–50.    [2] *Regement of Princes* (E.E.T.S. 1897), p. 71.
[3] *History of Troy* (E.E.T.S. 1906), p. 873.

real merits of his work were unappreciated. Judged by contemporary standards, his poetry was found lacking in the qualities then most admired; and although there were some to whom his simpler manner appealed, he was overshadowed for the time being by his disciple, Lydgate, and was hailed merely as the first great English poet and the reformer of the language. In the century that followed, his genius was more freely recognised by the Scottish poets; and with the publication of his works by William Thynne (1532) and others, his poetic reputation grew apace. Admired for the most part as a social and religious reformer, a satirist who had revealed the vices and follies of his contemporaries, he received, first from Thynne, a more adequate appreciation. In the dedication of his edition of the poet's works to Henry VIII that editor called attention to the poet's 'perfectyon in metre, his fresshnesse of inuencion, his compendyousnesse in narration, his sensible and open style'; and before the end of the century Spenser had sung his praise in no uncertain terms, while Sidney had declared that 'I know not whether to marvel more that he in that misty time could see so clearly, or that we in this clear age walk so stumblingly after him'.

## CHAPTER IX

## CONCLUSION

THE main lines of critical activity in medieval England have now been sketched; and it is necessary in concluding to attempt some estimate of the performance as a whole, and to suggest further its significance in the history of letters. The general character of the movement will have already emerged. It has been seen to be an unconscious exercise for the most part, intermittent in its workings and indirect in its methods, assuming throughout a variety of forms, and consisting largely of *obiter dicta* of writers engaged in their creative tasks. Yet in spite of this informal character, the movement, broadly speaking, is lacking in neither coherence nor growth. All comments, for instance, were attempts to pronounce on some aspect or other of literature; and the one aim throughout may not unfairly be described as that of groping for light in literary matters. Nor was the movement without its element of growth. There is evidence already, in the earliest stages, of a widening outlook on literature, when the teaching of John of Salisbury succeeded that of Bede and Alcuin. This was followed by a study of poetry, by systematic efforts to formulate a poetic technique; and it was the adaptation of this technique to vernacular requirements that from then on engaged the attention, though efforts were also made to pronounce on the nature of poetry itself, and to indulge in literary judgments of an elementary kind. As for the determining factors in the critical development, they have been found in the ever-changing national needs and conditions, and in certain foreign influences which provided inspiration from time to time. Thus the need for studying literature with a view to educating the clergy, the later demand for a yet wider culture, the vogue for verse writing in twelfth-century Western Europe, and the triumph of the vernacular in the fourteenth century, all these in turn gave rise to expositions of literary theory, and to comments on literature from various angles. In responding to these needs writers were aided from various quarters. Most important of all was the legacy inherited from ancient times, those post-classical doctrines modified by Christian tradition, which constituted the main basis of medieval theorising throughout. Further inspiration came subsequently from twelfth-century France, from the classical teaching of the school at Chartres, and still later from the cultured Italy of Petrarch and Boccaccio. And in this way was transformed the ancient teaching—a process in which, it should be added, the English native genius also played some part.

When we look for the results of these critical activities they will be seen to be varied and tentative in kind, though by no means wanting in interest. Of fundamental importance, in the first place, is the unbroken assimilation of literary theory derived from post-classical and patristic sources, that marks the whole period; for this accounts in large measure for the nature of medieval theorising generally. Not the least valuable, to begin with, are the various conceptions of poetry which come to light in the course of the development. Based on fragmentary hints drawn from various authorities, they represent attempts to formulate definite views concerning the nature of poetry, though in themselves of little permanent value. Early evidence of the vagueness that prevailed is provided by the twelfth-century controversy alluded to by John of Salisbury, in which the question was raised whether poetry was an independent art, or merely an art related to grammar or rhetoric. Then, too, there was the patristic tradition, according to which poetry was not so much an end in itself, as an instrument for revealing divine truth in human terms. This tradition it was, which, supported by Isidore's doctrine, gave rise to the theory that poetry was none other than a branch of theology; and yet later, Roger Bacon, influenced by Averroës's teaching, regarded poetry as little more than a higher and more persuasive logic. But while poetry was thus variously conceived of in terms of the Liberal Arts and theology, in actual practice, after the twelfth century, it was viewed mainly as a sort of versified rhetoric, in accordance with post-classical teaching; and this conception prevailed until the close of the medieval period—but not without modification.

Richard of Bury, for instance, was to claim for poetry the dignity of a *scientia* as opposed to a *facultas*, that is, a body of knowledge based on universal principles, as opposed to a mere technique founded on skill and experience. And further additions were made by Hawes, under Italian influence, when poetry was defined as truth set forth in allegorical and ornate fashion, or when Skelton attributed to poetry some measure of inspiration. These conceptions embodied ideas derived ultimately from post-classical and patristic authorities, notably the imparting of moral truth, the allegorical and verbal subtlety essential in an esoteric art, and the elevated diction of inspired utterance; while the rhetorical element remained an all-pervading influence. It can therefore be said that increased importance was being attached to poetic thought as distinct from form; a functional value was assigned to allegory; and the conception of poetry as 'a thing inspired' was also for the first time proclaimed. But all this at best was but theorising at second-hand; no real advance was made on the post-classical and patristic positions.

Of greater importance is the theory of the poetic art set forth, for instance, in Geoffrey of Vinsauf's *Poetria Nova*, according to which certain methods of enhancing literary effects were prescribed, including devices for amplifying a given theme (descriptions, apostrophes, personifications and the like), and an abundant use of figures for attaining an ornate and impressive style, to the neglect of the more important matters of structure and thought. This theory, again, which was based on the conception of poetry as versified rhetoric, owed its ultimate origin to post-classical teaching concerning the literary art. In it were comprised, for instance, the main characteristics of that earlier doctrine, namely, the absorption of poetic by rhetoric, the debasement of poetic (or rhetoric) to a mere study of style, and the limitation of style to ornamental details alone. Moreover its chief decorative devices, the figures, were drawn from an elementary school-rhetoric of pre-Ciceronian times, a work in which had been preserved Hellenistic teaching on oratory. Hence the distinguishing features of this medieval poetic—the triumph of decoration over form and function, the almost total neglect of structural principles, and the adoption of a fixed and elaborate technique—all of which were to lead poetic effort astray for generations to come. Such a theory is obviously of historical, rather than aesthetic, interest. It is, in fact, primarily an extension of second-century Sophistic, now applied to poetry. At the same time it is also something more than the mere reproduction of ancient doctrine. It involved some amount of constructive effort, the adaptation of earlier teaching to contemporary conditions; and as such it represents the first attempt at a systematic treatment of the poetic art in England, the first vague groping towards that sense of structure, in which the Middle Ages were conspicuously lacking. Apart from this it has the further interest of an *ars poetica* unique in kind, differing essentially from anything in classical antiquity or modern times, and peculiar to the Middle Ages alone. And since its teaching was extended to prose as well as to poetry, its influence may be said to have been widespread, and to have culminated in the poetic doctrine of the fifteenth century. Altogether it must be described as the central and representative doctrine of medieval literary theory. Rooted as it was in a decadent past, it gave direction to contemporary poetry, and its influence was not exhausted at the sixteenth-century Renascence.

Other elements of post-classical theory there were which, together with fragments drawn from classical antiquity, were appropriated and re-stated during this medieval period. Much of the material taken from post-classical rhetoricians and grammarians consisted of advice as to the choice of words, vices to be avoided in matters of expression, the classification of style as high, middle and low, distinctions drawn between *fabula*, *historia* and *argumentum*, as well as lists of the 'kinds', of figures and tropes, all of which were mere commonplaces of earlier teaching, and were mostly dead matter at this later date. Of special interest, however, are the Hellenistic definitions of tragedy and comedy, derived from the same sources, to which references were made by writers ranging from John of Salisbury to the poet Henryson. Most writers were content with incomplete and general statements. to the effect that whereas tragedy was a tale in verse (undramatic in form), which dealt with the fall of an exalted personage, comedy, on the other hand, was a tale which ended happily. By Chaucer, however, the conception of tragedy was further elaborated, and in significant fashion. The tragic catastrophe, unaccounted for by earlier authorities, was by him ascribed to the influence of Fortune, or else to moral forces; and with this addition a new stage in the history of tragedy was begun, though until the Elizabethan era the conception remained of academic interest only. Equally significant, however, are the fragments of the teaching of classical antiquity scattered here and there in these works, drawn mainly from the pages of Horace, the younger Seneca and Quintilian. Most are concerned with the art of expression in words; and, as in classical antiquity, the power of 'the word', that is, of effective speech, is specially emphasised. Then, too, the parts played by individual genius, a knowledge of artistic principles, as well as constant practice, are also explained. And among the precepts laid down are the primary needs for perspicuity and propriety of utterance, for the use in general of ordinary words, which however might acquire fresh values in new settings; or again, the matters dealt with are the virtues of brevity and variety of expression, and the effects of an injudicious use of figurative terms. Elsewhere attention is called to the basic need for taking thought in all artistic creation; and in matters of 'composition' special value is attached to effective arrangement and unity of effect, to the importance of regarding a work as a whole, and of avoiding irrelevant details. The necessity for presenting old and familiar themes in new and unfamiliar guise is also urged, as well as the need for a skilful concealment of all artistic devices. These were principles of value, calculated to correct the characteristic defects of medieval workmanship by the introduction of some amount of reasoned form into the literary art; but as yet they remained unassimilated, to be appreciated only in the fuller light of later ages.

While, however, the key to medieval theorising thus lies primarily in the transmission of doctrine derived from post-classical writers of the early centuries, not without their interest are the contributions due mainly to native initiative, which supply further evidence of the awakening of an artistic consciousness. They consist partly of protests made against the restrictive literary theories then current, partly of occasional ideas of some critical significance, partly also of attempts at 'practical' criticism which were to be developed at a later date; and their value lies not so much in their positive achievements as in the fact that they foreshadow in some measure the lines of later critical advance. Of the movement, to begin with, against an elaborate and a fixed technique where poetry was concerned, Chaucer provides the best example. His attitude is most clearly revealed in the development of his art, as he gradually breaks away from the fetters of external rules, and adopts to some extent more natural and convincing methods. But his views are also more or less explicitly stated in his casual remarks, as he ridicules the 'hauteyn' manner, with its 'subtilitee' and 'prolixitee', suggests that diction and style should be plain and in keeping with character, recognises the value of limitation and restraint, or prescribes methods of letter-writing based on psychological principles. It was in some sort a plea for reasoned artistic form, dictated, not by conventional and stereotyped rules, but by the simple demands of human nature. Then, too, in connexion with prose style the attitude of protest is equally visible and even more widespread; for, from the time of Aldhelm onwards, there persisted a marked tendency towards an affected and a pedantic eloquence, inspired originally by the false glamour of second-century Sophistic, but fostered also by the teaching of medieval poetic, which, itself a development of a false rhetorical tradition, in its turn gave wrong direction to medieval prose. Along with this, however, there existed a native prose tradition, less prominent but for all that deeply rooted, which attached prime value to a plain, clear style, one free from pedantry and affectation, straightforward, vivid and simple in the best sense. This tradition is already seen in the writings of Alfred and Aelfric, and later, in such works as the *Ancren Riwle* and the fourteenth-century devotional prose of Rolle, Hilton and others.[1] And it is the

[1] See R. W. Chambers, *On the Continuity of English Prose*, pp. lvii ff.

spirit of this tradition that animates the various pleas for simple
and intelligible writing set forth, often in casual fashion, by
Bede and Giraldus Cambrensis, Roger Bacon, Wiclif, Caxton
and Skelton. Their remarks constitute a striking manifestation
of literary taste, revealing a distrust of 'fine' and eccentric
writing, and embodying a demand for that element of directness
which the national temperament requires, as seen in the balance
between emotion and reserve attained by later masters of
English prose.

Of native additions to critical theory, more or less independent in kind, the traces are fewer; though such as occur are
worthy of mention. Alfred's original comments on the methods
of translation, for instance, marked the beginnings of a discussion which was to be continued, notably by Wiclif and
Caxton, as well as in later centuries; and Alfred's commendation
of both a literal and a free translation is not without its significance. By Roger Bacon, again, the problem was approached
from a different angle. Recognising the inherent difficulties of
all translation, and that something was inevitably lost in the
actual process, he requires from the translator an accurate
knowledge of languages as well as some acquaintance with the
subject-matter concerned, thus providing advice, the soundness
of which was only realised at a later date. Then, too, it is also
worth noting that something like the beginnings of a historical
sense as applied to literature were also present in the references
made by John of Garland, Roger Bacon and Richard of Bury
to the development of knowledge. This idea of intellectual
progress, it is true, was no medieval discovery, and in classical
antiquity it had been but dimly grasped. Its appearance at
this date was probably due to patristic influence, to the recognition of gradual development as the method of divine working.
And in the light of the tardy recognition in later criticism of the
historical point of view, even these slight indications are not
without their interest in the development of critical ideas.

It was in the attempts to bring about some appreciation of
literature, however, that native efforts made perhaps their most
obvious contribution to critical work. At this stage interpretation was necessarily of a general character, as when John of

Salisbury and Richard of Bury commended to their readers the intellectual and spiritual values of literature, using for that purpose ancient arguments, but presenting them anew with convincing charm and feeling. It was preliminary work confessedly; but it was also the work most needed at the time, a sort of introduction to literature revealing the intimate relations between life and letters. And as such, it prepared the way for future aesthetic appreciation; as did also indirectly Roger Bacon's advice on textual matters, and the crude defences of poetry put forward by Richard of Bury and Skelton. Notable also as marking the beginnings of a judicial attitude were the standards adopted for passing judgment on actual literary works; though here as a whole the results are of no great permanent value. John of Salisbury (following Quintilian) had suggested sound methods for forming literary judgment, in calling attention to the artistic values resulting from an appropriate treatment of subject-matter, from effective structure and ṛraces of expression. But his guidance in these matters passed ṇnheeded; and in the absence of definite ideas as to the nature of literature itself, various standards were in practice adopted. In general it may be said that the authority of the ancients counted for much, greater value being attached to the 'poesye' of antiquity than to the 'makyng' of vernacular poets. Yet, here too, the absence of artistic criteria was palpably felt. There was a want of discrimination in the appraisal of even these ancient works, Bede, for example, paying equal regard to classical and post-classical poets, whereas by others Dares is referred to on equal terms with Homer, Macrobius with Cicero, and Statius with Horace. This levelling of authors is in fact characteristic of the whole period, and it points to the lack of any serious literary judgment at this stage. For the rest, such tests as were applied were mainly of a non-aesthetic kind, being based on the literary doctrine prevailing at the time. Thus Bede makes use of purely rhetorical standards in elucidating the literary qualities of the Bible. Later on, didactic considerations provided the normal tests, with occasional suggestions however of the other Horatian requirement, as when reference is made in *The Owl and the Nightingale* to the pleasure-giving side of poetry, or when Chaucer recalls his aim of affording delight as well as instruction. Other tests resulted from the establishment of thirteenth-century poetic; and in the fifteenth century, when reasoned judgment of a sort began, the new standards were those of the earlier 'versified rhetoric', though now somewhat modified, the qualities commended being those bound up with moral teaching, conveyed in allegorical form, and adorned with the 'colours' of 'depured rethoryke', 'aureate diction' and the rest. Yet the period is not without its positive achievements in the sphere of judicial criticism. Among other things Bede's recognition of the significance of the new accentual verse, the welcome given in *The Owl and the Nightingale* to the new love-poetry, and Chaucer's sly comments on the degenerate romances of his day, all afford evidence of a judicial faculty at work, while all alike deal with developments of first-rate importance. Nor must the indirect nature of their critical methods pass unnoticed; for debate and parody were to prove effective instruments of later critical comment. Moreover the range of judgments is also worthy of note, embracing as they did estimates of Biblical, classical and native literatures. With Bede had begun some appreciation of Biblical literature, a field which was to be cultivated later by Colet and Lowth. From John of Salisbury came interesting pronouncements on classical literature, for which he was indebted to earlier authorities; while his independence of judgment is shown by his treatment of Seneca and certain of his own contemporaries. As for the fifteenth-century estimates of native poets, they are mainly valuable as revealing the limited aesthetic taste of the time; though already there are signs of a truer appreciation of Chaucer's merits, in spite of perverse theory and the many florid tributes paid to Lydgate and his school.

Such then are the main achievements of English medieval criticism—the assimilation and modification of some amount of post-classical and patristic theory, together with sundry attempts at theorising and judging—and it now remains to suggest its importance in the sphere of English letters. In general, it may at once be said, the results are somewhat slight and wanting in permanent value. Compared for instance with the searching inquiries of classical antiquity, or the imposing developments of later neo-classical doctrine, or again the varied approach to literary problems characteristic of a modern age, these medieval efforts are obviously limited in scope, elementary and unilluminating in character, providing but little that is of aesthetic value, or that helps to a better understanding of literature and the literary art. Of that speculative criticism which deals with literature in the abstract, its nature and functions, but few traces of any value are to be found. This, however, is not surprising, since the philosophical equipment for such treatment was lacking; and practical, rather than speculative, interests have always been characteristic of English thought. Nor again can it be said that many sound and original judgments on literature in the concrete were forthcoming. In the absence of clear ideas as to the nature of literature itself, no definite standards existed for forming reasoned judgment, or for pronouncing on the goodness or badness of literature as such. As for that subtler imaginative criticism characteristic of modern times, the age was manifestly not ripe for treatment of this kind. It was only in attempts at theorising on the literary art that something like substantial results were attained; and in the doctrines that emerged, relating to poetry and prose alike, lay the main contribution of medieval criticism. Yet here, too, it was for the most part preparatory work, often confused and misguided, with but little for the modern reader in search of positive artistic teaching or of aesthetic appreciation of literature in its various forms. The truth is, in short, that the primary value of this criticism lies not so much in its positive findings, as in its historical significance; and that will be seen to be considerable.

At the same time the positive results achieved are by no means negligible, and must first be noted. In the first place, this body of criticism is of value inasmuch as it provides a record of the successive notions held concerning literature during the Middle Ages, and is thus instrumental in throwing light on much of the literature produced. Some knowledge of the prevailing literary theory is, for instance, indispensable for the proper understanding of medieval poetic technique and the part it plays in medieval poetry. It also goes to explain some of the aberrations of contemporary prose; and thus conduces to a more intelligent reading of medieval literature generally. Then, again, not least valuable were the glimpses which had been afforded of the manifold possibilities of great literature in its bearing on human life—an inspiring introduction to literary study in an age of half-light. And at the same time new ground had been broken in the occasional accounts supplied of ancient writers and of classical artistic principles; all of which prepared the way for a wider outlook on literature, and for a more adequate treatment of its aesthetic qualities. Meanwhile conceptions of poetry as an independent art had also been tentatively formulated; and despite their inadequacy they marked an advance towards a more serious treatment of the subject. It was no longer possible, for instance, as in the twelfth century, to regard poetry as merely a branch of one of the Seven Liberal Arts, or solely as a form of versified rhetoric. For it had been claimed a technique of its own, besides qualities which afforded pleasure as well as instruction; and hints were even given that some sort of inspiration went to its making. If medieval criticism was unable to state definitely what poetry really was and what it aimed at, the failure was one that was to be shared by later ages. Nor was the technique prescribed entirely wanting in permanent interest; though its extreme elaboration and the mechanical method of its application impaired its value as an aid to composition. Yet here for the first time was introduced to English readers a host of artistic devices, amongst others the figures, by the skilful use of which poets in all ages have achieved an utterance transcending mere statement, and have added freshness and subtlety, illumination and charm, to their mode of expression. So that neither the meticulous nature of the teaching nor its flagrant abuse detracts wholly from the value of the underlying principles, or from their importance, more especially for criticism of a 'practical' kind. A fruitful approach to poetry must inevitably be in some measure both analytical and technical; and with this teaching the way had been prepared for a more intelligent appreciation of the literary art. For the rest, while interest must likewise be

attached to the growing practice of formulating literary judgment, perhaps the most outstanding characteristic of all, in the
light of later developments, was the tendency, already visible,
to protest against the tyranny of rules, and against various
forms of pedantic and affected writing. Thus attempts had been
made to escape from a false position by correcting theories
which were instinctively felt to be unsound; and this was
the tendency that was to determine largely the course of
later English criticism. It was in short an anticipation of the
protests subsequently made by Daniel, Dryden, and others
against the hampering restrictions of alien neo-classical rules,
and a characteristic assertion of the English genius where
literature was concerned.

It is, however, in its historical bearings that this medieval
criticism is mainly significant in the development of English
letters. And in the first place it has the interest that is attached
to all beginnings. Representing as it does the first troubling of
the waters, the earliest phase of those critical activities which
were to occupy so important a place in later English intellectual
life, it thus forms an integral part of the critical tradition in
England, a part without which the story of English criticism is
incomplete; and, in addition, it throws into clearer relief what
was actually done at the sixteenth-century Renascence. Apart
from this it is also notable as being the outcome of the first
impact of ancient learning on literary activities in England.
The revival of Latin scholarship in the seventh and eighth
centuries, with which critical studies began, was in effect no
less momentous than was the appearance of the Teutonic heroic
temper in literature at that date. But followed as that revival
was by the use subsequently made of ancient theory in the
critical development, it becomes yet more significant. Together they constitute the first phase of a decisive influence
on English criticism; an influence which was to become still
more active in the sixteenth century, and to culminate in the
recovery of the classical spirit at the end of the eighteenth.

As yet, however, it is important to note, the influence of
antiquity was mainly limited to theories representing a survival
of the Hellenistic culture of Imperial Rome, as distinct from

the classical teaching of the Greek and Graeco-Roman traditions; and the consequences of this fact are not without their interest. The main inspiration, as has been seen, was drawn from the New Sophistic and from doctrines current in the second and later centuries; and these doctrines were little more than a revival of Hellenistic theories, with their florid rhetorical tradition, and their sterile scholastic methods. In this same teaching were moreover embodied some of the glaring excesses against which classical theorists had inveighed from the time of Plato onwards, notably, heresies inaugurated by Gorgias and his followers, and fostered later by rhetoricians of the Asiatic schools; and these errors in due course were handed on to the Middle Ages. Thus, by an evil chance, Hellenistic teaching was instrumental in perpetuating, centuries later, some of the literary defects of classical antiquity, and that which was least valuable in ancient doctrine, in this way diverting medieval literature into inartistic channels. It is true that a tendency towards extravagance of expression would seem to be an ever-recurring phenomenon in the history of letters. But this much is certain, that the influence of antiquity at this stage was so far injurious, in that it gave authority for the time being to this species of defective art.

The full significance of this body of criticism is, however, not realised, unless its bearings on the views commonly held concerning the literary conditions of both the medieval and the Elizabethan periods are properly appreciated. For it modifies in some measure present-day notions concerning medieval conditions, and at the same time throws light on the literary activities of the period that followed. In the first place, it is usual to regard English medieval literature as essentially a spontaneous development, the product of conditions similar to those which prevailed in classical Greece, when fresh literary instincts and faculties of the human mind found fitting expression, free from systems and models which would have paralysed initiative and crippled original effort.[1] And this holds true of certain products of medieval literary activity. Unconscious originality created

[1] See Saintsbury, *History of Criticism*, I, 373, 472; Ker, *Forms of English Poetry*, pp. 105–7.

the romance, revolutionised the drama, and devised a new
lyric, thus inaugurating literary forms and motives hitherto
unknown, which not only enlarged the conception of literature,
but also opened up new channels along which the national
creative genius was in the future instinctively to work. Yet this
represents only half of the story. Apart from these developments there had come into being a considerable body of
literature, essentially different in kind, and more pretentious
in form, which was accepted by contemporaries as the characteristic utterance of the period, and as an embodiment of the
highest artistic culture then known. Such literature included
the poetry of Chaucer and Lydgate, Hawes and others; and
so far from being the product of unfettered genius, it represents
creative work which was the fruit of deliberate planning, and
of obedience to principles and rules systematically applied.
The principles and rules thus adopted were those set forth in
medieval theory; and to them must therefore be ascribed a
definite, if not a dominant, influence in contemporary literary
activities. The truth is, in fact, that medieval conditions after
all were not so very different from those which were to prevail
at the sixteenth-century Renaissance; though it is usual to
suggest that the use of systems and models began at the later
date, when the Latin spirit with its tradition of imitation
prevailed. Yet the evidence of medieval criticism goes to show
that the difference in conditions was in reality one of degree
rather than of kind, and that 'imitation of the ancients' had
already commenced in medieval times. In the fuller light of
sixteenth-century activities, inspiration was to come primarily
from the models and theories of classical antiquity, whereas in
the Middle Ages it was upon the decadent theories of Hellenistic
and post-classical times that theorists and artists consistently
drew.

Not less important is the bearing of this medieval criticism
on the literary theorising, as well as the literature, of the period
that followed. For it goes to explain much in the later activities,
and shows that while men of letters then drew increasingly on
classical and Italian sources for their ideas of art, they were
influenced to some extent also by English medieval traditions.

The fact is one that has been somewhat obscured in literary studies, owing not so much to a tacit acceptance of Humanistic scorn for things medieval, as to a concentration of interest on that classical and Italian teaching which constituted the main basis of the neo-classical system then forming. The result has been that Elizabethan criticism has seemed to be little more than a series of discussions on the 'kinds', the rules, the unities and the like; and this oversight has involved the neglect of not a little that is significant in the activities of Elizabethan times. Nor need the survival of medieval ideas at this later date occasion any great surprise. For one of the earliest effects of printing was to give new life to works characteristically medieval, as well as to post-classical writings which had been accepted as authoritative throughout the Middle Ages. Thus from the printing presses came not only new treasures in the form of recently discovered classics, but also a vast output of non-classical texts, including the school-books of Donatus, Diomedes and Martianus Capella, the rhetorical works of Hermogenes and others, the *Rhetorica ad Herennium* and *De Inventione*, and the writings of Aulus Gellius, Ausonius, Claudian and Sidonius, all of which had given direction to medieval thought and theorising. The acquaintance of the Tudor and Elizabethan ages with these texts cannot therefore be doubted. And for a time after their revival these post-classical works retained their earlier authority, until a sounder erudition and a more discriminating taste discerned the value of the genuine classical standards.

Of actual traces of the influence of this medieval criticism on later critical activities there is also abundant evidence; and one of the most obvious is the vigorous survival of the medieval cult of rhetoric which supplied the main impetus at the earlier stages of Renascence criticism. Having dominated literary studies of the medieval period, rhetorical influences continued to flourish until the end of the sixteenth century, and led to the appearance of a series of formal treatises on style, notably by Cox and Sherry, Wilson, Peacham and Fraunce. In these works the study of style, now regarded as an accomplishment, was limited as before to the art of decoration, the main interest being concentrated on those schemes and tropes which had played so great a part in medieval technique; and since the earlier confusion between poetic and rhetoric still persisted, these same devices are found occupying a prominent place in expositions of poetry by Puttenham and others.[1] Even in the tentative efforts at criticism of a judicial kind is this pre-occupation with rhetorical matters apparent; and this is illustrated, for instance, by "E.K.'s" comments on Spenser's *Shepherd's Calendar*, where the various figures are labelled, and attention is called to the poet's use of syncope, paronomasia, 'a pretty epanorthosis', 'an ingenious hyperbaton', and the rest. Apart from this, not a little of Renascence criticism is of the nature of unfinished controversies handed on from the Middle Ages. Thus questions relating to the constitution of the vernacular, to the nature of poetry and the poetic function, and the importance of allegory as an element of poetry, all these were matters which had been broached in medieval times, and were now being subjected to further and more detailed consideration. Moreover, there were the patristic objections to plays and literature generally which had been current throughout the Middle Ages. These still retained something of their earlier authority; and it was in reply to the ancient charges of unreality, immorality and futility that apologies of both poetry and the drama were now forthcoming. Nor, again, was medieval theory without its influence on later critical activities. Most notable perhaps was the continued survival of the medieval conceptions of tragedy and comedy, which maintained their ground with theorists in spite of Aristotelian teaching. Then, too, the earlier discussions on the methods of translation (both Biblical and secular) were now continued with even greater zest; so that translation came to be regarded as a form of literary activity with standards of its own. And in many other places in Renascence theorising on poetry can traces of fifteenth-century doctrine be detected, notably, in the demand for fine diction and for truths in poetry 'not affirmatively but allegorically and

---

[1] For a good account of the influence of the figures at this date see Puttenham, *Arte of English Poesie*, ed. G. D. Willcock and A. Walker, pp. lxxiv–lxxxiv.

figuratively written';[1] while not least significant was the occasional opposition to alien rules and standards, for which precedents had already existed in medieval times. In fact, it is only by appreciating the range and tenacity of medieval ideas and influences that the true position of the neo-classical element in Elizabethan criticism can be rightly understood.[2]

Nor were traces of medieval literary theory wholly wanting in the actual literature of the Elizabethan period; though the prime factors in determining the lines of literary progress were the workings of the national genius—already apparent in the romance, the medieval drama and lyric—together with some amount of classical and Italian influence. That the break with the earlier critical tradition was not complete is suggested by the retention of the medieval term 'poetry' (*poetria*), along with the classical 'poesy' (*poesis*), as terms descriptive of imaginative literature in verse. Or, again, there are the intricate stanza forms prescribed for medieval Latin verse, many of which are to be found in the metrical forms of the Tudor period. Apart from this, not without their significance are the prevalence of allegory in Elizabethan literature, the fondness for 'high-astounding terms' and figurative expression generally, as well as the adherence of dramatists in practice to the medieval conceptions of tragedy and comedy; while further reminiscences of medieval theory are found also in Elizabethan poetic technique. Thus traces of the earlier poetic are visible, for instance, in Spenser's work, in the sententious passages which open the cantos of his *Faerie Queene*; or again, in the Emblems with which each Eclogue of his *Shepherd's Calendar* is 'concluded full closely'. His *Complaints* moreover are merely developments of that earlier device, the apostrophe; and, for the rest, his treatment throughout is coloured by devices prescribed for medieval 'amplification', including *exempla*, digressions, repetitions, and above all, the separable decorative descriptions, while in addition there are few rhetorical figures that are not illustrated in his pages. Such details point unmistakably to the survival of some amount of medieval technique in Elizabethan poetry. And that the

---

[1] Sidney, *Apol. for Poetrie*, ed. Shuckburgh, p. 39.
[2] See D. L. Clark, *Rhetoric and Poetry in the Renaissance* (1922).

tradition was not unknown in the seventeenth century is suggested by one of Herrick's poems, *The Discription of a Woman*,[1] in which the treatment conforms in all its details with the technique required for a medieval 'description'.

These then are the main features of this first phase of critical activities in England, and their interest for modern readers. To all appearances little more than mere prolegomena or preliminary remarks on literature, the results nevertheless point to an expanding tradition, giving expression to new ideas and theories, and revealing an attitude of mind which was intensified, but not originated, at the sixteenth-century Renascence. The outstanding achievement was the establishment of a system of art based on ancient post-classical doctrine. But in addition to this the foundations of a critical tradition had also been laid, a tradition which not only began the practice of forming literary judgments, but also attempted to furnish the means for forming such judgments; and these after all are among the main functions of literary criticism. Much of the teaching, it is true, was of a decadent kind, intelligible only in the light of an earlier mode of thinking and misleading in its effects on the literature produced. It was further vitiated by a prevailing lack of the sense of form and an insensitiveness to those aesthetic qualities on which the true greatness of literature rests. Yet important questions had in the meantime been raised, some amount of theory established, and later problems anticipated; and in spite of shortcomings, expression had been given to a growing consciousness of literature, and to ideas of interest in critical history. To omit therefore such activities from a survey of English criticism is none other than to pass over the first phase in the critical development, and, incidentally, to ignore a chapter in the history of English thought which throws an interesting sidelight on medieval intellectual life.

[1] *Additional Poems*, no. 1.

## SUMMARY OF MEDIEVAL POETIC
### (Geoffrey of Vinsauf)

## A.   Methods of beginning and ending a poem[1]

(*a*)   Beginning:

    (1) *natural method (ab ovo)*, at the starting-point of the story, with events related in the order in which they occurred.

    (2) *artificial methods (in medias res)*:

        (i)   at the end of the story.

        (ii)   at the middle of the story.

        (iii)   at the end or the middle of the story, with an introductory proverb, *sententia*, or *exemplum*.

(*b*)   Ending:

    with a proverb or *sententia*.

## B.   Methods of amplification and abbreviation[2]

(*a*)   Amplification:

    (1) description (*effictio* and *notatio*).

    (2) apostrophe (*exclamatio*).

    (3) personification (*conformatio*).

    (4) repetition (*interpretatio, expolitio*).

    (5) periphrasis (*circuitio*).

    (6) contrast (*contrarium*).

    (7) comparison (*similitudo*).

    (8) digression.

(*b*)   Abbreviation:

    (1) exclusion of repetitions and descriptions.

    (2) use of ablative absolute.

    (3) *significatio* (or *emphasis*).

    (4) *occupatio* (or *occultatio*).

    (5) *dissolutio* (or *asyndeton*).

    (6) *articulus*.

    (7) fusion of clauses.

[1] *P.N.* (Faral), 87–154.        [2] *P.N.* (Faral), 219–736.

## C. Ornaments of Style

(a) 'DIFFICULT' ORNAMENTAL DEVICES (*ornatus difficilis*).[1]
Ten Tropes:

(1) *nominatio* (or *onomatopoeia*), formation of names or words from sounds that suggest the things signified.

(2) *pronominatio*, descriptive term or epithet used for a proper name.

(3) *denominatio* (or *metonymy*), substitution of an attributive or other suggestive word for the name of a thing.

(4) *circuitio* (or *periphrasis*), circumlocution.

(5) *transgressio* (or *hyperbaton*), transposition of words out of their normal order.

(6) *superlatio* (or *hyperbole*), use of exaggerated terms for emphasis.

(7) *intellectio* (or *synecdoche*), mention of a part when the whole is to be understood, or vice versa.

(8) *abusio* (or *catachresis*), use of words in wrong senses.

(9) *translatio*, metaphor.

(10) *permutatio*, expression with hidden meaning, allegorical or ironical.

(b) 'EASY' ORNAMENTAL DEVICES (*ornatus facilis*).

(α) Figures of speech (*figurae verborum*):[2]

(1) *repetitio*, repetition of a word at the beginning of successive clauses or sentences.

(2) *conversio*, repetition of a word at the close of successive clauses or sentences.

(3) *complexio*, combination of *repetitio* and *conversio*.

(4) *traductio*, repetition of a word elsewhere for emphasis.

(5) *conduplicatio*, repetition of a word to express emotion.

(6) *adnominatio*, repetition of the root of a word with a change of prefix or suffix: often represents a play upon words.

(7) *gradatio*, repetition of the closing word of one clause as the opening word of the next; a linking effect.

---

[1] *P.N.* (Faral), 765–1093. Cf. *Ad Her.* IV, 31–4, §§ 42–6.
[2] *P.N.* (Faral), 1094–1229. Cf. *Ad Her.* IV, 13–30, §§ 19–41.

(8) *interpretatio*, repetition of an idea in different words.

(9) *contentio*, antithesis of words.

(10) *contrarium*, denying the contrary of an idea before affirming it.

(11) *compar*, balancing of two clauses of equal length.

(12) *commutatio* (or *chiasmus*), in balanced clauses the reversal of the order of the first clause in the second clause.

(13) *similiter cadens*, two successive clauses ending in words with the same inflexional endings.

(14) *similiter desinens*, two successive clauses ending in words with similar sounds.

(15) *dissolutio* (or *asyndeton*), omission of connective words.

(16) *articulus*, succession of words without conjunctions; a staccato effect.

(17) *continuatio*, a rapid succession of words to complete a sentence.

(18) *praecisio* (or *aposiopesis*), a sentence unfinished; a significant or emotional break.

(19) *transitio*, a brief statement of what had been said and what was to follow.

(20) *conclusio*, a brief summing-up.

(21) *interrogatio*, a rhetorical question or summary challenge.

(22) *ratiocinatio*, a question addressed by a speaker to himself.

(23) *subjectio*, a suggested answer to a question.

(24) *definitio*, a brief explanation.

(25) *exclamatio*, exclamation (of anger, grief, etc.).

(26) *sententia*, a wise and pithy saying.

(27) *correctio* (or *epanorthosis*), substitution of a more suitable word for one previously used.

(28) *occupatio* (or *occultatio*), refusal to describe or narrate while referring briefly to a subject under cover of passing it over.

(29) *disjunctio*, use of different verbs to express similar ideas in successive clauses.

(30) *conjunctio*, use of one verb (interposed) for the expression of similar ideas in successive clauses.

(31) *adjunctio*, use of one verb (either at the beginning or end) for the expression of similar ideas in successive clauses.

(32) *permissio*, an admission or concession.
(33) *dubitatio*, expression of doubt; assumed embarrassment.
(34) *expeditio*, disproof of all but one of various alternatives.

(β) Figures of Thought (*figurae sententiarum*).[1]

    (1) *licentia*, bold or censorious speech.
    (2) *diminutio*, self-disparagement.
    (3) *descriptio*, clear and lucid explanation of a matter.
    (4) *divisio*, presenting a dilemma.
    (5) *frequentatio*, accumulation of arguments or facts.
    (6) *expolitio*, enlarging on a topic in different ways.
    (7) *commoratio*, emphasising an important point.
    (8) *contentio*, antithesis (of ideas).
    (9) *similitudo*, simile.
  (10) *exemplum*, illustrative story.
  (11) *imago*, a comparison.
  (12) *effictio*, personal description (outward appearance).
  (13) *notatio*, personal description (character).
  (14) *sermocinatio*, speech attributed to someone: imaginary discourse.
  (15) *conformatio* (or *prosopopoeia*), speech or action attributed to mute or inanimate things; personification.
  (16) *significatio* (or *emphasis*), suggestion of more than is actually said; innuendo.
  (17) *brevitas*, concise expression.
  (18) *demonstratio* (or *vision*), description which brings an event or scene vividly before one's eyes.
  (19) *distributio*, division: giving details.

[1] *P.N.* (Faral), 1230–1587. Cf. *Ad Her.* IV, 35–55, §§ 47–69.

# INDEX